ISBN: 9781313838009

Published by:
HardPress Publishing
8345 NW 66TH ST #2561
MIAMI FL 33166-2626

Email: info@hardpress.net
Web: http://www.hardpress.net

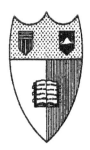

Chs. M. Lason
Yokohama Japan
April 4th
1903 —

CHINESE CHARACTERISTICS

UNG CHOU
PAGODA
AR PEKING.

A MEMORIAL ARCH.

NATIVE CHILDREN IN COURTYARD

TURTLE MONUMENT.

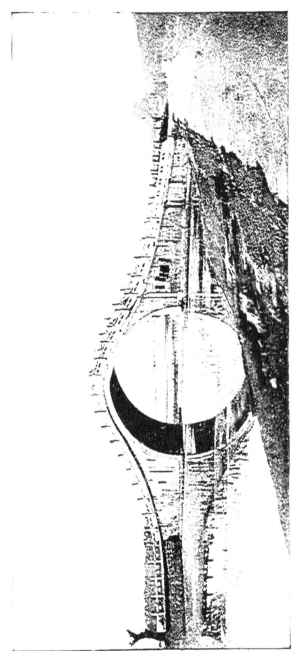

CAMEL'S-BACK BRIDGE IN THE GROUNDS OF THE EMPEROR'S SUMMER PALACE.

Chinese Characteristics

BY

Arthur H. Smith

Twenty-two Years a Missionary of the American Board in China

*Enlarged and Revised Edition with
Marginal and New Illustrations*

NEW YORK   CHICAGO   TORONTO

Fleming H. Revell Company

Publishers of Evangelical Literature

CONTENTS.

LIST OF ILLUSTRATIONS.*

* For the use of original photographs, from which engravings have been made
and here published for the first time, the author and publishers desire to acknowl-
edge their indebtedness to Miss J. G. Evans of Tung-Chou, for frontispiece and
illustrations facing pages 30, 44, 118, 171, 217, 242 and 300; and to the Rev. G. S.
Hays of Chefoo, for illustrations facing pages 19, 70, 200, and 251.

Within the Four Seas all are brethren.

Confucian Analects, XII., v. 4.

The scientific study of Man is the most difficult of all branches of knowledge.

O. W. Holmes.

We are firm believers in the maxim that for all right judgment of any man or thing it is useful—nay, essential—to see his good qualities before pronouncing on his bad.

Carlyle.

CHINESE CHARACTERISTICS.

INTRODUCTION.

A WITNESS when put upon the stand is expected to tell the truth, the whole truth, and nothing but the truth. Many witnesses concerning the Chinese have told the truth, but perhaps few of them have succeeded in telling nothing but the truth, and no one of them has ever told the whole truth. No single individual, whatever the extent of his knowledge, could by any possibility know the whole truth about the Chinese. The present volume of essays is therefore open to objection from three different points of view.

First, it may be said that the attempt to convey to others an idea of the real characteristics of the Chinese is vain. Mr. George Wingrove Cooke, the China correspondent of the London *Times* in 1857–58, enjoyed as good an opportunity of seeing the Chinese under varied circumstances, and through the eyes of those well qualified to help him to a just understanding of the people, as any writer on China up to that time. In the preface to his published letters, Mr. Cooke apologises as follows for his failure to describe the Chinese character: "1 have, in these letters, introduced no elaborate essay upon Chinese character. It is a great omission. No theme could be more tempting, no subject could afford wider scope for ingenious hypothesis, profound generalisation, and triumphant dogmatism. Every small critic will probably utterly despise me for not having made something out of such opportunities. The truth is, that I have written several very fine characters for the whole Chinese race, but having the misfortune to have the people under my eye at the same time with my essay, they were always saying something or doing something which rubbed so rudely against my hypothesis, that in the interest of truth I burnt several successive letters. I may add that I have often talked·over this matter with the most eminent and candid sinologues, and have always found them ready to agree with me as to the impossibility of a conception of Chinese character as a whole. These difficulties, however, occur only to those who know the Chinese practically ; a smart writer, entirely ignorant of the subject, might readily strike off a brilliant and antithetical analysis, which should leave nothing to be desired but truth. Some day, perhaps, we may acquire the necessary knowledge to give to each of the glaring inconsistencies of a Chinaman's mind its proper weight and influence in the general mass. At present, I, at least, must be content to avoid strict definitions, and to describe a Chinaman * by his most prominent qualities."

Within the past thirty years, the Chinese has made himself a factor in the affairs of many lands. He is seen to be irre-

* It is a matter of surprise, and even more of regret, that this barbarous compound seems to have rooted itself in the English language, to the exclusion of the proper word *Chinese*. We do not know of a foreign periodical in China in which natives of that country are not constantly called "Chinamen," nor of a single writer in the Empire who consistently avoids the use of the term.

pressible; is felt to be incomprehensible. He cannot, indeed, be rightly understood in any country but China, yet the impression still prevails that he is a bundle of contradictions who cannot be understood at all. But after all there is no apparent reason, now that several hundred years of our acquaintance with China have elapsed, why what is actually known of its people should not be co-ordinated, as well as any other combination of complex phenomena.

A more serious objection to this particular volume is that the author has no adequate qualifications for writing it. The circumstance that a person has lived for twenty-two years in China is no more a guarantee that he is competent to write of the characteristics of the Chinese, than the fact that another man has for twenty-two years been buried in a silver mine is a proof that he is a fit person to compose a treatise on metallurgy, or on bi-metallism. China is a vast whole, and one who has never even visited more than half its provinces, and who has lived in but two of them, is certainly not entitled to generalise for the whole Empire. These papers were originally prepared for the *North-China Daily News* of Shanghai, with no reference to any wider circulation. Some of the topics treated excited, however, so much interest, not only in China, but also in Great Britain, in the United States, and in Canada, that the author was asked to reproduce the articles in a permanent form.*

A third objection, which will be offered by some, is that parts of the views here presented, especially those which deal with the moral character of the Chinese, are misleading and unjust.

It should be remembered, however, that impressions are not like statistics which may be corrected to a fraction. They

* " Chinese Characteristics " was published in Shanghai in 1890; after being widely circulated throughout China and the East, the edition was exhausted more than two years ago.

rather resemble photographic negatives, no two of which may be alike, yet each of them may present truthfully something not observable in any of the rest.   The plates on which the photographs are taken differ ; so do the lenses, and the developers, and the resulting views differ too.

Many old residents of China, whose knowledge of the country is very much greater than that of the writer, have expressed themselves as in substantial agreement with his opinions, while others, whose judgment is entitled to equal respect, think that a somewhat lighter colouring in certain parts would increase the fidelity of the too "monochromatic" picture. With this undoubtedly just criticism in mind, the work has been revised and amended throughout.   While the exigencies of republication at this time have rendered convenient the omission of one-third of the characteristics originally discussed, those that remain contain nevertheless the most important portions of the whole, and the chapter on Content and Cheerfulness is altogether new.

There can be no valid excuse for withholding commendation from the Chinese for any one of the many good qualities which they possess and exhibit. At the same time, there is a danger of yielding to *à priori* considerations, and giving the Chinese credit for a higher practical morality than they can justly claim —an evil not less serious than indiscriminate condemnation. It is related of Thackeray, that he was once asked how it happened that the good people in his novels were always stupid, and the bad people clever.   To this the great satirist replied that he had no brains above his eyes.   There is a wood-cut representing an oak tree, in the outlines of which the observer is invited to detect a profile of Napoleon on the island of St. Helena, standing with bowed head and folded arms.   Protracted contemplation frequently fails to discover any such profile, and it would seem that there must be some mistake, but when once it is clearly pointed out, it is impossible to look at the picture and not see the Napoleon too. In like manner, many things are to be seen in China which do not at first appear, and many of them once seen are never forgotten.

While it has been impossible to introduce a qualifying clause into every sentence which is general in its form, the reader is expressly warned that these papers are not intended to be generalisations for a whole Empire, nor yet comprehensive abstracts of what foreigners have observed and experienced. What they are intended to be is merely a notation of the impression which has been made upon one observer, by a few out of many " Chinese Characteristics." They are not meant as a portrait of the Chinese people, but rather as mere outline sketches in charcoal of some features of the Chinese people, as they have been seen by that one observer. Taken together, they constitute only a single ray, of which an indefinite number are required to form a complete beam of white light. They may also be considered as studies in induction, in which many particulars taken from the experience not of the writer only, but of various other individuals at various times, are grouped. It is for this reason that the subject has been so largely treated by exemplification.

Mr. Meadows, the most philosophical of the many writers on China and the Chinese, expressed the opinion that the best way to convey to the mind of another person a correct idea of the genius of a foreign people would be to hand him for perusal a collection of notes, formed by carefully recording great numbers of incidents which had attracted one's attention, particularly those that seemed at all extraordinary, together with the explanation of the extraordinary parts as given by natives of the country.

From a sufficient number of such incidents a general principle is inferred. The inferences may be doubted or denied, but such particulars as are cited cannot, for that reason alone, be set aside, being so far as they go truthful, and they must ultimately be reckoned with in any theory of the Chinese character.

The difficulty of comparing Chinese with Anglo-Saxons will be most strongly felt by those who have attempted it. To such it will soon become evident that many things which seem " characteristic " of the Chinese are merely Oriental traits ; but to what extent this is true, each reader in the light of his own experience must judge for himself.

It has been said that in the present stage of our intercourse with Chinese there are three ways in which we can come to some knowledge of their social life—by the study of their novels, their ballads, and their plays. Each of these sources of information doubtless has its worth, but there is likewise a fourth, more valuable than all of them combined, a source not open to every one who writes on China and the Chinese. It is the study of the family life of the Chinese in their own homes. As the topography of a district can be much better understood in the country than in the city, so it is with the characteristics of the people. A foreigner may live in a Chinese city for a decade, and not gain as much knowledge of the interior life of the people as he can acquire by living twelve months in a Chinese village. Next to the Family we must regard the Village as the unit of Chinese social life, and it is therefore from the standpoint of a Chinese village that these papers have been written. They are of purpose not intended to represent the point of view of a missionary, but that of an observer not consciously prejudiced, who simply reports what he sees. For this reason no reference is made to any characteristics of the Chinese as they may be modified by Christianity. It is not assumed that the Chinese need Christianity at all, but if it appears that there are grave defects in their character, it is a fair question how those defects may be remedied.

The " Chinese question," as already remarked, is now far more than a national one. It is international. There is reason to think that in the twentieth century it will be an even more pressing question than at present. The problem of the means by which so vast a part of the human race may be improved cannot be without interest to any one who wishes well to mankind. If the conclusions to which we may find ourselves led are correct, they will be supported by a line of argument heretofore too much neglected. If these conclusions are wrong, they will, however supported, fall of themselves.

It is many years since Lord Elgin's reply to an address from the merchants of Shanghai, but his words are true and pertinent to-day. "When the barriers which prevent free access to the interior of the country shall have been removed, Christian civilisation of the West will find itself face to face not with barbarism, but with an ancient civilisation in many respects effete and imperfect, but in others not without claims to our sympathy and respect. In the rivalry which will then ensue, Christian civilisation will have to win its way among a sceptical and ingenious people, by making it manifest that a faith which reaches to heaven furnishes better guarantees for public and private morality than one which does not rise above the earth."

CHAPTER I.

FACE.

AT first sight nothing can be more irrational than to call that which is shared with the whole human race a "characteristic" of the Chinese. But the word "face" does not in China signify simply the front part of the head, but is literally a compound noun of multitude, with more meanings than we shall be able to describe, or perhaps to comprehend.

In order to understand, however imperfectly, what is meant by "face," we must take account of the fact that as a race the Chinese have a strongly dramatic instinct. The theatre may almost be said to be the only national amusement, and the Chinese have for theatricals a passion like that of the Englishman for athletics, or the Spaniard for bull-fights. Upon very slight provocation, any Chinese regards himself in the light of an actor in a drama. He throws himself into theatrical attitudes, performs the salaam, falls upon his knees, prostrates himself and strikes his head upon the earth, under circumstances which to an Occidental seem to make such actions superfluous, not to say ridiculous. A Chinese thinks in theatrical terms. When roused in self-defence he addresses two or three persons as if they were a multitude. He exclaims: "I say this in the presence of You, and You, and You, who are all here present." If his troubles are adjusted he speaks of himself as having "got off the stage" with credit, and if they are not adjusted he finds no way to "retire from the stage." All this, be it clearly understood, has nothing to do with realities.

The question is never of facts, but always of form. If a fine speech has been delivered at the proper time and in the proper way, the requirement of the play is met. We are not to go behind the scenes, for that would spoil all the plays in the world. Properly to execute acts like these in all the complex relations of life, is to have " face." To fail of them, to ignore them, to be thwarted in the performance of them, this is to " lose face." Once rightly apprehended, " face " will be found to be in itself a key to the combination lock of many of the most important characteristics of the Chinese.

It should be added that the principles which regulate "face" and its attainment are often wholly beyond the intellectual apprehension of the Occidental, who is constantly forgetting the theatrical element, and wandering off into the irrelevant regions of fact. To him it often seems that Chinese "face" is not unlike the South Sea Island taboo, a force of undeniable potency, but capricious, and not reducible to rule, deserving only to be abolished and replaced by common sense. At this point Chinese and Occidentals must agree to disagree, for they can never be brought to view the same things in the same light. In the adjustment of the incessant quarrels which distract every hamlet, it is necessary for the " peace-talkers " to take as careful account of the balance of " face " as European statesmen once did of the balance of power. The object in such cases is not the execution of even-handed justice, which, even if theoretically desirable, seldom occurs to an Oriental as a possibility, but such an arrangement as will distribute to all concerned " face " in due proportions. The same principle often obtains in the settlement of lawsuits, a very large percentage of which end in what may be called a drawn game.

To offer a person a handsome present is to " give him face." But if the gift be from an individual it should be accepted only in part, but should seldom or never be altogether refused. A few examples of the thirst for keeping face will suffice for illustration.   To be accused of a fault is to "lose face," and the fact must be denied, no matter what the evidence, in order to save face.   A tennis-ball is missed, and it is more than suspected that a coolie picked it up.   He indignantly denies it, but goes to the spot where the ball disappeared, and soon finds it lying there (dropped out of his sleeve), remarking, "Here is your 'lost' ball."   The waiting-woman who secreted the penknife of a guest in her master's house afterwards discovers it under the table-cloth, and ostentatiously produces it. In each case "face" is saved.   The servant who has carelessly lost an article which he knows he must replace or forfeit an equivalent from his wages, remarks loftily, as he takes his dismissal, "The money for that silver spoon I do not want," and thus his "face" is intact.   A man has a debt owing to him which he knows that he shall not collect; but going to the debtor, he raises a terrible disturbance, by which means he shows that he knows what ought to be done.   He does not get the money, but he saves his "face," and thus secures himself from imposition in the future.   A servant neglects or refuses to perform some duty.   Ascertaining that his master intends to turn him off, he repeats his former offence, dismisses himself, and saves his "face."

To save one's face and lose one's life would not seem to us very attractive, but we have heard of a Chinese District Magistrate who, as a special favour, was allowed to be beheaded in his robes of office in order to save his face!

CHAPTER II.

ECONOMY.

THE word "economy" signifies the rule by which the house should be ordered, especially with reference to the relation between expenditure and income. Economy, as we understand the term, may be displayed in three several ways: by limiting the number of wants, by preventing waste, and by the adjustment of forces in such a manner as to make a little represent a great deal. In each of these ways the Chinese are pre-eminently economical.

One of the first things which impress the traveller in China is the extremely simple diet of the people. The vast bulk of the population seems to depend upon a few articles, such as rice, beans in various preparations, millet, garden vegetables, and fish. These, with a few other things, form the staple of countless millions, supplemented it may be on the feast-days, or other special occasions, with a bit of meat.

Now that so much attention is given in Western lands to the contrivance of ways in which to furnish nourishing food to the very poor, at a minimum cost, it is not without interest to learn the undoubted fact that, in ordinary years, it is in China quite possible to furnish wholesome food in abundant quantity at a cost for each adult of not more than two cents a day. Even in famine times, thousands of persons have been kept alive for months on an allowance of not more than a cent and a half a day. This implies the general existence in

China of a high degree of skill in the preparation of food. Poor and coarse as their food often is, insipid and even repulsive as it not infrequently seems to the foreigner, it is impossible not to recognise the fact that, in the cooking and serving of what they have, the Chinese are past-masters of the culinary art. In this particular, Mr. Wingrove Cooke ranked them below the French, and above the English (and he might have added the Americans). Whether they are really below any one of these nationalities we are by no means so certain as Mr. Cooke may have been, but their superiority to some of them is beyond dispute. In the few simple articles which we have mentioned, it is evident that even from the point of view of the scientific physiologist, the Chinese have made a wise choice of their staple foods. The thoroughness of their mode of preparing food, and the great variety in which these few constituents are constantly presented, are known to all who have paid the least attention to Chinese cookery.

Another fact of extreme significance does not force itself upon our notice, but can easily be verified. There is very little waste in the preparation of Chinese food, and everything is made to do as much duty as possible. What there is left after an ordinary Chinese family have finished one of their meals would represent but a fraction of the net cost of the food. In illustration of this general fact, it is only necessary to glance at the physical condition of the Chinese dog or cat. On the leavings of human beings it is the unhappy function of these animals to "live," and their lives are uniformly protracted at "a poor dying rate." The populations of new countries are proverbially wasteful, and we have not the least doubt that it would be possible to support sixty millions of Asiatics in comparative luxury with the materials daily wasted in a land like the United States, where a living is easily to be had. But we should like to see how many human beings could be fattened from what there is left after as many Chinese have "eaten to repletion," and the servants or children have all had their turn at the remains! Even the tea left in the cups is poured back into the teapot to be heated again.

It is a fact which cannot fail to force itself upon our notice at every turn, that the Chinese are not as a race gifted with that extreme fastidiousness in regard to food which is frequently developed in Western lands. All is fish that comes to their net, and there is very little which does not come there first or last. In the northern parts of China the horse, the mule, the ox, and the donkey are in universal use, and in large districts the camel is made to do full duty. Doubtless it will appear to some of our readers that economy is carried too far, when we mention that it is the general practice to eat *all* of these animals as soon as they expire, no matter whether the cause of death be an accident, old age, or disease. This is done as a matter of course, and occasions no remark whatever, nor is the habit given up because the animal may chance to have died of some epidemic malady, such as the pleuro-pneumonia in cattle. Such meat is not considered so wholesome as that of animals which have died of other diseases, and this truth is recognised in the lower scale of prices asked for it, but it is all sold, and is all eaten. Certain disturbances of the human organisations into which such diseased meat has entered are well recognised by the people, but it is doubtless considered more economical to eat the meat at the reduced rates, and run the risk of the consequences, which, it should be said, are by no means constant. Dead dogs and cats are subject to the same processes of absorption as dead horses, mules, and donkeys. We have been personally cognisant of several cases in which villagers cooked and ate dogs which had been purposely poisoned by strychnine to get rid of them. On one of these occasions some one was thoughtful enough to consult a foreign physician as to the probable results, but as the animal was "already in the pot," the survivors could not make up their minds to forego the luxury of a feast, and no harm appeared to come of their indulgence!

Another example of Chinese economy in relation to the preparation of food is found in the nice adjustment of the material of the cooking-kettles to the exigencies of the requisite fuel. The latter is scarce and dear, and consists generally of nothing but the leaves, stalks, and roots of the crops, making a rapid blaze which quickly disappears. To meet the needs of the case the bottoms of the boilers are made as thin as possible, and require very careful handling. The whole business of collecting this indispensable fuel is an additional example of economy in an extreme form. Every smallest child, who can do nothing else, can at least gather fuel. The vast army of fuel-gatherers, which in the autumn and winter overspread all the land, leave not a weed behind the hungry teeth of their bamboo rakes. Boys are sent into the trees to beat off with clubs the autumnal leaves, as if they were chestnuts, and even straws are scarcely allowed leisure to show which way the wind blows, before some enterprising collector has " seized " them.

Every Chinese housewife knows how to make the most of her materials. Her dress is not in its pattern or its construction wasteful like those of her sisters in Occidental countries, but all is planned to save time, strength, and material. The tiniest scrap of foreign stuff is always welcome to a Chinese woman, who will make it reappear in forms of utility if not of beauty, of which a whole parliament of authoresses of " Domestic Economies " would never have dreamed. What cannot be employed in one place is sure to be just the thing for another, and a mere trifle of bias stuff is sufficient for the binding of a shoe. The benevolent person in London or New York who gives away the clothing for which he has no further use entertains a wild hope that it may not be the means of making the recipients paupers, and so do more harm than good. But whoever bestows similar articles upon the Chinese, though the stuffs which they use and the style of wear are so radically different from ours, has a well-grounded confidence that the usefulness of those particular articles has now at last begun, and will not be exhausted till there is nothing left of them for a base with which other materials can unite.

The Chinese often present their friends with complimentary inscriptions written on paper loosely *basted* upon a silk background. Basting is adopted instead of pasting, in order that the recipient may, if he chooses, eventually remove the inscription, when he will have a very serviceable piece of silk!

Chinese economy is exhibited in the transactions of retail merchants, to whom nothing is too small for attention. A dealer in odds and ends, for example, is able to give the precise number of matches in a box of each of the different kinds, and he knows to a fraction the profit on each box.

Every scrap of a Chinese account-book is liable to be utilised in pasting up windows, or in the covering of paper lanterns.

The Chinese constantly carry their economy to the point of depriving themselves of food of which they are really in need. They see nothing irrational in this, but do it as a matter of course. A good example is given in Dr. B. C. Henry's "The Cross and the Dragon." He was carried by three coolies for five hours a distance of twenty-three miles, his bearers then returning to Canton to get the breakfast which was furnished them. Forty-six miles before breakfast, with a heavy load half the way, to save five cents!

In another case two chair coolies had gone with a chair thirty-five miles, and were returning by boat, having had nothing to eat since 6 A.M., rather than pay three cents for two large bowls of rice. The boat ran aground, and did not reach Canton till 2 P.M. next day. Yet these men, having gone twenty-seven hours without food, carrying a load thirty-five miles, offered to take Dr. Henry fifteen miles more to Canton, and but for his baggage would have done so!

Many of the fruits of Chinese economy are not at all pleasing to the Westerners, but we cannot help admitting the genuine nature of the claim which may be built on them. In parts of the Empire, especially (strange to say) in the north, the children of both sexes roam around in the costume of the Garden of Eden, for many months of the year. This comes to be considered more comfortable for them, but the primary motive is economy. The stridulous squeak of the vast army of Chinese wheelbarrows is due to the absence of the few drops of oil which might stop it, but which never do stop it, because to those who are gifted with "an absence of nerves" the squeak is cheaper than the oil.

If a Japanese emigrates, it is specified in his contract that he is to be furnished daily with so many gallons of hot water, in which he may, according to custom, parboil himself. The Chinese have their bathing-houses too, but the greater part of the Chinese people never go near them, nor indeed ever saw one. "Do you wash your child every day?" said an inquisitive foreign lady to a Chinese mother, who was seen throwing shovelfuls of dust over her progeny, and then wiping it off with an old broom. "Wash him every day!" was the indignant response; "he was never washed since he was born!" To the Chinese generally, the motto could never be made even intelligible which was put in his window by a dealer in soap, "Cheaper than dirt."

The Chinese doubtless regard the average foreigner as it is said the Italians do the English, whom they term "soapwasters." Washing of clothes in China by and for the Chinese there certainly is, but it is on a very subdued scale, and in comparison with what we call cleanliness it might almost be left out of account. Economy of material has much to do with this, as we cannot help thinking, for many Chinese appreciate clean things as much as we do, and some of them are models of neatness, albeit under heavy disadvantages.

It is due to the instinct of economy that it is generally impossible to buy any tool ready-made. You get the parts in a "raw" shape, and adjust the handles, etc., yourselves. It is generally cheaper to do this for one's self than to have it done, and as every one takes this view of it, nothing is to be had ready-made.

We have spoken of economical adjustments of material, such as that found in ordinary houses, where a dim light, which costs next to nothing, is made to diffuse its darkness over two apartments by being placed in a hole in the dividing wall. The best examples of such adjustments are to be found in Chinese manufactures, such as the weaving of all kinds of fabrics, working in pottery, metal, ivory, etc. Industries of this sort do not seem to us to exemplify ingenuity so much as they illustrate Chinese economy. Many better ways can be devised of doing Chinese work than the ways which they adopt, but none which make insignificant materials go further than they do with the Chinese. They seem to be able to do almost everything by means of almost nothing, and this is a characteristic generally of their productions, whether simple or complex. It applies as well to their iron-foundries, on a minute scale of completeness in a small yard, as to a cooking-range of strong and perfect draft, made in an hour out of a pile of mud bricks, lasting indefinitely, operating perfectly, and costing nothing.

No better and more characteristic example of economy of materials in accomplishing great tasks could be found, even in China, than the arrangements, or rather the entire lack of arrangements, for the handling of the enormous amount of grain which is sent as tribute to Peking. This comes up the Peiho from Tientsin, and is discharged at T'ung-chou. It would surprise a "Corn Exchange" merchant to find that all

Doubtless this is more or less true of farming everywhere, but the Chinese farmer is industrious with an industry which it would be difficult to surpass.

That which is true of the farmer class, is true with still greater emphasis of the mere labourer, who is driven by the constant and chronic reappearance of the wolf at his door to spend his life in an everlasting grind. As the farmer bestows the most painstaking thought and care upon every separate stalk of cabbage, picking off carefully each minute insect, thus at last tiring out the ceaseless swarms by his own greater perseverance, so does the labourer watch for the most insignificant job, that he may have something for his stomach and for his back, and for other stomachs and backs that are wholly dependent upon him. Those who have occasion to travel where cart-roads exist, will often be obliged to rise soon after midnight and pursue their journey, for such, they are told, is the custom. But no matter at what hour one is on the way, there are small bodies of peasants patrolling the roads, with fork in hand and basket on their back, watching for opportunities to collect a little manure. When there is no other work pressing, this is an invariable and an inexhaustible resource.

It is by no means uncommon to see those who are hard pressed to find the means of support, following two different lines of occupation which dovetail into each other. Thus the boatmen of Tientsin, whose business is spoiled by the closing of the rivers, take to the swift ice-sled, by which means it is possible to be transported rapidly at a minimum cost. In the same way, most of the rural population of some districts spend all the time which can be spared from the exigencies of farm work in making hats or in plaiting the braid, now so large an article of export. Chinese women are not often seen without a shoe-sole in their hands on which they are perpetually taking stitches, even while talking gossip at the entrance of their

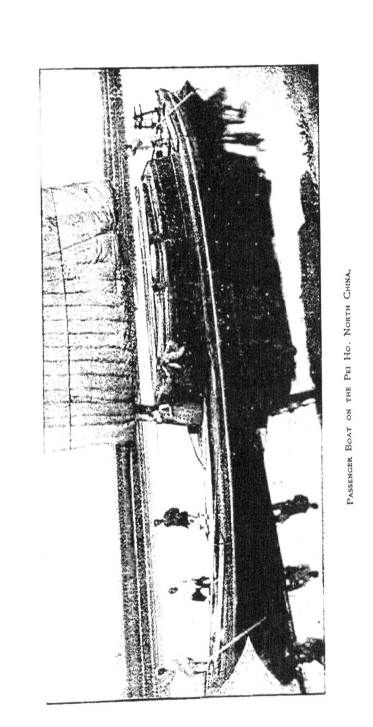

PASSENGER BOAT ON THE PEI HO. NORTH CHINA.

alleys ; or perhaps it is a reel of cotton which they are spinning. But idle they are not.

The indefatigable activity of the classes which have been named is well matched by that of the merchants and their employés. The life of a merchant's clerk, even in Western lands, is not that of one who holds a sinecure, but as compared with that of a Chinese clerk it is comparative idleness. For to the work of the latter there is no end. His holidays are few and his tasks heavy, though they may be interspersed with periods of comparative torpor.

Chinese shops are always opened early, and they close late. The system of bookkeeping by a species of double entry appears to be so minute that the accountants are often kept busy till a very late hour recording the sales and balancing the entries. When nothing else remains to be done, clerks can be set to sorting over the brass cash taken in, in quest of rare coins which may be sold at a profit.

It is a matter of surprise that the most hard-worked class of the Chinese race is that class which is most envied, and into which every ambitious Chinese strives to raise himself—to wit, the official. The number and variety of transactions with which a Chinese official of any rank must occupy himself, and for the success of which he is not only theoretically but very practically responsible, is likewise surprising. How would our Labour Unions, who are so strenuous about the coming Eight Hours a Day, relish a programme of a day's work such as the following, which is taken from a statement made to an interpreter in one of the Foreign Legations in Peking by an eminent Chinese statesman? " I once asked a member of the Chinese cabinet, who was complaining of fatigue and overwork, for an account of his daily routine. He replied that he left home every morning at two o'clock, as he was on duty at the Palace from three to six. As a member of the Privy Council, he was engaged in that body from six until nine.

From nine until eleven he was at the War Department, of which he was President. Being a member of the Board of Punishment, he was in attendance at the office of that body daily from twelve until two, and, as one of the senior Ministers of the Foreign Office, he spent every day, from two till five or six in the afternoon, there. These were his regular daily duties. In addition to them he was frequently appointed to serve on special boards or commissions, and these he sandwiched in between the others as he could. He seldom reached home before seven or eight o'clock in the evening." It is not strange to be told that this officer died six months after this conversation, from overwork and exhaustion, nor is it at all unlikely that the same state of things may put an end to many careers in China the continuance of which would have been valuable to the interests of the government.

The quality of extension, of which we have spoken, applies to the number of those who are industrious, but it also applies to the extent of time covered by that industry, which, as we have seen, is very great. The Chinese day begins at a dim period, often not at a great remove from midnight. The Emperor holds his daily audiences at an hour when every Court of Europe is wrapped in the embrace of Morpheus. To an Occidental this seems simply inexplicable, but to a Chinese it doubtless appears the most natural thing in the world. And the conduct of the Son of Heaven is imitated more or less closely by the subjects of the Son of Heaven, in all parts of his Empire. The copper workers of Canton, the tinfoil workers of Foochow, the wood-carvers of Ningpo, the rice-mill workers of Shanghai, the cotton-cleaners and workers in the treadmill for bolting flour in the northern provinces, may all be heard late at night, and at a preposterous hour in the morning. Long before daylight the traveller comes upon a countryman who has already reached a distance of many miles from his home, where he is posted in the darkness waiting for the coming of daylight, when he will begin the sale of his cabbages!

By the time an Occidental has had his breakfast, a Chinese market is nearly over. There are few more significant contrasts than are suggested by a stroll along the principal street in Shanghai, at the hour of half-past five on a summer's morning. The lordly European, who built those palaces which line the water-front, and who does his business therein, is conspicuous by his total absence, but the Asiatic is on hand in full force, and has been on hand for a long time. It will be hours before the Occidentals begin to jostle the Chinese from the sidewalks, and to enter with luxurious ease on their round of work, and by that time the native will have finished half his day's labour.

Sir John Davis was quite right in his comments on *the cheerful labour* of the Chinese, as a sign that their government has succeeded in securing them great content with their condition. This quality of their labour is one of its most striking characteristics, and to be comprehended must be long observed and well weighed.

It remains to say a word of the quality of *intension* in Chinese industry. The Chinese are Asiatics, and they work as such. It is in vain to attempt to make over this virile race on the model of our own. To us they certainly appear lacking in the heartiness which we esteem so highly. The Anglo-Saxon needs no scriptural hint to enable him to see the importance of doing with his might what his hand finds to do, but the Chinese cannot be made to change his pace, though the combined religions and philosophy of the ages were brought to bear upon him. He has profited by the accumulated experience of millenniums, and, like the gods of Homer, he is never in a hurry.

One cannot help forecasting a time when the white and the yellow races will come into a keener competition than any yet known. When that inevitable day shall have arrived, which of them will have to go to the wall?

Surely if Solomon was right in his economic maxim that

the hand of the diligent maketh rich, the Chinese ought to be among the most prosperous of the peoples of the earth. And so they doubtless would be, if there were with them a balance of virtues, instead of a conspicuous absence of some of those fundamental qualities which, however they may be enumerated as "constant virtues," are chiefly "constant" in their absence. When, by whatever means, these qualities of honesty and sincerity shall have been restored to their theoretical place in the Chinese moral consciousness, then (and not sooner) will the Chinese reap the full reward of their unmatched Industry.

CHAPTER IV.

POLITENESS.

THERE are two quite different aspects in which the politeness of the Chinese, and of Oriental peoples generally,
may be viewed—the one of appreciation, the other of criticism. The Anglo-Saxon, as we are fond of reminding ourselves, has, no doubt, many virtues, and among them is to be
found a very large percentage of *fortiter in re*, but a very small
percentage of *suaviter in modo*. When, therefore, we come to
the Orient, and find the vast populations of the immense Asiatic continent so greatly our superiors in the art of lubricating
the friction which is sure to arise in the intercourse of man
with man, we are filled with that admiration which is the tribute
of those who cannot do a thing to those who can do it easily
and well. The most bigoted critic of the Chinese is forced to
admit that they have brought the practice of politeness to a
pitch of perfection which is not only unknown in Western
lands, but, previous to experience, is unthought of and almost
unimaginable.

The rules of ceremony, we are reminded in the Classics, are
three hundred, and the rules of behaviour three thousand.
Under such a load as this, it would seem unreasonable to hope
for the continuance of a race of human beings, but we very
soon discover that the Chinese have contrived to make their
ceremonies, as they have made their education, an instinct
rather than an acquirement. The genius of this people has
made the punctilio, which in Occidental lands is relegated to

but denote as well all the time covered by the twelfth part of a day which each of them connotes. In this way the term "noon," which would seem as definite as any, is employed of the entire period from eleven to one o'clock. "What time is it," a Chinese inquired in our hearing, "when it is noon by the moon?" Phrased in less ambiguous language, the question which he intended to propound was this: "What is the time of night when the moon is at the meridian?"

Similar uncertainties pervade almost all the notes of time which occur in the language of everyday life. "Sunrise" and "sunset" are as exact as anything in Chinese can be expected to be, though used with much latitude (and much longitude as well), but "midnight," like "noon," means nothing in particular, and the ordinary division of the night by "watches" is equally vague, with the exception of the last one, which is often associated with the appearance of daylight. Even in the cities the "watches" are of more or less uncertain duration. Of the portable time-pieces which we designate by this name, the Chinese as a people know nothing, and few of those who really own watches govern their movements by them, even if they have the watches cleaned once every few years and ordinarily keep them running, which is not often the case. The common people are quite content to tell their time by the altitude of the sun, which is variously described as one, two, or more "flagstaffs," or if the day is cloudy a general result can be arrived at by observing the contraction and dilatation of the pupil of a cat's eye, and such a result is quite accurate enough for all ordinary purposes.

The Chinese use of time corresponds to the exactness of their measures of its flight. According to the distinction described by Sydney Smith, the world is divided into two classes of persons, the antediluvians and the post-diluvians. Among the latter the discovery has been made that the age of man no longer runs into the centuries which verge on a millennium, and accordingly they study compression, and adaptation to their environment. The antediluvians, on the contrary, cannot be made to realise that the days of Methusaleh have gone by, and they continue to act as if life were still laid out on the patriarchal plan.

Among these "antediluvians" the Chinese are to be reckoned. A good Chinese story-teller, such as are employed in the tea-shops to attract and retain customers, reminds one of Tennyson's "Brook." Men may come and men may go, but *he* goes on "forever ever." The same is true of theatrical exhibitions, which sometimes last for days, though they fade into insignificance in comparison with those of Siam, where we are assured by those who claim to have survived one of them that they are known to hold for two months together! The feats of Chinese jugglers when well done are exceedingly clever and very amusing, but they have one fatal defect—they are so long drawn out by the prolix and inane conversation of the participants, that long before the jugglers finish, the foreign spectator will have regretted that he ever weakly consented to patronise them. Not less formidable, but rather far more so, are the interminable Chinese feasts, with their almost incredible number and variety of courses, the terror and despair of all foreigners who have experienced them, although to the Chinese these entertainments seem but too short. One of their most pensive sayings observes that "there is no feast in the world which must not break up at last," though to the unhappy barbarian lured into one of these traps this hopeful generality is often lost in despair of the particular.

From his earliest years, the Chinese is thoroughly accustomed to doing everything on the antediluvian plan. When he goes to school, he generally goes for the day, extending to all the period from sunrise to dark, with one or two intermissions for food. Of any other system, neither pupils nor master have ever heard. The examinations for degrees are protracted through several days and nights, with all grades of severity, and while most of the candidates experience much inconvenience from such an irrational course, it would be difficult to convince any of them of its inherent absurdity as a test of intellectual attainments.

The products of the minds of those thus educated are redolent of the processes through which they have passed. The Chinese language itself is essentially antediluvian, and to overtake it requires the lifetime of a Methusaleh. It is as just to say of the ancient Chinese as of the ancient Romans, that if they had been obliged to learn their own language they would never have said or written anything worth setting down! Chinese histories are antediluvian, not merely in their attempts to go back to the ragged edge of zero for a point of departure, but in the interminable length of the sluggish and turbid current which bears on its bosom not only the mighty vegetation of past ages, but wood, hay, and stubble past all reckoning. None but a relatively timeless race could either compose or read such histories ; none but the Chinese memory could store them away in its capacious " abdomen."

Chinese disregard of time is manifested in their industry, the quality of intension in which we have already remarked to be very different from that in the work of Anglo-Saxons.

How many of those who have had the pleasure of building a house in China, with Chinese contractors and workmen, thirst to do it again? The men come late and go early. They are perpetually stopping to drink tea. They make long journeys to a distant lime-pit carrying a few quarts of liquid mud in a cloth bag, when by using a wheelbarrow one man could do the work of three ; but this result is by no means the one aimed at. If there is a slight rain all work is suspended. There is generally abundant motion with but little progress, so that it is often difficult to perceive what it is which represents the day's " labour " of a gang of men. We have known

CARPENTERS SAWING LARGE TIMBER.

a foreigner, dissatisfied with the slow progress of his carpenters in lathing, accomplish while they were eating their dinner as much work as all four of them had done in half a day. The mere task of keeping their tools in repair is for Chinese workmen a serious matter in expenditure of time. If the tools belong to the foreigner, however, there is no embarrassment on this score. They are broken mysteriously, and yet no one has touched them. *Non est inventus* is the appropriate motto for them all. Poles and small rafters are pitched over the wall, and all the neighbourhood loins appear to be girded with the rope which was purchased for supporting the staging. During the entire progress of the work, each day is a crisis. All previous experience goes for nothing. The sand, the lime, the earth of *this* place will not do for any of the uses for which sand, lime, and earth are in general supposed to be adapted. The foreigner is helpless. He is aptly represented by Gulliver held down by threads, which, taken together, are too much for him. Permanently have we enshrined in our memory a Cantonese contractor, whose promises, like his money, vanished in smoke, for he was unfortunately a victim of the opium pipe. At last, forbearance having ceased to be a virtue, he was confronted with a formidable bill of particulars of the things wherein he had come short. " You were told the size of the glass. You measured the windows three several times. Every one of those you have made is wrong, and they are useless. Not one of your doors is properly put together. There is not an ounce of glue about them. The flooring-boards are short in length, short in number, full of knot-holes, and wholly unseasoned." After the speaker had proceeded in this way for some time, the mild-mannered Cantonese gazed at him sadly, and when he brought himself to speak he remarked, in a tone of gentle remonstrance: " Don't say dat! Don't say dat! *No gentleman talk like dat !* "

To the Chinese the chronic impatience of the Anglo-Saxon

is not only unaccountable, but quite unreasonable. It has been wisely suggested that they consider this trait in our character as objectionable as we do their lack of sincerity.

In any case, appreciation of the importance of celerity and promptness is difficult to cultivate in a Chinese. We have known a bag full of foreign mail detained for some days between two cities twelve miles apart, because the carrier's donkey was ailing and needed rest! The administration of the Chinese telegraph system is frequently a mere travesty of what it might be and ought to be.

But in no circumstances is Chinese indifference to the lapse of time more annoying to a foreigner than when the occasion is a mere social call. Such calls in Western lands are recognised as having certain limits, beyond which they must not be protracted. In China, however, there are no limits. As long as the host does not offer his guest accommodations for the night, the guest must keep on talking, though he be expiring with fatigue. In calling on foreigners the Chinese can by no possibility realise that there is an element of time, which is precious. They will sit by the hour together, offering few or no observations of their own, and by no means offering to depart. The excellent pastor who had for his motto the saying, "The man who wants to see me is the man I want to see," would have modified this dictum materially had he lived for any length of time in China. After a certain experience of this sort, he would not improbably have followed the example of another busy clergyman, who hung conspicuously in his study the scriptural motto, "The Lord bless *thy goings out!*" The mere enunciation of his business often seems to cost a Chinese a mental wrench of a violent character. For a long time he says nothing, and he can endure this for a period of time sufficient to wear out the patience of ten Europeans. Then, when he begins to speak, he realises the truth of the adage which declares that "it is easy to go on the mountains to fight tigers, but to open your mouth and out with a thing—this is hard!" Happy is the foreigner situated like the late lamented Dr. Mackenzie, who, finding that his incessant relays of Chinese guests, the friends "who come but never go," were squandering the time which belonged to his hospital work, was wont to say to them, "Sit down and make yourselves at home; I have urgent business, and must be excused." And yet more happy would he be if he were able to imitate the naïve terseness of a student of Chinese who, having learned a few phrases, desired to experiment with them on the teacher, and who accordingly filled him with stupefaction by remarking at the end of a lesson, "Open the door! Go!"

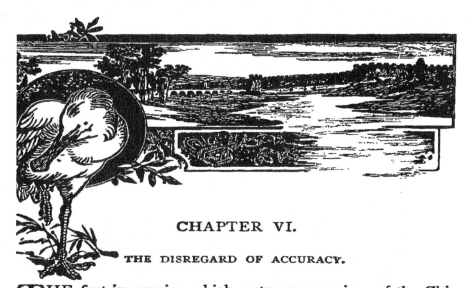

CHAPTER VI.

THE DISREGARD OF ACCURACY.

THE first impression which a stranger receives of the Chinese is that of uniformity. Their physiognomy appears to be all of one type, they all seem to be clad in one perpetual blue, the "hinges" of the national eye do not look as if they were "put on straight," and the resemblance between one Chinese cue and another is the likeness between a pair of peas from the same pod. But in a very brief experience the most unobservant traveller learns that, whatever else may be predicated of the Chinese, a dead level of uniformity cannot be safely assumed. The speech of any two districts, no matter how contiguous, varies in some interesting and perhaps unaccountable ways. Divergences of this sort accumulate until they are held to be tantamount to a new "dialect," and there are not wanting those who will gravely assure us that in China there are a great number of different "languages" spoken, albeit the written character is the same. The same variations, as we are often reminded, obtain in regard to customs, which, according to a saying current among the Chinese, do not run uniform for ten *li* together, a fact of which it is impossible not to witness singular instances at every turn. A like diversity is found to prevail in those standards of quantity upon the absolute invariability of which so much of the comfort of life in Western lands is found to depend.

The existence of a double standard of any kind, which is

often so keen an annoyance to an Occidental, is an equally keen joy to the Chinese. Two kinds of cash, two kinds of weights, two kinds of measures, these seem to him natural and normal, and by no means open to objection. A man who made meat dumplings for sale was asked how many of these dumplings were made in a day; to which he replied that they used about " one hundred [Chinese] pounds of flour," the un-known relation between this amount of flour and the number of resultant dumplings being judiciously left to the inquirer to conjecture for himself. In like manner, a farmer who is asked the weight of one of his oxen gives a figure which seems much too low, until he explains that he has omitted to estimate the bones! A servant who was asked his height mentioned a measure which was ridiculously inadequate to cover his length, and upon being questioned admitted that he had left out of account all above his shoulders! He had once been a soldier, where the height of the men's clavicle is important in assign-ing the carrying of burdens. And since a Chinese soldier is to all practical purposes complete without his head, this was omitted. Of a different sort was the measurement of a rustic who affirmed that he lived "ninety *li* from the city," but upon cross-examination he consented to an abatement, as this was reckoning both to the city and back, the real distance being, as he admitted, only "forty-five *li* one way!"

The most conspicuous instance of this variability in China is seen in the method of reckoning the brass cash, which con-stitute the only currency of the Empire. The system is every-where a decimal one, which is the easiest of all systems to be reckoned, but no one is ever sure, until he has made particular inquiries, what number of pieces of brass cash are expected in any particular place to pass for a hundred. He will not need to extend his travels over a very large part of the eighteen provinces to find that this number varies, and varies with a lawlessness that nothing can explain, from the full hundred which is the theoretical "string," to 99, 98, 96, 83 (as in the capital of Shansi), down to 33, as in the eastern part of the province of Chihli, and possibly to a still lower number' elsewhere.   The same is true, but in a more aggravated degree, of the weight by which silver is sold.   No two places have the same "ounce," unless by accident, and each place has a great variety of different ounces, to the extreme bewilderment of the stranger, the certain loss of all except those who deal in silver, and the endless vexation of all honest persons, of whom there are many, even in China.   The motive for the perpetuation of this monetary chaos is obvious, but we are at present concerned only with the fact of its existence.

The same holds true universally of measures of all sorts. The bushel of one place is not the same as that of any other, and the advantage which is constantly taken of this fact in the exactions connected with the grain tax would easily cause political disturbances among a less peaceable people than the Chinese.   So far is it from being true that "a pint is a pound the world around," in China a "pint" is not a pint, nor is a "pound" a pound.   Not only does the theoretical basis of each vary, but it is a very common practice (as in the salt monopoly, for example) to fix some purely arbitrary standard, such as twelve ounces, and call that a pound (catty).   The purchaser pays for sixteen ounces and receives but twelve, but then it is openly done and is done by all dealers within the same range, so that there is no fraud, and if the people think of it at all, it is only as an "old-time custom" of the salt trade.   A similar uncertainty prevails in the measurement of land.   In some districts the "acre" is half as large again as in others, and those who happen to live on the boundary are obliged to keep a double set of measuring apparatus, one for each kind of "acre."

It is never safe to repeat any statement (as travellers in China are constantly led to do) in regard to the price of each "catty" of grain or cotton, until one has first informed himself what kind of "catty" they have at that point. The same holds as to the amount of any crop yielded per "acre," statistics of which are not infrequently presented in ignorance of the vital fact that "acre" is not a fixed term. That a like state of things prevails as to the terms employed to measure distance, every traveller in China is ready to testify. It is always necessary in land travel to ascertain, when the distance is given in "miles" (*li*), whether the "miles" are "large" or not! That there is *some* basis for estimates of distances we do not deny, but what we do deny is that these estimates or measurements are either accurate or uniform. It is, so far as we know, a universal experience that the moment one leaves a great imperial highway the "miles" become "long." If 120 *li* constitute a fair day's journey on the main road, then on country roads it will take fully as long to go 100 *li*, and in the mountains the whole day will be spent in getting over 80 *li*. Besides this, the method of reckoning is frequently based, not on absolute distance, even in a Chinese sense, but on the relative difficulty of getting over the ground. Thus it will be "ninety *li*" to the top of a mountain the summit of which would not actually measure half that distance from the base, and this number will be stoutly held to, on the ground that it is as much trouble to go this "ninety *li*" as it would be to do that distance on level ground. Another somewhat peculiar fact emerges in regard to linear measurements, namely, that the distance from A to B is not necessarily the same as the distance from B to A! It is vain to cite Euclidian postulates that "quantities which are equal to the same quantity are equal to each other." In China this statement requires to be modified by the insertion of a negative. We could name a section of one of the most important highways in China, which from north to south is 183 *li* in length, while from south to north it is 190 *li*, and singularly enough, this holds true no matter how often you travel it or how carefully the tally is kept!*

Akin to this is another intellectual phenomenon, to wit, that in China it is not true that the "whole is equal to the sum of all its parts." This is especially the case in river travel. On inquiry you ascertain that it is "forty *li*" to a point ahead. Upon more careful analysis, this "forty" turns out to be composed of two "eighteens," and you are struck dumb with the statement that "four nines are forty, are they not ?" In the

---

* Since this was written, we have met in Mr. Baber's "Travels in Western China" with a confirmation of the view here taken. "We heard, for instance, with incredulous ears, that the distance between two places depended upon which end one started from; and all the informants, separately questioned, would give the same differential estimate. Thus from A to B would be unanimously called one mile, while from B to A would, with equal unanimity, be set down as three. An explanation of this offered by an intelligent native was this : Carriage is paid on a basis of so many cash per mile, it is evident that a coolie ought to be paid at a higher rate if the road is uphill. Now it would be very troublesome to adjust a scale of wages rising with the gradients of the road. It is much more convenient for all parties to assume that the road in difficult or precipitous places is longer. This is what has been done, and these conventional distances are now all that the traveller will succeed in ascertaining. ' But,' I protested, ' on the same principle, wet weather must elongate the road, and it must be farther by night than by day.' ' Very true, but a little extra payment adjusts that.' This system may be convenient for the natives, but the traveller finds it a continual annoyance. The scale of distances is something like this : On level ground, one statute mile is called two *li* ; on ordinary hill roads, not very steep, one mile is called five *li* ; on very steep roads, one mile is called fifteen *li*. The natives of Yunnan, being good mountaineers, have a tendency to underrate the distance on level ground, but there is so little of it in their country, that the future traveller need scarcely trouble himself with the consideration. It will be sufficient to assume five local *li*, except in very steep places, as being one mile."

In Mr. Little's "Through the Yang-tse Gorges," he mentions a stage which down the river was called ninety *li*, while up-stream it was 120 *li*. He estimates 3.62 *li* to a statute mile, or 250 to a degree of latitude.

same manner, "three eighteens" make "sixty," and so on generally. We have heard of a case in which an imperial courier failed to make a certain distance in the limits of time allowed by rule, and it was set up in his defence that the "sixty *li*" were "large." As this was a fair plea, the magistrate ordered the distance measured, when it was found that it was in reality "eighty-three *li*," and it has continued to be so reckoned ever since.

Several villages scattered about at distances from a city varying from one *li* to six, may each be called "The Three-Li Village." One often notices that a distance which would otherwise be reckoned as about a *li*, if there are houses on each side of the road, is called five *li*, and every person in that hamlet will gravely assure us that such is the real length of the street.

Under these circumstances, it cannot be a matter of surprise to find that the regulation of standards is a thing which each individual undertakes for himself. The steel-yard maker perambulates the street, and puts in the little dots (called "stars") according to the preferences of each customer, who will have not less than two sets of balances, one for buying and one for selling. A ready-made balance, unless it might be an old one, is not to be had, for the whole scale of standards is in a fluid condition, to be solidified only by each successive purchaser.

The same general truth is illustrated by the statements in regard to age, particularity in which is a national trait of the Chinese. While it is easy to ascertain one's age with exactness, by the animal governing the year in which he was born, and to which he therefore "belongs," nothing is more common than to hear the wildest approximation to exactness. An old man is "seventy or eighty years of age," when you know to a certainty that he was seventy only a year ago. The fact is, that in China a person becomes "eighty" the moment he stops being seventy, and this "general average" must be allowed for, if precision is desired. Even when a Chinese intends to be exact, it will often be found that he gives his age as it will be after the next New-Year's day—the national birthday in China. The habit of reckoning by "tens" is deepseated, and leads to much vagueness. A few people are "ten or twenty," a "few tens," or perhaps "ever so many tens," and a strictly accurate enumeration is one of the rarest of experiences in China. The same vagueness extends upwards to "hundreds," "thousands," and "myriads," the practical limit of Chinese counting. For greater accuracy than these general expressions denote, the Chinese do not care.

An acquaintance told the writer that two men had spent "200 strings of cash" on a theatrical exhibition, adding a moment later, "It was 173 strings, but that is the same as 200 —is it not?"

Upon their departure for the home land, a gentleman and his wife who had lived for several years in China, were presented by their Chinese friends with two handsome scrolls, intended not for themselves but for their aged mothers—the only surviving parents—who happened to be of exactly the same age. One of the inscriptions referred to "Happiness, great as the sea," and to "Old age, green as the perpetual pines," with an allusion in smaller characters at the side to the fact that the recipient had attained "seven decades of felicity." The other scroll contained flowery language of a similar character, but the small characters by the side complimented the lady on having enjoyed "six decades of glory." After duly admiring the scrolls, one of the persons whose mother was thus honoured, ventured to inquire of the principal actor in the presentation, why, considering the known parity of ages of the two mothers, one was assigned seventy years, and the other only sixty. The thoroughly characteristic reply was given, that to indite upon each of two such scrolls the identi-

Chinese Performers in Stage Dress.

cal legend, "seven decades," would look as if the writers were entirely destitute of originality !

Chinese social solidarity is often fatal to what we mean by accuracy. A man who wished advice in a lawsuit told the writer that he himself "lived" in a particular village, though it was obvious from his narrative that his abode was in the suburbs of a city. Upon inquiry, he admitted that he did not *now* live in the village, and further investigation revealed the fact that the removal took place nineteen generations ago ! "But do you not almost consider yourself a resident of the city now ? " he was asked. "Yes," he replied simply, "we do live there now, but the old root is in that village !"

Another individual called the writer's attention to an ancient temple in his own native village, and remarked proudly, "*I* built that temple." Upon pursuing the subject, it appeared that the edifice dated from a reign in the Ming Dynasty, more than three hundred years ago, when " I " only existed in the potential mood.

One of the initial stumbling-blocks of the student of Chinese is to find a satisfactory expression for identity, as distinguished from resemblance. The whole Chinese system of thinking is based on a line of assumptions different from those to which we are accustomed, and they can ill comprehend the mania which seems to possess the Occidental to ascertain everything with unerring exactness. The Chinese does not know how many families there are in his native village, and he does not wish to know. What any human being can want to know this number for is to him an insoluble riddle. It is " a few hundreds," " several hundreds," or " not a few," but a fixed and definite number it never was and never will be.

The same lack of precision which characterises the Chinese use of numbers, is equally conspicuous in their employment of written and even of printed characters. It is not easy to procure a cheap copy of any Chinese book which does not abound in false characters. Sometimes the character which is employed is more complex than the one which should have been used, showing that the error was not due to a wish to economise work, but it is rather to be credited to the fact that ordinarily accuracy is considered as of no importance. A like carelessness of notation is met with in far greater abundance in common letters, a character being often represented by another of the same sound, the mistake being due as much to illiteracy as to carelessness.

Indifference to precision is nowhere more flagrantly manifested than in the superscription of epistles. An ordinary Chinese letter is addressed in bold characters, to " My Father Great Man," " Compassionate Mother Great Man," " Ancestral Uncle Great Man," " Virtuous Younger Brother Great Man," etc., etc., generally with no hint as to the *name* of the " Great Man " addressed.

It certainly appears singular that an eminently practical people like the Chinese should be so inexact in regard to their own personal names as observation indicates them to be. It is very common to find these names written now with one character and again with another, and either one, we are informed, will answer. But this is not so confusing as the fact that the same man often has several different names, his family name, his "style," and, strange to say, a wholly different one, used only on registering for admission to literary examinations. It is for this reason not uncommon for a foreigner to mistake one Chinese for two or three. The names of villages are not less uncertain, sometimes appearing in two or even three entirely different forms, and no one of them is admitted to be more "right" than another. If one should be an acknowledged corruption of another, they may be employed interchangeably, or the correct name may be used in official papers and the other in ordinary speech, or yet again, the corruption may be used as an adjective, forming with the original appellation a compound title.

The Chinese are unfortunately deficient in the education which comes from a more or less intimate aquaintance with chemical formulæ, where the minutest precision is fatally necessary. The first generation of Chinese chemists will probably lose many of its number as a result of the process of mixing a "few tens of grains" of something with "several tens of grains" of something else, the consequence being an unanticipated earthquake. The Chinese are as capable of learning minute accuracy in all things as any nation ever was—nay, more so, for they are endowed with infinite patience—but what we have to remark of this people is that, as at present constituted, they are free from the quality of accuracy and that they do not understand what it is. If this is a true statement, two inferences would seem to be legitimate. First, much allowance must be made for this trait in our examination of Chinese historical records. We can readily deceive ourselves by taking Chinese statements of numbers and of quantities to be what they were never intended to be—exact. Secondly, a wide margin must be left for all varieties of what is dignified with the title of a Chinese "census." The whole is not greater than its parts, Chinese enumeration to the contrary notwithstanding. When we have well considered all the bearings of a Chinese "census," we shall be quite ready to say of it, as was remarked of the United States Supreme Court by a canny Scotchman who had a strong realisation of the "glorious uncertainty of the law," that it has "the last guess at the case!"

CHAPTER VII.

THIS remarkable gift of the Chinese people is first observed when the foreigner knows enough of the language to employ it as a vehicle of thought. To his pained surprise, he finds that he is not understood. He therefore returns to his studies with augmented diligence, and at the end of a series of years is able to venture with confidence to accost the general public, or any individual thereof, on miscellaneous topics. If the person addressed is a total stranger, especially if he has never before met a foreigner, the speaker will have opportunity for the same pained surprise as when he made his maiden speech in this tongue. The auditor evidently does not understand. He as evidently does not expect to understand. He visibly pays no attention to what is said, makes no effort whatever to follow it, but simply interrupts you to observe, "When you speak, we do not understand." He has a smile of superiority, as of one contemplating the struggles of a deaf-mute to utter articulate speech, and as if he would say, "Who supposed that you could be understood? It may be your misfortune and not your fault that you were not born with a Chinese tongue, but you should bear your disabilities, and not worry us with them, for when you speak we do not understand you." It is impossible to retain at all times an unruffled serenity in situations like this, and it is natural to turn fiercely on your adversary, and inquire, "Do you understand what I

58

am saying at this moment ? " " No," he replies, " I do not understand you! "

Another stage in the experience of Chinese powers of misunderstanding is reached when, although the words are distinctly enough apprehended, through a disregard of details the thought is obscured even if not wholly lost. The " Foreigner in Far Cathay " needs to lay in a copious stock of phrases which shall mean, " on this condition," " conditionally," " with this understanding," etc., etc. It is true that there do not appear to be any such phrases, nor any occasion for them felt by the Chinese, but with the foreigner it is different. The same is true in regard to the notation of tenses. The Chinese do not care for them, but the foreigner is compelled to care for them.

Of all subjects of human interest in China, the one which most needs to be guarded against misunderstanding is *money.* If the foreigner is paying out this commodity (which often appears to be the principal function of the foreigner as seen from the Chinese standpoint) a future-perfect tense is " a military necessity." " When you shall have done your work, you will receive your money." But there is no future-perfect tense in Chinese, or tense of any description. A Chinese simply says, " Do work, get money," the last being the principal idea which dwells in his mind, the " time relation " being absent. Hence when he is to do anything for a foreigner he wishes his money at once, in order that he may " eat," the presumption being that if he had not stumbled on the job of this foreigner he would never have eaten any more! Eternal vigilance, we must repeat, is the price at which immunity from misunderstandings about money is to be purchased in China. Who is and who is not to receive it, at what times, in what amounts whether in silver ingots or brass cash, what quality and weight of the former, what number of the latter shall pass as a " string "—these and other like points are those in regard to which it is morally impossible to have a too definite and fixed understanding. If the matter be a contract in which a builder, a compradore, or a boatman is to do on his part certain things and furnish certain articles, no amount of preliminary precision and exactness in explanations will come amiss.

To "cut off one's nose to spite one's face" is in China a proceeding too common to attract the least attention. A boatman or a carter who is engaged to go wherever the foreigner who hires his boat may direct, sometimes positively refuses to fulfil his contract. The inflexible obstinacy of a Chinese carter on such occasions is aptly illustrated by the behaviour of one of his mules, which, on coming to a particularly dusty place in the road, lies down with great deliberation to its dust-bath. The carter meantime lashes the mule with his whip to the utmost limit of his strength, but in vain. The mule is as indifferent as if a fly were tickling it. In considering the phenomena to which this is analogous, we have been frequently reminded of the caustic comments of De Quincey, in which, with a far too sweeping generalisation, he affirms that the Chinese race is endued with "an obstinacy like that of mules." The Chinese are not obstinate like mules, for the mule does not change his mood, while the same obstreperous carter who defies his employer in the middle of his journey, though expressly warned that his " wine-money " will be wholly withheld should he persist, is at the end of the journey ready to spend half a day in pleading and in prostrations for the favour which at a distance he treated with contemptuous scorn. That a traveller should have a written agreement with his carters, boatmen, etc., is a matter of ordinary prudence. No loophole for a possible misconstruction must be left open.

" Plain at first, afterwards no dispute " is the prudent aphorism of the Chinese. Yet the chances are that, after exhausting one's ingenuity in preliminary agreements, some occasion for misunderstanding will arise. And whatever be his care on

A Peking Cart.

this point, money will probably make the foreigner in China more trouble than any other single cause. Whether the Chinese concerned happen to be educated scholars or ignorant coolies, makes little difference. All Chinese are gifted with an instinct for taking advantage of misunderstandings. They find them as a January north wind finds a crack in a door, as the water finds a leak in a ship, instantly and without apparent effort. The Anglo-Saxon race is in some respects singularly adapted to develop this Chinese gift. As the ancient Persians were taught principally the two arts of drawing the long bow and speaking the truth, so the Anglo-Saxon is soon perceived by the Chinese to have a talent for veracity and doing justice as well towards enemies as towards friends. To the Chinese these qualities seem as singular as the Jewish habit of suspending all military operations every seventh day, no matter how hard-pressed they might be, must have appeared to the Romans under Titus, and the one eccentricity proves as useful to the Chinese as the other did to the Romans.

Foreign intercourse with China for the century preceding 1860 was one long illustration of the Chinese talent for misunderstanding, and the succeeding years have by no means exhausted that talent. The history of foreign diplomacy with China is largely a history of attempted explanations of matters which have been deliberately misunderstood. But in these or in other cases, the initial conviction that a foreigner will do as he has promised is deeply rooted in the Chinese mind, and flourishes in spite of whatever isolated exceptions to the rule are forced upon observation. The confidence, too, that a foreigner will act justly (also in spite of some private and many national examples to the contrary) is equally firm. But given these two fixed points, the Chinese have a fulcrum from which they may hope to move the most obstinate foreigner. " You said thus and thus." " No, I did not say so." " But I understood you to say so. We all understood you to say so.

Please excuse our stupidity, and please pay the money, as you said you would." Such is the substance of thousands of arguments between Chinese and foreigners, and in ninety-seven cases out of a hundred the foreigner pays the money, just as the Chinese knew he would, in order to seem strictly truthful as well as strictly just. In the remaining three cases some other means must be devised to accomplish the result, and of these three two will succeed.

Examples of the everyday misunderstanding on all subjects will suggest themselves in shoals to the experienced reader, for their name is legion. The coolie is told to pull up the weeds in your yard, but to spare the precious tufts of grass just beginning to sprout, and in which you see visions of a longed-for turf. The careless buffalo takes a hoe and chops up every green thing he meets, making a wilderness and calling it peace. He did not "understand" you. The cook was sent a long distance to the only available market, with instructions to buy a carp and a young fowl. He returns with no fish, and three tough geese, which were what he thought you ordered. He did not "understand" you. The messenger that was sent just before the closing of the mail with an important packet of letters to the French Consulate returns with the information that the letters could not be received. He has taken them to the Belgian Consulate, and the mail has closed. He did not "understand" you.

How easy it is for the poor foreigner both to misunderstand and to be misunderstood is well illustrated in the experience of a friend of the writer, who visited a Chinese bank with the proprietors of which he was on good terms, and in the neighbourhood of which there had recently been a destructive conflagration. The foreigner congratulated the banker that the fire had not come any nearer to his establishment. On this the person addressed grew at once embarrassed and then angry, exclaiming: "What sort of talk is this? This is not a

proper kind of talk!" It was not till some time afterwards
that the discovery was made that the point of the offence
against good manners lay in the implied hint that if the fire
had come too near it might have burned the cash-shop, which
would have been most unlucky, and the very contemplation of
which, albeit in congratulatory language, was therefore taboo!
A foreigner who was spending a short time in the capital met
a drove of camels, among which was a baby camel. Turning
to the driver of the cart, who had been for many years in the
employ of foreigners, he said: "When you come back to the
house, tell my little boy to come out and look at this little
camel, as he has never seen one, and it will amuse him very
much." After a considerable lapse of time, during which, as
in the last case, the idea was undergoing slow fermentation,
the carter replied thoughtfully: "If you should *buy* the camel,
you could not *raise* it—it would be sure to die!"

The writer was once present at a service in Chinese, when
the speaker treated the subject of the cure of Naaman. He
pictured the scene as the great Syrian general arrived at the
door of Elisha's house, and represented the attendants striv-
ing to gain admittance for their master. Struggling to make
this as pictorial as possible, the speaker cried out dramatically,
on behalf of the Syrian servants, "Gatekeeper, open the door;
the Syrian general has come!" To the speaker's surprise a
man in the rear seat disappeared at this point as if he had
been shot out, and it subsequently appeared that this person
had laboured under a misunderstanding. He was the gatekeeper of the premises, and oblivious of what had gone before,
on hearing himself suddenly accosted he had rushed out with
commendable promptness to let in Naaman!

Not less erroneous were the impressions of another auditor
of a missionary in one of the central provinces, who wished to
produce a profound impression upon his audience by showing
with the stereopticon a highly magnified representation of a

very common parasite. As the gigantic body of this reptile, much resembling an Egyptian crocodile, was thrown athwart the canvas, one of the spectators present was heard to announce in an awed whisper the newly gained idea, " See, this is the great Foreign Louse!"

CHAPTER VIII.

THE TALENT FOR INDIRECTION.

ONE of the intellectual habits upon which we Anglo-Saxons pride ourselves most is that of going directly to the marrow of a subject, and when we have reached it saying exactly what we mean. Considerable abatements must no doubt be made in any claim set up for such a habit, when we consider the usages of polite society and those of diplomacy, yet it still remains substantially true that the instinct of recti-linearity is the governing one, albeit considerably modified by special circumstances. No very long acquaintance is required with any Asiatic race, however, to satisfy us that their instincts and ours are by no means the same—in fact, that they are at opposite poles. We shall lay no stress upon the redundancy of honorific terms in all Asiatic languages, some of which in this respect are indefinitely more elaborate than the Chinese. Neither do we emphasise the use of circumlocutions, peri-phrases, and what may be termed aliases, to express ideas which are perfectly simple, but which no one wishes to express with simplicity. Thus a great variety of terms may be used in Chinese to indicate that a person has died, and not one of the expressions is guilty of the brutality of saying so ; nor does the periphrasis depend for its use upon the question whether the person to whom reference is made is an emperor or a coolie, however widely the terms employed may differ in the two cases. Nor are we at present concerned, except in a very general way, with the quality of veracity of language. When every one agrees to use words in "a Pickwickian sense," and every one understands that every one else is doing so, the questions resulting are not those of veracity but of method.

No extended experience of the Chinese is required to enable a foreigner to arrive at the conclusion that it is impossible, from merely hearing what a Chinese says, to tell what he means. This continues to be true, no matter how proficient one may have become in the colloquial—so that he perhaps understands every phrase, and might possibly, if worst came to worst, write down every character which he has heard in a given sentence; and yet he might be unable to decide exactly what the speaker had in mind. The reason of this must of course be that the speaker did not express what he had in mind, but something else more or less cognate to it, from which he wished his meaning or a part of it to be inferred.

Next to a competent knowledge of the Chinese language, large powers of inference are essential to any one who is to deal successfully with the Chinese, and whatever his powers in this direction may be, in many instances he will still go astray, because these powers were not equal to what was required of them. In illustration of this all-pervading phenomenon of Chinese life, let us take as an illustration a case often occurring among those who are the earliest, and often by no means the least important, representatives to us of the whole nation —our servants. One morning the "Boy" puts in an appearance with his usual expressionless visage, merely to mention that one of his "aunts" is ailing, and that he shall be obliged to forego the privilege of doing our work for a few days while he is absent prosecuting his inquiries as to her condition. Now it does not with certainty follow from such a request as this that the "Boy" has no aunt, that she is not sick, and that he has not some more or less remote idea of going to see about her, but it is, to put it mildly, much more probable that the "Boy" and the cook have had some misunderstanding, and that as the prestige of the latter happened in this case to be the greater of the two, his rival takes this oblique method of intimating that he recognises the facts of the case, and retires to give place to another.

The individual who has done you a favour, for which it was impossible to arrange at the time a money payment, politely but firmly declines the gratuity which you think it right to send him in token of your obligation. What he says is that it would violate all the Five Constant Virtues for him to accept anything of you for such an insignificant service, and that you wrong him by offering it, and would disgrace him by insisting on his acceptance of it. What does this mean? It means that his hopes of what you would give him were blighted by the smallness of the amount, and that, like Oliver Twist, he "wants more." And yet it may not mean this after all, but may be an intimation that you do now, or will at some future time, have it in your power to give him something which will be even more desirable, to the acquisition of which the present payment would be a bar, so that he prefers to leave it an open question till such time as his own best move is obvious.

If the Chinese are thus guarded when they speak of their own interests, it follows from the universal dread of giving offence that they will be more cautious about speaking of others, when there is a possibility of trouble arising in consequence. Fond as they are of gossip and all kinds of small-talk, the Chinese distinguish with a ready intuition cases in which it will not do to be too communicative, and under these circumstances, especially where foreigners are concerned, they are the grave of whatever they happen to know. In multitudes of instances the stolid-looking people by whom we are surrounded could give us "points," the possession of which would cause a considerable change in our conduct towards others. But unless they clearly see in what way they are to be benefited by the result, and protected against the risks, the instinct of reticence will prevail, and our friends will maintain an agnostic silence.

Nothing is more amusing than to watch the demeanour of a Chinese who has made up his mind that it is best for him to give an intimation of something unfavourable to some one else. Things must have gone very far indeed when, even under these conditions, the communication is made in plain and unmistakable terms. What is far more likely to occur is the indirect suggestion, by oblique and devious routes, of a something which cannot, which *must* not be told. Our informant glances uneasily about as though he feared a spy in ambush. He lowers his voice to a mysterious whisper. He holds up three fingers of one hand, to shadow dimly forth the notion that the person about whom he is not speaking, but gesturing, is the third in the family. He makes vague introductory remarks, leading up to a revelation of apparent importance, and just as he gets to the climax of the case he suddenly stops short, suppresses the predicate upon which everything depends, nods significantly, as much as to say, "*Now* you see it, do you not?" when all the while the poor unenlightened foreigner has seen nothing, except that there is nothing whatever to see. Nor will it be strange if, after working things up to this pitch, your " informant " (falsely so called) leaves you as much in the dark as he found you, intimating that at some other time you will perceive that he is right!

It is a trait which the Chinese share with the rest of the race, to wish to keep back bad news as long as possible, and to communicate it in a disguised shape. But " good form " among Chinese requires this deception to be carried to an extent which certainly seems to us at once surprising and futile. We have known a fond grandmother, having come unexpectedly upon the whispered consultation of two friends, who had arrived expressly to break to her the news of the sad death of a grandchild away from home, to be assured with the emphasis of iteration that they were only discussing a bit of gossip, though within half an hour the whole truth came out. We have known a son, returning to his home after an absence of several months, advised by a friend in the last village at which he called before reaching his home *not* to stay and see a theatrical exhibition, from which he inferred, and rightly, that his mother was dead! We once had a Chinese letter entrusted to us for transmission to a person at a great distance from home, the contents of the missive being to the effect that during his absence the man's wife had died suddenly, and that the neighbours, finding that no one was at hand to prevent it, had helped themselves to every article in the house, which was literally left unto him desolate. Yet on the exterior of this epistle were inscribed in huge characters the not too accurate words, " A peaceful family letter "!

The Chinese talent for indirection is often exhibited in refraining from the use of numerals where they might reasonably be expected. Thus the five volumes of a book will be labelled Benevolence, Justice, Propriety, Wisdom, Confidence, because this is the invariable order in which the Five Constant Virtues are named. The two score or more volumes of K'ang Hsi's Dictionary are often distinguished, not, as we should anticipate, by the radicals which indicate their contents, but by the twelve " time-cycle characters." At examinations students occupy cells designated by the thousand successive characters of the millenary classic, which has no duplicates.

Another illustration of this subject is found in the oblique terms in which references are made, both by members of her family and others, to married women. Such a woman literally has no name, but only two surnames, her husband's and that of her mother's family. She is spoken of as " the mother of so-and-so." Thus a Chinese with whom you are acquainted, talks of the illness of " the Little Black One his mother." Perhaps you never heard in any way that he had a " Little

Black One " in his household, but he takes it for granted that you must know it.   If, however, there are no children, then the matter is more embarrassing.   Perhaps the woman is called the "Aunt" of a "Little Black One," or by some other periphrasis.   Elderly married women have no hesitation in speaking of their " Outside," meaning the one who has the care of things out of the house ; but a young married woman not blessed with children is sometimes put to hard straits in the attempt to refer to her husband without intimating the connection in words.   Sometimes she calls him her " Teacher," and in one case of which we have heard she was driven to the desperate expedient of dubbing her husband by the name of his business—" Oilmill says thus and so! "

A celebrated Chinese general, on his way to the war, bowed low to some frogs in a marsh which he passed, wishing his soldiers to understand that valour like that of these reptiles is admirable.   To an average Occidental it might appear that this general demanded of his troop somewhat "large powers of inference," but not greater, perhaps, than will be called for by the foreigner whose lot is cast in China.   About the time of a Chinese New-Year when the annual debt-paying season had arrived, an acquaintance, upon meeting the writer, made certain gestures which seemed to have a deep significance. He pointed his finger at the sky, then at the ground, then at the person whom he was addressing, and last at himself, all without speaking a word.   There was certainly no excuse for misapprehending this proposition, though we are ashamed to say that we failed to take it in at its full value.   He thought that there would be no difficulty in one's inferring from his pantomime that he wished to borrow a little money, and that he wished to do it so secretly that only "Heaven," "Earth," "You," and " I " would know !   The phrase " eating [gluttony], drinking [of wine], lust, and gambling " denotes the four most common vices, to which is now added opium smoking.   A speaker

CHINESE CARD PLAYERS.

sometimes holds up the fingers of one hand and remarks, " He absorbed them all," meaning that some one was guilty in all these ways.

It is an example of the Chinese talent for indirection, that owing to their complex ceremonial code one is able to show great disrespect for another by methods which to us seem preposterously oblique. The manner of folding a letter, for example, may embody a studied affront. The omission to raise a Chinese character above the line of other characters may be a greater indignity than it would be in English to spell the name of a person without capital letters. In social intercourse rudeness may be offered without the utterance of a word to which exception could be taken, as by not meeting an entering guest at the proper point, or by neglecting to escort him the distance suited to his condition. The omission of any one of a multitude of simple acts may convey a thinly disguised insult, instantly recognised as such by a Chinese, though the poor untutored foreigner has been thus victimised times without number, and never even knew that he had not been treated with distinguished respect! All Chinese revile one another when angry, but those whose literary talents are adequate to the task delight to convey an abusive meaning by such delicate innuendo that the real meaning may for the time quite escape observation, requiring to be digested like the nauseous core of a sugar-coated pill. Thus, the phrase *tung-hsi*—literally " east-west "—means a thing, and to call a person " a thing " is abusive. But the same idea is conveyed by indirection, by saying that one is *not* " north-south," which implies that he *is* " east-west," that is, " a thing "!

Every one must have been struck by the wonderful fertility of even the most illiterate Chinese in the impromptu invention of plausible excuses, each one of which is in warp and woof fictitious. No one but a foreigner ever thinks of taking them seriously, or as any other than suitable devices by which to keep one's "face." And even the too critical foreigner requires no common ability to pursue, now in air, now in water, and now in the mud, those to whom most rigid economy of the truth has become a fixed habit. And when driven to close quarters, the most ignorant Chinese has one firm and sure defence which never fails, he can fall back on his ignorance in full assurance of escape. He "did not know," he "did not understand," twin propositions, which, like charity, cover a multitude of sins.

No more fruitful illustration of our theme could be found than that exhibited in the daily issues of the Peking *Gazette*. Nowhere is the habit of what, in classical language, is styled "pointing at a deer and calling it a horse" carried to a higher pitch, and conducted on a more generous scale. Nowhere is it more true, even in China, that "things are not what they seem," than in this marvellous lens, which, semi-opaque though it be, lets in more light on the real nature of the Chinese government than all other windows combined. If it is a general truth that a Chinese would be more likely than not to give some other than the real reason for anything, and that nothing requires more skill than to guess what is meant by what is said, this nowhere finds more perfect exemplification than in Chinese official life, where formality and artificiality are at their maximum. When a whole column of the "leading journal" of China is taken up with a description of the various aches and pains of some aged mandarin who hungers and thirsts to retire from His Majesty's service, what does it all mean? When his urgent prayer to be relieved is refused, and he is told to go back to his post at once, what does that mean? What do the long memorials reporting as to matters of fact really connote? When a high official accused of some flagrant crime is ascertained—as per memorial printed—to be innocent, but guilty of something else three shades less blameworthy, does it mean that the writer of the memorial was not influenced to a sufficient extent, or has the official in question really done those particular things ?   Who can decide ?

Firmly are we persuaded that the individual who can peruse a copy of the Peking *Gazette* and, while reading each document, can form an approximately correct notion as to what is really behind it, knows more of China than can be learned from all the works on this Empire that ever were written. But is there not reason to fear that by the time any outside barbarian shall have reached such a pitch of comprehension of China as this implies, we shall be as much at a loss to know what *he* meant by what *he* said, as if he were really Chinese?

CHAPTER IX.

THE first knowledge which we acquire of the Chinese is derived from our servants. Unconsciously to themselves, and not always to our satisfaction, they are our earliest teachers in the native character, and the lessons thus learned we often find it hard to forget. But in proportion as our experience of the Chinese becomes broad, we discover that the conclusions to which we had been insensibly impelled by our dealings with a very narrow circle of servants are strikingly confirmed by our wider knowledge, for there is a sense in which every Chinese may be said to be an epitome of the whole race. The particular characteristic with which we have now to deal, although not satisfactorily described by the paradoxical title which seems to come nearest to an adequate expression, can easily be made intelligible by a very slight description.

Of all the servants employed in a foreign establishment in China, there is no one who so entirely holds the peace of the household in the hollow of his hands, as the cook. His aspect is the personification of deference as he is told by his new mistress what are the methods which she wishes him to employ, and what methods she most emphatically does *not* wish employed. To all that is laid down as the rule of the establishment he assents with a cordiality which is prepossessing, not to say winning. He is, for example, expressly warned that the late cook had a disagreeable habit of putting the

74

bread into the oven before it was suitably raised, and that as this is one of the details on which a mistress feels bound to insist, he and his mistress parted. To this the candidate responds cheerfully, showing that whatever his other faults may be, obstinacy does not seem to be one of them. He is told that dogs, loafers, and smoking will not be tolerated in the kitchen; to which he replies that he hates dogs, has never learned to smoke, and being a comparative stranger, has but few friends in the city, and none of them are loafers. After these preliminaries his duties begin, and it is but a few days before it is discovered that this cook is a species of "blood brother" of the last one in the item of imperfectly risen bread, that there is an unaccountable number of persons coming to and departing from the kitchen, many of them accompanied by dogs, and that a not very faint odour of stale tobacco is one of the permanent assets of the establishment. The cook cordially admits that the bread is not quite equal to his best, but is sure that it is *not* due to imperfect kneading. He is particular on that point. The strangers seen in the kitchen are certain "yard brothers" of the coolie, but none of them had dogs, and they are all gone now and will not return— though they are seen again next day. Not one of the servants ever smokes, and the odour must have come over the wall from the establishment of a man whose servants are dreadful smokers. The cook is the personification of reasonableness, but as there is nothing to change he does not know how to change it.

The same state of things holds with the coolie who is set to cut the grass with a foreign sickle, bright and sharp. He receives it with a smile of approval, and is seen later in the day doing the work with a Chinese reaping-machine, which is a bit of old iron about four inches in length, fitted to a short handle. "The old," he seems to say, "is better." The washerman is provided with a foreign washing-machine, which economises time, soap, labour, and, most of all, the clothing to be washed. He is furnished with a patent wringer which requires no strength, and does not damage the fabrics. The washing-machine and the wringer are alike suffered to relapse into "innocuous desuetude," and the washerman continues to scrub and wrench the garments into holes and shreds as in former days. Eternal vigilance is the price at which innovations of this nature are to be defended.

The gardener is told to repair a decayed wall by using some adobe bricks which are already on hand, but he thinks it better to use the branches of trees buried a foot deep in the top of the wall, and accordingly does so, explaining, if he is questioned, the superiority of his method. The messenger who is employed to take an important mail to a place several days' journey distant, receives his packages late in the evening, that he may start the next morning by daylight. The next afternoon he is seen in a neighbouring alley, and on being sent for and asked what he means, he informs us that he was obliged to take a day and wash his stockings! It is the same experience with the carter whom you have hired by the day. He is told to go a particular route, to which, like all others in the cases supposed, he assents, and takes you by an entirely different one, because he has heard from some passing stranger that the other was not so good. Cooks, coolies, gardeners, carters—all agree in distrusting *our* judgment, and in placing supreme reliance upon their own.

Phenomena illustrating our subject are constantly observed wherever there is a foreign dispensary and hospital. The patient is examined carefully and prescribed for, receives his medicine in a specified number of doses, with directions thrice repeated to avoid mistakes, as to the manner in which and times at which it is to be taken. Lest he should forget the details, he returns once or twice to make sure, goes home and swallows the doses for two days at a gulp, because the excellence of the cure *must* be in the direct ratio of the dose. The most minute and emphatic cautions against disturbing a plaster jacket are not sufficient to prevent its summary removal, because the patient does not wish to become a "turtle," and have a hard shell grow to his skin.

It is not a very comforting reflection, but it is one which seems to be abundantly justified by observation, that the opinion of the most ignorant assistant in a dispensary seems (and therefore is) to the average patient as valuable as that of the physician in charge, though the former may not be able to read a character, does not know the name of a drug or the symptoms of any disease, and though the latter may have been decorated with all the letters in the alphabet of medical titles, and have had a generation of experience. Yet a hint from the gatekeeper or the coolie may be sufficient to secure the complete disregard of the directions of the physician, and the adoption of something certainly foolish, and possibly fatal.

Thus far, we have spoken of instances of inflexibility in which foreigners are concerned, for those are the ones to which our attention is soonest drawn, and which possess for us the most practical interest. But the more our observation is directed to the relations of the Chinese to one another, through which if anywhere their true dispositions are to be manifested, the more we perceive that the state of things indicated by the expressive Chinese phrase " Outwardly is, inwardly is not," is not exceptional. Chinese servants are yielding and complaisant to Chinese masters, as Chinese servants are to foreign masters, but they have no idea of not doing things in their own way, and it is not unlikely that their masters never for a moment suppose that their orders will be literally obeyed. A foreign employer requires his employés to do exactly as they are told, and because they do not do so he is in a state of chronic hostility to some of them. A friend of the writer who had one of that numerous class of servants who combine extreme faithfulness with extreme mulishness—thus making themselves an indispensably necessary nuisance—happily expressed a dilemma into which the masters of such servants are often brought, when he remarked that as regarded that particular "Boy," he was in a condition of chronic indecision, whether to kill him or to raise his wages! The Chinese master knows perfectly well that his commands will be ignored in various ways, but he anticipates this inevitable result as one might set aside a reserve for bad debts, or allow a margin for friction in mechanics.

The same greater or less disregard of orders appears to prevail through all the various ranks of Chinese officials in their relations to one another, up to the very topmost round. There are several motives any one of which may lead to the contravening of instructions, such as personal indolence, a wish to oblige friends, or, most potent of all, the magnetic influence of cash. A district magistrate who lived in a place where the water is brackish, ordered his servant to take a water-cart and draw water from a river several miles distant. The servant did nothing of the kind, but merely went to a village where he knew the water to be sweet, and provided the magistrate with as much as he wanted of this fluid, to the saving of two thirds the distance and to the entire satisfaction of all parties. If the magistrate had known to a certainty that he was disobeyed, it is not probable that he would have uttered a whisper on the subject so long as the water was good. In China "the cat that catches the rat is the good cat." Nothing succeeds like success. The dread of giving offence and the innate Chinese instinct of avoiding a disturbance would prevent misdemeanours of disobedience from being reported, though five hundred people might be in the secret. That was a typical Chinese servant who, having been told to empty the water from a cistern into something which would save it for future use, was found to have poured it all into a well! Thus he contrived to preserve the shell of conformity, with the most absolute negation of any practical result. Dr. Rennie mentions the case of an official at Amoy, who cut in two an Imperial proclamation, posting the last part first, so that it could not easily be read. Such devices are common in matters concerning foreigners, whom mandarins seldom wish to please.

It is easy to see how such a policy of evasion may come into collision with the demands of justice. The magistrate sentences a criminal to wear a heavy wooden collar for a period of two months, except at night, when it is to be removed. By the judicious expenditure of cash " where it will do the most good," this order is only so far carried out that the criminal is decorated with the cangue at such times as the magistrate is making his entrance to and his exit from the yamên. At all other times the criminal is quite free from the obnoxious burden. Does the magistrate not suspect that his sentence will be defeated by bribery, and will he slip out the back way in order to come upon the explicit proof of disobedience? By no means. The magistrate is himself a Chinese, and he knew when the sentence was fixed that it would not be regarded, and with this in mind he made the term twice as long as it might otherwise have been. This seems to be a sample of the intricacies of official intercourse in all departments, as exemplified by what foreigners continually observe. The higher officer orders the lower to see that a certain step is taken. The lower official reports respectfully that it has been done. Meanwhile nothing has been done at all. In many cases this is the end of the matter. But if there is a continued pressure from some quarter, and the orders are urgent, the lower magistrate transmits the pressure to those still lower, and throws the blame upon them, until the *momentum* of the pressure is exhausted, and then things go on just as they were before. This is called " reform," and is often seen on a great scale, as in the spasmodic suppression of the sale of opium, or of the cultivation of the poppy, with results which are known to all.

There are doubtless those to whom the Chinese seem the most "obstinate" of peoples, and to such the adjective "flexible," which we have employed to characterise the "inflexibility" of the Chinese, will appear singularly inappropriate. Nevertheless, we must repeat the conviction that the Chinese are far from being the most obstinate of peoples, and that they are in fact far less obstinate than the Anglo-Saxons. We call them "flexible" because, with a "firmness" like that of mules, they unite a capacity of bending of which the Anglo-Saxon is frequently destitute.

No better illustration of this talent of the Chinese for "flexibility" can be cited, than their ability to receive *gracefully* a reproof. Among the Anglo-Saxon race it is a lost art, or rather it is an art that was never discovered. But the Chinese listens patiently, attentively, even cordially, while you are exposing to him his own shortcomings, assents cheerfully, and adds, "I am in fault, I am in fault." Perhaps he even thanks you for your kindness to his unworthy self, and promises that the particulars which you have specified shall be immediately, thoroughly, permanently reformed. These fair promises you well know to be "flowers in the mirror, and the bright moon in the water," but despite their unsubstantial nature, it is impossible not to be mollified therewith, and this, be it noted, is the object for which they were designed.

Few comparisons of the sort hit the mark more exactly than that which likens the Chinese to the bamboo. It is graceful, it is everywhere useful, it is supple, and it is hollow. When the east wind blows it bends to the west. When the west wind blows it bends to the east. When no wind blows it does not bend at all. The bamboo plant is a grass. It is easy to tie knots in grasses. It is difficult, despite its suppleness, to tie knots in the bamboo plant. Nothing in nature is more flexible than a human hair. It can be drawn out a large percentage of its own length, and when the tractile force is withdrawn, it at once contracts. It bends in any direction by its own weight alone. There is a certain growth of hair on many human heads which consists of definite tufts, quite per-sistent in the direction of their growth, and generally incapa-ble of any modification. Such a growth is vulgarly called a "cow-lick," and as it cannot be controlled, the remaining hairs, however numerous they may be, must be arranged with reference thereto. If the planet on which we dwell be con-sidered as a head, and the several nations as the hair, the Chinese race is a venerable cow-lick, capable of being combed, clipped, and possibly shaved, but which is certain to grow again just as before, and the general direction of which is not likely to be changed.

CHAPTER X.

IN speaking of "intellectual turbidity" as a Chinese charac-teristic, we do not wish to be understood as affirming it to be a peculiarity of the Chinese, or that all Chinese possess it. Taken as a whole, the Chinese people seem abundantly able to hold their own with any race now extant, and they certainly exhibit no weakness of the intellectual powers, nor any tend-ency to such a weakness. At the same time it must be borne in mind that education in China is restricted to a very narrow circle, and that those who are but imperfectly educated, or who are not educated at all, enjoy in the structure of the Chi-nese language what is called by the lawyers an "accessory before the fact" to any most flagrant intellectual turbidity of which they may be disposed to be guilty.

Chinese nouns, as is by this time known to several, appear to be indeclinable. They are quite free from "gender" and "case." Chinese adjectives have no degrees of comparison. Chinese verbs are not hampered by any "voice," "mode," "tense," "number," or "person." There is no recognisable distinction between nouns, adjectives, and verbs, for any char-acter may be used indiscriminately in either capacity (or in-capacity), and no questions asked. We are not about to com-plain that the Chinese language cannot be made to convey human thought, nor that there are wide ranges of human thought which it is difficult or impossible to render intelligible in the Chinese language (though this appears to be a truth), but only to insist that such a language, so constructed, invites to "intellectual turbidity" as the incandescent heats of summer gently woo to afternoon repose.

Nothing is more common in conversation with an uneducated Chinese than to experience extreme difficulty in ascertaining what he is talking about. At times his remarks appear to consist exclusively of predicates, which are woven together in an intricate manner, the whole mass seeming, like Mohammed's coffin, to hang in the air, attached to nothing whatever. To the mind of the speaker, the omission of a nominative is a point of no consequence. *He* knows what he is talking about, and it never occurs to him that this somewhat important item of information is not conveyed to the mind of his auditor by any kind of intuition. It is remarkable what expert guessers long practice has made most Chinese, in reading a meaning into words which do not convey it, by the simple practice of supplying subjects or predicates as they happen to be lacking. It is often the most important word in the whole sentence which is suppressed, the clue to which may be entirely unknown. There is very frequently nothing in the form of the sentences, the manner of the speaker, his tone of voice, nor in any concomitant circumstance, to indicate that the subject has changed, and yet one suddenly discovers that the speaker is not now speaking of himself as he was a moment ago, but of his grandfather, who lived in the days of Tao Kuang. How the speaker got there, and also how he got back again, often remains an insoluble mystery, but we see the feat accomplished every day. To a Chinese there is nothing more remarkable in a sudden, invisible leap, without previous notice, from one topic, one person, one century to another, than in the ability of a man who is watching an insect on the windowpane to observe at the same time and without in the least deflecting his eyes, a herd of cattle situated in the same line of vision on a distant hill.

The fact that Chinese verbs have no tenses, and that there is nothing to mark transitions of time, or indeed of place, does not tend to clarify one's perceptions of the inherently turbid. Under such circumstances the best the poor foreigner can do, who wishes to keep up the appearance at least of following in the train of the vanished thought, is to begin a series of catechetical inquiries, like a frontier hunter " blazing " his way through a pathless forest with a hatchet. " Who was this person that you are talking about now? " This being ascertained, it is possible to proceed to inquire, "Where was this?" "When was it? " "What was it that this man did? " "What was it that they did about it? " " What happened then?" At each of these questions your Chinese friend gazes at you with a bewildered and perhaps an appealing look, as if in doubt whether you have not parted with all your five senses. But a persistent pursuit of this silken thread of categorical inquiry will make it the clue of Ariadne in delivering one from many a hopeless labyrinth.

To the uneducated Chinese any idea whatever comes as a surprise, for which it is by no means certain that he will not be totally unprepared. He does not understand, because he does not expect to understand, and it takes him an appreciable time to get such intellectual forces as he has into a position to be used at all. His mind is like a rusty old smooth-bore cannon mounted on a decrepit carriage, which requires much hauling about before it can be pointed at anything, and then it is sure to miss fire. Thus when a person is asked a simple question, such as " How old are you? " he gazes vacantly at the questioner, and asks in return, " I ? " To which you respond, " Yes, you." To this he replies with a summoning up of his mental energies for the shock, " How old? " " Yes, how old ? " Once more adjusting the focus, he inquires, " How old am I ? " " Yes," you say, "how old are you ? "

" Fifty-eight," he replies, with accuracy of aim, his piece being now in working order.

A prominent example of intellectual turbidity is the prevalent habit of announcing as a reason for a fact, the fact itself. " Why do you not put salt into bread-cakes ? " you ask of a Chinese cook. " We do not put salt into bread-cakes," is the explanation. " How is it that with so much and such beautiful ice in your city none of it is stored up for winter ? " " No, we do not store up ice for winter in our city." If the Latin poet who observed, " Happy is he who is able to know the reasons of things," had lived in China, he might have modified his dictum so as to read, " Unhappy is the man who essays to find out the reasons of things."

Another mark of intellectual torpor is the inability of an ordinary mind to entertain an idea, and then pass it on to another in its original shape. To tell A something which he is to tell B, in order that C may govern his actions thereby, is in China one of the most fatuous of undertakings. Either the message will never be delivered at all, because the parties concerned did not understand that it was of importance, or it reaches C in such a shape that he cannot comprehend it, or in a form totally at variance with its original. To suppose that three cogs in so complicated a piece of machinery are capable of playing into each other without such friction as to stop the works, is to entertain a very wild hope. Even minds of considerable intelligence find it hard to take in and then give out an idea without addition or diminution, just as clear water is certain to refract the image of a straight stick as if it were a broken one.

Illustrations of these peculiarities will meet the observant foreigner at every turn. " Why did he do so ? " you inquire in regard to some preposterous act. " Yes," is the compendious reply. There is a certain numeral word in constant use,

which is an aggravating accessory to vague replies. It signifies both interrogatively, " How many? " and affirmatively,
" Several." " How many days have you been here? " you
ask. " Yes, I have been here several days," is the reply. Of
all the ambiguous words in the Chinese language, probably
the most ambiguous is the personal (or impersonal) pronoun
t'a, which signifies promiscuously " he," "she," or " it." Sometimes the speaker designates the subject of his remarks by
vaguely waving his thumb in the direction of the subject's
home, or towards the point where he was last heard of. But
more frequently the single syllable *t'a* is considered wholly
sufficient as a relative, as a demonstrative pronoun, and as a
specifying adjective. Under these circumstances, the talk of
a Chinese will be like the testimony of a witness in an English
court, who described a fight in the following terms : " He'd a
stick, and he'd a stick, and he w'acked he, and he w'acked
he, and if he'd a w'acked he as hard as he w'acked he, he'd a
killed he, and not he he."

" Why did you not come when you were called? " you
venture to inquire of a particularly negligent servant. " Not
on account of any reason," he answers, with what appears to
be frank precision. The same state of mental confusion leads
to a great variety of acts, often embarrassing, and to a well-
ordered Occidental intellect always irritating. The cook
makes it a matter of routine practice to use up the last of
whatever there may be in his charge, and then serves the next
meal minus some invariable concomitant. When asked what
he means by it, he answers ingenuously that *there was no more.*
" Then why did you not ask for more in time? " " I did not
ask for any more," is his satisfactory explanation. The man
to whom you have paid a sum of cash in settlement of his
account, going to the trouble of unlocking your safe and
making change with scrupulous care, sits talking for " an old
half-day " on miscellaneous subjects, and then remarks with

nonchalance, " I have still another account besides this one."
" But why did you not tell me when I had the safe open, so
that I could do it all at once ? "   " Oh, I thought that account
and this one had nothing to do with each other! "   In the
same way a patient in a dispensary who has taken a liberal
allowance of the time of the physician, retires to the waiting-
room, and when the door is next opened advances to re-enter.
Upon being told that his case has been disposed of, he observes, with delightful simplicity, " But I have got another
different disease besides that one! "

An example of what seems to us immeasurable folly, is the
common Chinese habit of postponing the treatment of diseases because the patient happens to be busy, or because the
remedy would cost something.   It is often considered cheaper
to undergo severe and repeated attacks of intermittent fever,
than to pay ten cash—about one cent—for a dose of quinia,
morally certain to cure.   We have seen countless cases of the
gravest diseases sometimes nourished to the point where they
became fatal simply to save time, when they might have been
cured gratuitously.

A man living about half a mile from a foreign hospital,
while away from home contracted some eye trouble, and
waited in agony for more than two weeks after his return
before coming for treatment, hoping each day that the pain
would stop, instead of which, one eye was totally destroyed
by a corneal ulcer.

Another patient, who had been under daily treatment for a
deeply ulcerated neck, mentioned *on the eighteenth day* that
his leg prevented his sleeping.   Upon examination he was
found to have there another ulcer about the size and depth
of a teacup!   When his neck was well he was intending to
speak about his leg!

Many such phenomena of Chinese life may serve to remind
one of a remark in one of the novels of Charles Reade, that

" Mankind are not lacking in intelligence, but they have one intellectual defect—they are Muddleheads!"

A Chinese education by no means fits its possessors to grasp a subject in a comprehensive and practical manner. It is popularly supposed in Western lands that there are certain preachers of whom it can be truthfully affirmed that if their text had the smallpox, the sermon would not catch it. The same phenomenon is found among the Chinese in forms of peculiar flagrance. Chinese dogs do not as a rule take kindly to the pursuit of wolves, and when a dog is seen running after a wolf it is not unlikely that the dog and the wolf will be moving, if not in opposite directions, at least at right angles to each other. Not without resemblance to this oblique chase, is the pursuit by a Chinese speaker of a perpetually retreating subject. He scents it often, and now and then he seems to be on the point of overtaking it, but he retires at length, much wearied, without having come across it in any part of his course.

China is the land of sharp contrasts, the very rich and the wretchedly poor, the highly educated and the utterly ignorant, living side by side. Those who are both very poor and very ignorant, as is the fate of millions, have indeed so narrow a horizon that intellectual turbidity is compulsory. Their existence is merely that of a frog in a well, to which even the heavens appear only as a strip of darkness. Ten miles from their native place many such persons have never been, and they have no conception of any conditions of life other than those by which they have always been surrounded. In many of them even that instinctive curiosity common to all races seems dormant or blighted. Many Chinese, who know that a foreigner has come to live within a mile from their homes, never think to inquire where he came from, who he is, or what he wants. They know how to struggle for an existence, and they know nothing else. They do not know whether they have three souls, as is currently supposed, or one, or none, and so long as the matter has no relation to the price of grain, they do not see that it is of any consequence whatever. They believe in a future life in which the bad will be turned into dogs and insects, and they also believe in annihilation pure and simple, in which the body becomes dirt, and the soul—if there be one—fades into the air. They are the ultimate outcome of the forces which produce what is in Western lands called a " practical man," whose life consists of two compart-ments, a stomach and a cash-bag. Such a man is the true positivist, for he cannot be made to comprehend anything which he does not see or hear, and of causes as such he has no conception whatever. Life is to him a mere series of facts, mostly disagreeable facts, and as for anything beyond, he is at once an atheist, a polytheist, and an agnostic. An occa-sional prostration to he knows not what, or perhaps an offer-ing of food to he knows not whom, suffices to satisfy the instinct of dependence, but whether this instinct finds even this expression will depend largely upon what is the custom of those about him. In him the physical element of the life of man has alone been nourished, to the utter exclusion of the psychical and the spiritual. The only method by which such beings can be rescued from their torpor is by a transfusion of a new life, which shall reveal to them the sublime truth uttered by the ancient patriarch, " There is a spirit in man," for only thus is it that " the inspiration of the Almighty giveth them understanding."

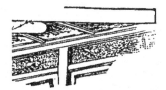

CHAPTER XI.

THE ABSENCE OF NERVES.

IT is a very significant aspect of modern civilisation which is expressed in the different uses of the word "nervous." Its original meaning is "possessing nerve; sinewy; strong; vigorous." One of its derivative meanings, and the one which we by far most frequently meet, is, "Having the nerves weak or diseased; subject to, or suffering from, undue excitement of the nerves; easily excited; weakly." The varied and complex phraseology by which the peculiar phases of nervous diseases are expressed has become by this time familiar in our ears as household words. There is no doubt that civilisation, as exhibited in its modern form, tends to undue nervous excitement, and that nervous diseases are relatively more common than they were a century ago.

But what we have now to say does not concern those who are specially subject to nervous diseases, but to the general mass of Occidentals, who, while not in any specific condition of ill health, are yet continually reminded in a great variety of ways that their nervous systems are a most conspicuous part of their organisation. We allude, in short, to people who are "nervous," and we understand this term to include *all* our readers. To the Anglo-Saxon race, at least, it seems a matter of course that those who live in an age of steam and of electricity must necessarily be in a different condition, as to their nerves, from those who lived in the old slow days of sailing-packets and of mail-coaches. Ours is an age of extreme activity. It is an age of rush. There is no leisure so much as to eat, and the nerves are kept in a state of constant tension, with results which are sufficiently well known.

Business men in our time have an eager, restless air (at least those who do their business in Occidental lands), as if they were in momentary expectation of a telegram—as they often are—the contents of which may affect their destiny in some fateful way. We betray this unconscious state of mind in a multitude of acts. We cannot sit still, but we must fidget. We finger our pencils while we are talking, as if we ought at this particular instant to be rapidly inditing something ere it be forever too late. We rub our hands together as if preparing for some serious task, which is about to absorb all our energies. We twirl our thumbs, we turn our heads with the swift motion of the wild animal which seems to fear that something dangerous may have been left unseen. We have a sense that there is something which we ought to be doing now, and into which we shall proceed at once to plunge as soon as we shall have despatched six other affairs of even more pressing importance. The effect of overworking our nerves shows itself not mainly in such affections as "fiddler's cramp," "telegrapher's cramp," "writer's cramp," and the like, but in a general tension. We do not sleep as we once did, either as regards length of time or soundness of rest. We are wakened by slight causes, and often by those which are exasperatingly trivial, such as the twitter of a bird on a tree, a chance ray of light straggling into our darkened rooms, the motion of a shutter in the breeze, the sound of a voice, and when sleep is once interrupted it is banished. We have taken our daily life to rest with us, and the result is that we have no real rest. In an age when it has become a kind of aphorism that a bank never succeeds until it has a president who takes it to bed with him, it is easy to understand that, while the shareholders reap the advantage, it is bad for the president.

We have mentioned thus fully these familiar facts of our everyday Western life, to point the great contrast to them which one cannot help seeing, and feeling too, when he begins to become acquainted with the Chinese.   It is not very common to dissect dead Chinese, though it has doubtless been done, but we do not hear of any reason for supposing that the nervous anatomy of the " dark-haired race " differs in any essential respect from that of the Caucasian.   But though the nerves of a Chinese as compared with those of the Occidental may be, as the geometricians say, " similar and similarly situated," nothing is plainer than that they are nerves of a very different sort from those with which we are familiar.

It seems to make no particular difference to a Chinese how long he remains in one position.   He will write all day like an automaton.   If he is a handicraftsman, he will stand in one place from dewy morn till dusky eve, working away at his weaving, his gold-beating, or whatever it may be, and do it every day without any variation in the monotony, and apparently with no special consciousness that there is any monotony to be varied.   In the same way Chinese school-children are subjected to an amount of confinement, unrelieved by any recesses or change of work, which would soon drive Western pupils to the verge of insanity.   The very infants in arms, instead of squirming and wriggling as our children begin to do almost as soon as they are born, lie as impassive as so many mud gods.   And at a more advanced age, when Western children would vie with the monkey in its wildest antics, Chinese children will often stand, sit, or squat in the same posture for a great length of time.

It seems to be a physiological fact that to the Chinese exercise is superfluous.   They cannot understand the desire which seems to possess all classes of foreigners alike, to walk when there is no desire to go anywhere; much less can they comprehend the impulse to race over the country at the risk of one's life, in such a singular performance as that known as a "paper hunt," representing "hare and hounds"; or the motive which impels men of good social position to stand all the afternoon in the sun, trying to knock a base-ball to some spot where it shall be inaccessible to some other persons, or, on the other hand, struggling to catch the same ball with celerity, so as to "kill" another person on his "base"! A Cantonese teacher asked a servant about a foreign lady whom he had seen playing tennis: "How much is she *paid* for rushing about like that?" On being told "Nothing," he would not believe it. Why any mortal should do acts like this, when he is abundantly able to hire coolies to do them for him, is, we repeat, essentially incomprehensible to a Chinese, nor is it any more comprehensible to him because he has heard it explained.

In the item of sleep, the Chinese establishes the same difference between himself and the Occidental as in the directions already specified. Generally speaking, he is able to sleep anywhere. None of the trifling disturbances which drive us to despair annoy him. With a brick for a pillow, he can lie down on his bed of stalks or mud bricks or rattan and sleep the sleep of the just, with no reference to the rest of creation. He does not want his room darkened, nor does he require others to be still. The "infant crying in the night" may continue to cry for all he cares, for it does not disturb him. In some regions the entire population seem to fall asleep, as by a common instinct (like that of the hibernating bear), during the first two hours of summer afternoons, and they do this with regularity, no matter where they may be. At two hours after noon the universe at such seasons is as still as at two hours after midnight. In the case of most working-people, at least, and also in that of many others, position in sleep is of no sort of consequence. It would be easy to raise in China an army of a million men—nay, of ten millions—tested by competitive examination as to their capacity to go to sleep across three wheelbarrows, with head downwards, like a spider, their mouths wide open and a fly inside!

Beside this, we must take account of the fact that in China breathing seems to be optional. There is nowhere any ventilation worth the name, except when a typhoon blows the roof from a dwelling, or when a famine compels the owner to pull the house down to sell the timbers. We hear much of Chinese overcrowding, but overcrowding is the normal condition of the Chinese, and they do not appear to be inconvenienced by it at all, or in so trifling a degree that it scarcely deserves mention. If they had an outfit of Anglo-Saxon nerves, they would be as wretched as we frequently suppose them to be.

The same freedom from the tyranny of nerves is exhibited in the Chinese endurance of physical pain. Those who have any acquaintance with the operations in hospitals in China, know how common, or rather how almost universal, it is for the patients to bear without flinching a degree of pain from which the stoutest of us would shrink in terror. It would be easy to expand this topic alone into an essay, but we must pass it by, merely calling attention to a remark of George Eliot's, in one of her letters. " The highest calling and election," she says—irritated, no doubt, by theological formulas for which she had no taste—" is to do without opium, and to bear pain with clear-eyed endurance." If she is right, there can be little doubt that most Chinese, at least, have made their calling and election sure.

It is a remark of Mrs. Browning's, that " Observation without sympathy is torture." So it doubtless is to persons of a sensitive organisation like the distinguished poetess, as well as to a multitude of others of her race. An Occidental does not like to be watched, especially if he is doing any delicate or difficult work. But perhaps a Chinese does his best work under close observation. We all of us grow rapidly weary of being stared at by the swarms of curious Chinese who crowd about a foreigner, in every spot to which foreigners do not commonly resort. We often declare that we shall " go wild " if we cannot in some way disperse those who are subjecting us to no other injury than that of unsympathetic observation. But to the Chinese this instinctive feeling of the Occidental is utterly incomprehensible. He does not care how many people see him, nor when, nor for how great a length of time, and he cannot help suspecting that there must be something wrong about persons who so vehemently resent mere inspection.

It is not alone when he sleeps that an Occidental requires quiet, but most of all when he is sick. Then, if never before, he demands freedom from the annoyance of needless noises. Friends, nurses, physicians, all conspire to insure this most necessary condition for recovery; and if recovery is beyond hope, then more than ever is the sufferer allowed to be in as great peace as circumstances admit. Nothing in the habits of the Chinese presents a greater contrast to those of Westerners, than the behaviour of the Chinese to one another in cases of sickness. The notification of the event is a signal for all varieties of raids upon the patient from every quarter, in numbers proportioned to the gravity of the disease. Quiet is not for a moment to be thought of, and, strange to say, no one appears to desire it. The bustle attendant upon the arrival and departure of so many guests, the work of entertaining them, the wailings of those who fear that a death is soon to take place, and especially the pandemonium made by priests, priestesses, and others to drive away the malignant spirits, constitute an environment from which death would be to most Europeans a happy escape. Occidentals cannot fail to sympathise with the distinguished French lady who sent word to a caller that she " begged to be excused, as she was engaged in dying." In China such an excuse would never be offered, nor, if it were offered, would it be accepted.

It remains to speak of the worries and anxieties to which humanity is everywhere subjected in this distracted world. The Chinese are not only as accessible to these evils as any other people, but far more so. The conditions of their social life are such that in any given region there is a large proportion who are always on the ragged edge of ruin. A slight diminution of the rainfall means starvation to hundreds of thousands. A slight increase in the rainfall means the devastation of their homes by destructive floods, for which there is no known remedy. No Chinese is safe from the entanglement of a lawsuit, which, though he be perfectly innocent, may work his ruin. Many of these disasters are not only seen, but their stealthy and steady approach is perceived, like the gradual shrinking of the iron shroud. To us nothing is more dreadful than the momentary expectation of a calamity which cannot be forefended, and which may bring all that is horrible in its train. The Chinese face these things, perhaps because they seem to be inevitable, with a "clear-eyed endurance," which is one of the most remarkable phenomena of the race. Those who have witnessed the perfectly quiet starvation of millions in times of devastating famine will be able to understand what is here meant. To be fully appreciated, it must be seen, but seen on no matter what scale, it is as difficult for an Occidental really to understand it as it is for a Chinese truly to understand the idea of personal and social liberty, which the Anglo-Saxon has inherited and developed.

In whatever aspect we regard them, the Chinese are and must continue to be to us more or less a puzzle, but we shall make no approach to comprehending them until we have it settled firmly in our minds that, as compared with us, they are gifted with the "absence of nerves." What the bearing of this pregnant proposition may be on the future impact of this race with our own—an impact likely to become more violent as the years go by—we shall not venture to conjecture. We have come to believe, at least in general, in the survival of the most fit. Which is the best adapted to survive in the struggles of the twentieth century, the "nervous" European, or the tireless, all-pervading, and phlegmatic Chinese?

CHAPTER XII.

IT is difficult for the European traveller who visits the city of Canton for the first time, to realise the fact that this Chinese emporium has enjoyed regular intercourse with Europeans for a period of more than three hundred and sixty years. During much the greater part of that time there was very little in the conduct of any Western nation in its dealings with the Chinese of which we have any reason to be proud. The normal attitude of the Chinese towards the people of other lands who chose to come to China for any purpose whatever, has been the attitude of the ancient Greeks to every nation not Grecian, considering and treating them as "barbarians." It is only since 1860, by a special clause in the treaties, that a character which signifies "barbarian," and which the Chinese had been in the habit of employing in official documents as synonymous with the word "foreign," was disallowed.

It must always be remembered in connection with the behaviour of the Chinese towards outside nations of the West, that the Chinese had for ages been surrounded only by the most conspicuous inferiority, and had thus been flattered in the most dangerous because the most plausible and therefore the most effective, way. Finding, as they did, that the foreigners with whom they came into contact could be alternately cajoled and bullied into conforming to the wishes of the Chinese, the latter were but confirmed in their conviction of their

98

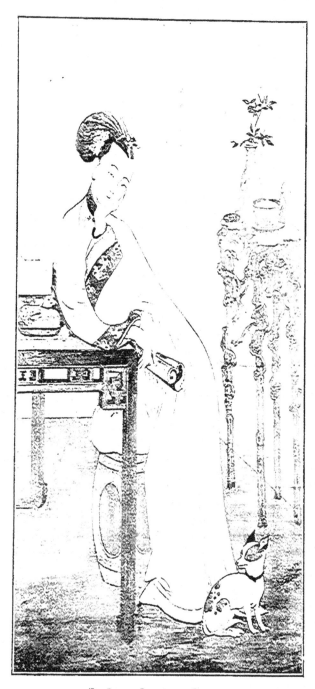

THE EMPRESS DOWAGER OF CHINA.

own unspeakable superiority, and invariably acted upon this theory, until compelled by the capture of Peking to do otherwise. Since that time, although only a generation has passed away, great changes have come over China, and it might be supposed that now at length foreign civilisation and foreigners would be appreciated by the Chinese at their full value. No very extended or intimate acquaintance with the Chinese people is needed, however, to convince any candid observer that the present normal attitude of the Chinese mind, official and unofficial, towards foreigners, is not one of respect. If the Chinese do not feel for us an actual contempt, they do feel condescension, and often unintentionally manifest it. It is this phenomenon with which we have now to deal.

The first peculiarity which the Chinese notice in regard to foreigners is their dress, and in this we think no one will claim that we have much of which we can be proud. It is true that all varieties of the Oriental costume seem to us to be clumsy, pendulous, and restrictive of "personal liberty," but that is because our requirements in the line of active motion are utterly different from those of any Oriental people. When we consider the Oriental modes of dress as adapted to Orientals, we cannot help recognising the undoubted fact that for Orientals this dress is exactly suited. But when Orientals, and especially Chinese, examine our costume, they find nothing whatever to admire, and much to excite criticism, not to say ridicule. It is a postulate in Oriental dress that it shall be loose, and shall be draped in such a way as to conceal the contour of the body. A Chinese gentleman clad in a short frock would not venture to show himself in public, but numbers of foreigners are continually seen in every foreign settlement in China, clad in what are appropriately styled "monkey jackets." The foreign sack-coat, the double-breasted frock-coat (not a single button of which may be in use), and especially the hideous and amorphous abortion called a "dress-coat," are all equally incomprehensible to the Chinese, particularly as some of these garments do not pretend to cover the chest, which is the most exposed part of the body, made still more exposed by the unaccountable deficiencies of a vest cut away so as to display a strip of linen. Every foreigner in China is seen to have two buttons securely fastened to the tail of his coat, where there is never anything to button, and where they are as little ornamental as useful.

If the dress of the male foreigner appears to the average Chinese to be essentially irrational and ridiculous, that of the foreign ladies is far more so. It violates Chinese ideas of propriety, not to say of decency, in a great variety of ways. Taken in connection with that freedom of intercourse between the sexes which is the accompaniment of Occidental civilisation, it is not strange that the Chinese, who judge only from traditional standards of fitness, should thoroughly misunderstand and grossly misconstrue what they see.

Foreign ignorance of the Chinese language is a fertile occasion for a feeling of superiority on the part of the Chinese. It makes no difference that a foreigner may be able to converse fluently in every language of modern Europe, if he cannot understand what is said to him by an ignorant Chinese coolie, the coolie will despise him in consequence. It is true that in so doing the coolie will only still further illustrate his own ignorance, but his feeling of superiority is not the less real on account of its inadequate basis. If the foreigner is struggling with his environment, and endeavouring to master the language of the people, he will be constantly stung by the air of disdain with which even his own servants will remark in an audible " aside," " Oh, he does not *understand!* " when the sole obstacle to understanding lies in the turbid statement of the Chinese himself. But the Chinese does not recognise this fact, nor if he should do so would it diminish his sense of innate superiority. This general state of things continues indefinitely for all students of Chinese, for no matter how much one knows, there is always a continental area which he does not know. It seems to be a general experience, though not necessarily a universal one, that the foreigner in China, after the preliminary stages of his experience are passed, gets little credit for anything which he happens to know, but rather discredit for the things which he does not know. The Chinese estimate of the value of the knowledge which foreigners display of the Chinese language and Chinese literature is frequently susceptible of illustration by a remark of Dr. Johnson's in regard to woman's preaching, which he declared to be like a dog's walking on its hind legs—it is not well done. but then it is a surprise to find it done at all!

Foreign ignorance of the customs of the Chinese is another cause of a feeling of superiority on the part of the Chinese. That any one should be ignorant of what they have always known, seems to them to be almost incredible.

The fact that a foreigner frequently does not know when he has been snubbed by indirect Chinese methods, leads the Chinese to look upon their unconscious victim with conscious contempt. Scornful indifference to what "the natives" may think of us, brings its own appropriate and sufficient punishment.

Many Chinese unconsciously adopt towards foreigners an air of amused interest, combined with depreciation, like that with which Mr. Littimer regarded David Copperfield, as if mentally saying perpetually, "So young, sir, so young!" This does not apply equally to all stages of one's experience in China, for experience accumulates more or less rapidly for shrewd observers, as foreigners in China are not unlikely to be. Still, whatever the extent of one's experience, there are multitudes of details, in regard to social matters, of which one must necessarily be ignorant for the reason that he has never heard of them, and there must be a first time for every acquisition.

Foreign inability to do what any ordinary Chinese can do with the greatest ease, leads the Chinese to look down upon us. We cannot eat what they eat, we cannot bear the sun, we cannot sleep in a crowd, in a noise, nor without air to breathe. We cannot scull one of their boats, nor can we cry "Yi! yi!" to one of their mule-teams in such a way that the animals will do anything which we desire. It is well known ' that the artillery department of the British army, on the way to Peking in 1860, was rendered perfectly helpless near Ho-hsi-wu by the desertion of the native carters, for not a man in the British forces was able to persuade the Chinese animals to take a single step!

Inability to conform to Chinese ideas and ideals in ceremony, as well as in what we consider more important matters, causes the Chinese to feel a thinly disguised contempt for a race whom they think will not and cannot be made to understand "propriety." It is not that a foreigner cannot make a bow, but he generally finds it hard to make a Chinese bow in a Chinese way, and the difficulty is as much moral as physical. The foreigner feels a contempt for the code of ceremonials, often frivolous in their appearance, and he has no patience, if he has the capacity, to spend twenty minutes in a polite scuffle, the termination of which is foreseen by both sides with absolute certainty. The foreigner does not wish to spend his time in talking empty nothings for "an old half-day." To him time is money, but it is very far from being so to a Chinese, for in China every one has an abundance of time, and very few have any money. No Chinese has ever yet learned that when he kills time it is well to make certain that it is time which belongs to him, and not that of some one else.

With this predisposition to dispense as much as possible with superfluous ceremony because it is distasteful, and because the time which it involves can be used more agreeably in other ways, it is not strange that the foreigner, even in his

own eyes, makes but a poor figure in comparison with a cere-
monious Chinese. Compare the dress, bearings, and action
of a Chinese official, his long, flowing robes and his graceful
motions, with the awkward genuflections of his foreign visitor.
It requires all the native politeness of the Chinese to prevent
them from laughing outright at the contrast. In this connection it must be noted that nothing contributes so effectively to
the instinctive Chinese contempt for the foreigner as the evident disregard which the latter feels for that official display so
dear to the Oriental. What must have been the inner thought
of the Chinese who were told that they were to behold the
" great American Emperor," and who saw General Grant in
citizen's costume with a cigar in his mouth, walking along the
open street? Imagine a foreign Consul, who ranks with a
Chinese Taotai, making a journey to a provincial capital to
interview the Governor, in order to settle an international dispute. Thousands are gathered on the city wall to watch the
procession of the great foreign magnate, a procession which is
found to consist of two carts and riding horses, the attendants
of the Consul being an interpreter, a Chinese acting as messenger, and another as cook! Is it any wonder that Orientals, gazing on such a scene, should look with a curiosity
which changes first to indifference and then to contempt?
The particulars in which we consider ourselves to be unquestionably superior to the Chinese do not make upon them
the impression which we should expect, and which we could
desire. They recognise the fact that we are their superiors
in mechanical contrivances, but many of these contrivances
are regarded in the light in which we should look upon feats
of sleight-of-hand—curious, inexplicable, and useless. Our
results appear to them to be due to some kind of supernatural
power, and it is remembered that Confucius refused to talk of
magic. How profoundly indifferent the Chinese are to the
wonders of steam and electricity practically applied, an army

of disappointed contractors who have been in China have discovered. With few exceptions, the Chinese do not wish (though they may be forced to take) foreign models for anything whatever. They care nothing for sanitation, for ventilation, nor for physiology. They would like some, but by no means all, of the results of Western progress without submitting to Western methods, but rather than submit to Western methods they will cheerfully forego the results. Whatever has a direct, unmistakable tendency to make China formidable as a "power," that they want and will have, but the rest must wait; and if there were not a *Zeitgeist*, or Spirit-of-the-Age, superior to any Chinese, other improvements might wait long. Some Chinese scholars and statesmen, apparently realising the inferiority of China, claim that Western nations have merely used the data accumulated by ancient Chinese who cultivated mathematical and natural science to a high degree, but whose modern descendants have unfortunately allowed the secrets of nature to be stolen by the men of the West.

The Chinese do not appear to be much impressed by the undoubted ability of individual foreigners in practical lines. Saxons admire the man who "can," and, as Carlyle was so fond of remarking, they make and call him "king." The skill of the foreigner is to the Chinese amusing and perhaps amazing, and they will by no means forget or omit to make demands upon it the next time they chance to want anything done; but so far from regarding the foreigner in this respect as a model for imitation, it is probable that the idea does not even enter the skull of one Chinese in ten thousand. To them the ideal scholar continues to be the literary fossil who has learned everything, forgotten nothing, taken several degrees, has hard work to keep from starvation, and with claws on his hands several inches in length, cannot do any one thing (except to teach school) by which he can keep soul and body together, for "the Superior Man is not a Utensil."

Western nations, taken as a whole, do not impress educated Chinese with a sense of the superiority of such nations to China. This feeling was admirably exemplified in the reply of His Excellency Kuo, former Chinese Minister to Great Britain, when told, in answer to a question, that in Dr. Legge's opinion the moral condition of England is higher than that of China. After pausing to take in this judgment in all its bearings, His Excellency replied, with deep feeling, " I am very much surprised." Comparisons of this sort cannot be successfully made in a superficial way, and least of all from a diplomatic point of view. They involve a minute acquaintance with the inner life of both nations, and an ability to appreciate the operations of countless causes in the gradual multiplication of effects. Into any such comparison it is far from being our purpose now to enter. It is now well recognised that the Literati of China are the chief enemies of the foreigner, who, though he may have sundry mechanical mysteries at his disposal, is held to be wholly incapable of appreciating China's moral greatness. This feeling of jealous contempt is embodied in the typical Chinese scholar, " with his head in the Sung Dynasty and his feet in the present." It is men of this class who prepared and put in circulation the flood of bitter anti-foreign literature with which in recent years central China has been inundated.

It was once thought that with Western inventions China could be taken by storm. Knives, forks, stockings, and pianos were shipped to China from England, under the impression that this Empire was about to be " Europeanised." If there ever had been a time when the Chinese Empire was to be taken by storm in this way, that time would have been long ago, but there never was such a time. China is not a country, and the Chinese are not a people, to be taken by storm with anything whatsoever. The only way to secure the solid and permanent respect of the Chinese race for Western peoples as a whole is by convincing object lessons, showing that Christian civilisation in the mass and in detail accomplishes results which cannot be matched by the civilisation which China already possesses.   If this conviction cannot be produced, the Chinese will continue, and not without reason, to feel and to display in all their relation to foreigners both condescension and contempt.

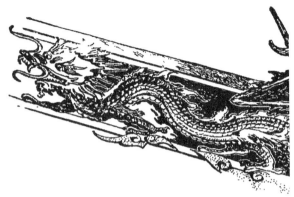

CHAPTER XIII.

THE Book of Odes, one of the most ancient of the Chinese Classics, contains the following prayer, supposed to be uttered by the husbandmen : " May it rain first on our public fields, and afterwards extend to our private ones." Whatever may have been true of the palmy days of the Chou Dynasty and of those which preceded it, there can be no doubt that very little praying is done in the present day, either by husbandmen or any other private individuals, for rain which is to be applied "first" on the "public fields." The Chinese government, as we are often reminded, is patriarchal in its nature, and demands filial obedience from its subjects. A plantation negro who had heard the saying, " Every man for himself, and God for us all," failed to reproduce the precise shade of its thought in his own modified version, as follows, " Every man for himself, and *God for himself!* " This new form of an old adage contains in a nutshell the substance of the views of the average Chinese with regard to the powers that be. " I, for my part, am obliged to look out for myself," he seems to think, if indeed he bestows any thought whatever on the government, and "the government is old enough and strong enough to take care of itself without any help of mine." The government, on the other hand, although patriarchal, is much more occupied in looking after the Patriarch, than in caring for the Patriarch's family. Generally speaking, it will do very little to which it is not impelled by the danger, if it does nothing at first, of having to do all the more at a later date. The people recognise distinctly that the prospective loss of taxes is the motive force in government efforts to mitigate disasters such as the continual outbreaks of irrepressible rivers. What the people do for themselves in endeavouring to prevent calamities of this sort, is due to the instinct of self-preservation, for the people thus make sure that the work is done, and also escape the numberless exactions which are sure to be the invariable concomitants of government energy locally applied.

No more typical example could be selected of the neglect of public affairs by the government, and the absence of public spirit among the people, than the condition of Chinese roads. There are abundant evidences in various parts of the Empire that there once existed great imperial highways connecting many of the most important cities, and that these highways were paved with stone and bordered with trees. The ruins of such roads are found not only in the neighbourhood of Peking, but in such remote regions as Hunan and Szechuen. Vast sums must have been expended on their construction, and it would have been comparatively easy to keep them in repair, but this has been uniformly neglected, so that the ruins of such highways present serious impediments to travel, and the tracks have been abandoned from sheer necessity. It has been supposed that this decay of the great lines of traffic took place during the long period of disturbances before the close of the Ming Dynasty, and at the beginning of the present Manchu line; but making all due allowance for political convulsions, a period of two hundred and fifty years is surely sufficiently long in which to restore the arteries of the Empire. No such restoration has either taken place or been attempted, and the consequence is the state of things with which we are but too familiar.

The attitude of the government is handsomely matched by

THE ABSENCE OF PUBLIC SPIRIT

that of the people, who each and all are in the position of one who has no care or responsibility for what is done with the public property so long as he personally is not the loser. In fact, the very conception that a road, or that anything, belongs to " the public " is totally alien to the Chinese mind. The " streams and mountains " (that is, the Empire) are supposed to be the property in fee simple of the Emperor for the time, to have and to hold as long as he can. The roads are his too, and if anything is to be done to them let him do it. But the greater part of the roads do not belong to the Emperor in any other sense than that in which the farms of the peasants belong to him, for these roads are merely narrow strips of farms devoted to the use of those who wish to use them, not with the consent of the owner of the land, for that was never asked, but from the force of necessity. The entire road belongs to some farm, and pays taxes like any other land, albeit the owner derives no more advantage from its use than does any one else. Under these circumstances, it is evidently the interest of the farmer to restrict the roads as much as he can, which he does by an extended system of ditches and banks designed to make it difficult for any one to traverse any other than the narrow strip of land which is indispensable for communication. If the heavy summer rains wash away a part of the farm into the road, the farmer goes to the road and digs his land out again, a process which, combined with natural drainage and the incessant dust-storms, results eventually in making the road a canal. Of what we mean by "right of way" no Chinese has the smallest conception.

Travellers on the Peiho River between Tientsin and Peking have sometimes noticed in the river little flags, and upon inquiry have ascertained that they indicated the spots where torpedoes had been planted, and that passing boats were expected to avoid them! A detachment of Chinese troops engaged in artillery practice has been known to train their cannon directly across one of the leading highways of the Empire, to the great interruption of traffic and to the terror of the animals attached to carts, the result being a serious runaway accident.

A man who wishes to load or to unload his cart leaves it in the middle of the roadway while the process is going on, and whoever wishes to use the road must wait until the process is completed. If a farmer has occasion to fell a tree he allows it to fall across the road, and travellers can tarry until the trunk is chopped up and removed.

The free and easy ways of the country districts are well matched by the encroachments upon the streets of cities. The wide streets of Peking are lined with stalls and booths which have no right of existence, and which must be summarily removed if the Emperor happens to pass that way. As soon as the Emperor has passed, the booths are in their old places. The narrow passages which serve as streets in most Chinese cities are choked with every form of industrial obstruction. The butcher, the barber, the peripatetic cook with his travelling-restaurant, the carpenter, the cooper, and countless other workmen, plant themselves by the side of the tiny passage which throbs with the life of a great metropolis, and do all they can to form a strangulating clot. Even the women bring out their quilts and spread them on the road, for they have no space so broad in their exiguous courts. There is very little which the Chinese do at all which is not at some time done on the street.

Nor are the obstructions to traffic of a movable nature only. The carpenter leaves a pile of huge logs in front of his shop, the dyer hangs up his long bolts of cloth, and the flour-dealer his strings of vermicelli across the principal thoroughfare, for the space opposite to the shop of each belongs not to an imaginary " public," but to the owner of the shop. The idea

that this alleged ownership of the avenues of locomotion en-
tails any corresponding duties in the way of repair, is not one
which the Chinese mind, in its present stage of development,
is capable of taking in at all. No one individual, even if he
were disposed to repair a road (which would never happen),
has the time or the material wherewith to do it, and for many
persons to combine for this purpose would be totally out of
the question, for each would be in deep anxiety lest he should
do more of the work, and receive less of the benefit, than
some other person. It would be very easy for each local
magistrate to require the villages lying along the line of the
main highways, or within a reasonable distance thereof, to
keep them passable at almost all seasons, but it is doubtful
whether this idea ever entered the mind of any Chinese
official.

Not only do the Chinese feel no interest in that which
belongs to the "public," but all such property, if unprotected
and available, is a mark for theft. Paving-stones are carried
off for private use, and square rods of the brick facing to city
walls gradually disappear. A wall enclosing a foreign cemetery in one of the ports of China was carried away till not a
brick remained, as soon as it was discovered that the place
was in charge of no one in particular. It is not many years
since an extraordinary sensation was caused in the Imperial
palace in Peking by the discovery that extensive robberies had
been committed on the copper roofs of some of the buildings
within the forbidden city. It is a common observation among
the Chinese that, within the Eighteen Provinces, there is no
one so imposed upon and cheated as the Emperor.

The question is often raised whether the Chinese have any
patriotism, and it is not a question which can be answered in
a word. There is undoubtedly a strong national feeling, especially among the literary classes, and to this feeling much of
the hostility exhibited to foreigners and their inventions is to

be traced. Within recent years the province of Hunan has been flooded with streams of anti-foreign literature full of malignant calumniations, and designed to cause riots which shall drive the foreign devil out of the Celestial Empire. From the Chinese point of view the impulse which leads to these publications is as praiseworthy as we should consider resistance to anarchists to be. The charges are partly due to misapprehension, and in part also to that race hatred from which Western nations are by no means free. Probably many Chinese consider these attacks thoroughly patriotic. But that any considerable body of Chinese are actuated by a desire to serve their country, because it is their country, aside from the prospect of emolument, is a proposition which will require much more proof than has yet been offered to secure its acceptance by any one who knows the Chinese. It need not be remarked that a Chinese might be patriotic without taking much interest in the fortunes of a Tartar Dynasty like the present, but there is the best reason to think that, whatever the dynasty might happen to be, the feeling of the mass of the nation would be the same as it is now—a feeling of profound indifference. The key-note to this view of public affairs was sounded by Confucius himself, in a pregnant sentence found in the "Analects": "The Master said: He who is not in an office has no concern with plans for the administration of its duties." To our thought these significant words are partly the result, and to a very great degree the cause, of the constitutional unwillingness of the Chinese to interest themselves in matters for which they are in no way responsible.

M. Huc gives an excellent example of this spirit. "In 1851, at the period of the death of the Emperor Tao Kuang, we were travelling on the road from Peking, and one day when we had been taking tea at an inn, in company with some Chinese citizens, we tried to get up a little political discussion. We spoke of the recent death of the Emperor, an

important event which of course must have interested everybody. We expressed our anxiety on the subject of the suc-
cession to the Imperial throne, the heir to which was not yet
publicly declared. 'Who knows,' said we, 'which of the three
sons of the Emperor will have been appointed to succeed
him? If it should be the eldest, will he pursue the same system of government? If the younger, he is still very young,
and it is said that there are contrary influences, two opposing
parties at court; to which will he lean?' We put forward,
in short, all kinds of hypotheses, in order to stimulate these
good citizens to make some observation. But they hardly
listened to us. We came back again and again to the charge,
in order to elicit some opinion or other on questions that really
appeared to us of great importance. But to all our piquant
suggestions they replied by shaking their heads, puffing out
whiffs of smoke, and taking great gulps of tea. This apathy
was really beginning to provoke us, when one of these worthy
Chinese, getting up from his seat, came and laid his two hands
on our shoulders in a manner quite paternal, and said, smiling
rather ironically: 'Listen to me, my friend! Why should you
trouble your heart and fatigue your head by all these vain
surmises? The mandarins have to attend to affairs of state;
they are paid for it. Let them earn their money, then. But
don't let us torment ourselves about what does not concern
us. We should be great fools to want to do political business
for nothing.' 'That is very conformable to reason,' cried the
rest of the company; and thereupon they pointed out to us
that our tea was getting cold and our pipes were out."

When it is remembered that in the attack on Peking, in
1860, the British army was furnished with mules bought of
the Chinese in the province of Shantung; that Tientsin and
Tungchow made capitulations on their own account, agreeing
to provide the British and French with whatever was wanted
if these cities were not disturbed; that most indispensable

coolie work was done for the foreign allies by Chinese subjects hired for the purpose in Hongkong; and that when these same coolies were captured by the Chinese army they were sent back to the British ranks with their cues cut off—it is not difficult to perceive that patriotism and public spirit, if such things exist at all in China, do not mean what these words imply to Anglo-Saxons.

Upon the not infrequent occasions when it is necessary for the people to rise and resist the oppressions and exactions of their rulers, it is always indispensable that there should be a few men of capacity to take the lead. Under them the movement may gather such momentum that the government must make some practical concessions. But whatever it does with the mass of the "stupid people," the leaders are invariably marked men, and nothing less than their heads will satisfy the demands of justice. To be willing not merely to risk but almost certainly to lose one's life in such a cause is the highest possible example of public spirit.

At critical epochs in Chinese history, especially when there is likely to be a change of dynasties, single-hearted and resolute men have often thrown themselves into the breach, with a chivalrous devotion to the cause which they espoused worthy of the highest praise. Such men are not only true patriots, but are irrefragable proofs that the Chinese are capable of being stirred to the most heroic exertions in following public-spirited leaders.

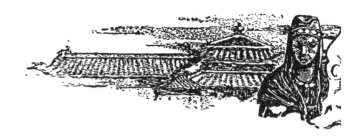

CHAPTER XIV.

IT is true of the Chinese, to a greater degree than of any other nation in history, that their Golden Age is in the past. The sages of antiquity themselves spoke with the deepest reverence of more ancient " ancients." Confucius declared that he was not an originator, but a transmitter. It was his mission to gather up what had once been known, but long neglected or misunderstood. It was his painstaking fidelity in accomplishing this task, as well as the high ability which he brought to it, that gave the Master his extraordinary hold upon the people of his race. It is his relation to the past, as much as the quality of what he taught, that constitutes the claim of Confucius to the front rank of holy men. It is the Confucian theory of morals that a good ruler will make a good people. The prince is the dish, the people are the water; if the dish is round, the water is round, if the dish is square, the water will be square also. Upon this theory, it is not strange that all the virtues are believed to have flourished in the days when model rulers existed. The most ignorant coolie will upon occasion remind us that in the days of " Yao and Shun " there was no necessity for closing the doors at night, for there were no thieves; and that if an article was lost on the highway it was the duty of the first comer to stand as a nominal guard over it until the next one happened along, who took his turn until the owner arrived, who always found his property perfectly intact. It is a common saying that the present is infe-

115

rior to the past in the items of benevolence and justice; but that in violations of conscience the past cannot compete with the present.

This tendency to depreciate the present time is by no means confined to China or to the Chinese, but is found with impartiality all over the earth; yet in the Celestial Empire it seems to have attained a sincerity of conviction not elsewhere equalled. All that is best in the ancient days is believed to have survived in the *literature* to which the present day is the heir, and it is for this reason that this literature is regarded with such unmixed idolatry. The orthodox Chinese view of the Chinese Classics appears to be much the same as the orthodox Christian view in regard to the Hebrew Scriptures; they are supposed to contain all that is highest and best of the wisdom of the past, and to contain all that is equally adapted to the present time and to the days of old. That anything is needed to supplement the Chinese Classics is no more believed by a good Confucianist, than it is believed by a good Christian that supplementary additions to the Bible are desirable or to be expected. Both Christians and Confucianists agree in the general proposition that when a thing is as good as it can be, it is idle to try to make it any better.

Just as many good Christians make some Bible "text" a pretext for something which the biblical writers never had in mind, so Confucian scholars are upon occasion able to find in " the old masters " not only authority for all the modern proceedings of the government, but the real roots of ancient mathematics, and even of modern science.

The literature of antiquity is that which has moulded the Chinese nation, and has brought about a system of government which, whatever its other qualities, has been proved to possess that of persistence. Since self-preservation is the first law of nations as of individuals, it is not singular that a form of rule which an experience of unmatched duration has shown to be

so well adapted to its end should have come to be regarded
with a reverence akin to that felt for the Classics. It would
be a curious discovery if some learned student of Chinese
history should succeed in ascertaining and explaining the processes by which the Chinese government came to be what it
is. If ever those processes should be discovered, we think it
certain that it will then be clearly seen why there have been
in China so few of those interior revolutions to which all other
peoples have been subject. There is a story of a man who
built a stone wall six feet wide and only four feet high, and
on being asked his reasons for so singular a proceeding, he
replied that it was his purpose that when the wall blew over,
it should be higher than it was before! The Chinese government is by no means incapable of being blown over, but it is
a cube, and when it capsizes, it simply falls upon some other
face, and to external appearance, as well as to interior substance, is the same that it has always been. Repeated experience of this process has taught the Chinese that this result is
as certain as that a cat will fall upon its feet, and the conviction is accompanied by a most implicit faith in the divine wisdom of those who planned and built so wisely and so well.
To suggest improvements would be the rankest heresy. Hence
it has come about that the unquestioned superiority of the
ancients rests upon the firm basis of the recognised inferiority
of those who come after them.

With these considerations clearly in mind, it is not difficult
to perceive the *rationale* of what seems at first the blind
and obstinate adherence of the Chinese to the ways of the
past. To the Chinese, as to the ancient Romans, manners and
morals are interchangeable ideas, for they have the same root
and are in their essence identical. To the Chinese an invasion of their customs is an invasion of the regions which are
most sacred. It is not necessary for this effect that the customs should be apprehended in their ultimate relations, or in-

deed, strictly speaking, apprehended at all. They are resolutely defended by an instinct similar to that which leads a she-bear to protect her cubs. This is not a Chinese instinct merely, but it belongs to human nature. It has been profoundly remarked that millions of men are ready to die for a faith which they do not comprehend, and by the tenets of which they do not regulate their lives.

Chinese customs, like the Chinese language, have become established in some way to us unknown. Customs, like human speech, once established resist change. But the conditions under which Chinese customs and language crystallised into shape are in no two places exactly the same. Hence we have those perplexing variations of usage indicated in the common proverb that customs differ every ten miles. Hence, too, we have the bewildering dialects. When once the custom or the dialect has become fixed, it resembles plaster-of-Paris which has set, and while it may be broken, it cannot be changed. This, at least, is the theory, but, like other theories, it must be made sufficiently elastic to suit the facts, which are that no mere custom is necessarily immortal, and, given certain conditions, a change can be effected.

No better illustration of this truth could be given than one drawn from the experience of the present dynasty in introducing an entirely new style of tonsure among their Chinese subjects. It was inevitable that such a conspicuous and tangible mark of subjection should have been bitterly resisted, even to the death, by great numbers of the Chinese. But the Manchus showed how well they were fitted for the high task which they had undertaken, by their persistent adherence to the requirement, compliance with which was made at once a sign and a test of loyalty. The result is what we see. The Chinese people are now more proud of their cues than of any other characteristic of their dress, and the rancorous hostility to the edict of the Manchus survives only in the turbans of

A CHINESE BARBER.

the natives of the provinces of Canton and Fukien, coverings once adopted to hide the national disgrace.

The introduction of the Buddhist religion into China was accomplished only at the expense of a warfare of the most determined character; but once thoroughly rooted, it appears as much like a native as Taoism, and not less difficult to supplant.

The genesis of Chinese customs being what it is, it is easy to perceive that it is the underlying assumption that whatever is is right. Thus a long-established usage is a tyranny. Of the countless individuals who conform to the custom, not one is at all concerned with the origin or the reason of the acts. His business is to conform, and he conforms. The degree of religious faith in different parts of the Empire doubtless differs widely, but nothing can be more certain than that all the rites of the " three religions " are performed by millions who are as destitute of anything which ought to be called faith, as they are of an acquaintance with Egyptian hieroglyphics. To any inquiry as to the reason for any particular act of religious routine, nothing is more common than to receive two answers: the first, that the whole business of communication with the gods has been handed down from the ancients, and must therefore be on the firmest possible basis; the second, that " everybody " does so, and therefore the person in question *must* conform. In China the machinery moves the cogs, and not the cogs the machinery. While this continues to be always and everywhere true, it is also true that the merest shell of conformity is all that is demanded.

It is a custom in Mongolia for every one who can afford it to use snuff, and to offer it to his friends. Every one is provided with a little snuff-box, which he produces whenever he encounters a friend. If the person with the snuff-box happens to be out of snuff, that does not prevent the passing of the snuff-box, of which each guest takes a deliberate, though an imaginary pinch, and returns the box to its owner. To seem to notice that the box is empty would not be "good form," but by compliance with the proper usages the "face" of the host is saved, and all is according to well-settled precedent. In many important particulars it is not otherwise with the Chinese. The life may have long departed, but there remains the coral reef, the avenues to which, in order to avoid shipwreck, must be diligently respected.

The fixed resolution to do certain acts in certain ways, and in no other, is not peculiar to China. The coolies in India habitually carried burdens upon their heads, and applied the same principle to the removal of earth for railways. When the contractors substituted wheelbarrows, the coolies merely transferred the barrows to the tops of their skulls. The coolies in Brazil carry burdens in the same way as those of India. A foreign gentleman in the former country gave a servant a letter to be posted, and was surprised to see him put the letter on his head and weight it with a stone to keep it in place. The exact similarity of mental processes reveals a similarity of cause, and it is a cause very potent in Chinese affairs. It leads to those multiplied instances of imitativeness with which we are all so familiar, as when the cook breaks an egg and throws it away each time that he makes a pudding, because on the first occasion when he was shown how to make a pudding an egg happened to be bad; or when the tailor puts a patch on a new garment because an old one given him as a measure chanced to be thus decorated. Stories of this sort are doubtless often meant as harmless exaggerations of a Chinese characteristic, but they represent the reality with great fidelity.

Every one acquainted with Chinese habits will be able to adduce instances of a devotion to precedent which seems to us unaccountable, and which really is so until we apprehend the postulate which underlies the act. In a country which stretches through some twenty-five degrees of latitude, but in which winter furs are taken off and straw hats are put on according to a fixed rule for the whole Empire, it would be strange if precedent were not a kind of divinity. In regions where the only heat in the houses during the cold winter comes from the scanty fire under the "stove-bed," or *k'ang*, it is not uncommon for travellers who have been caught in a sudden "cold snap" to find that no arguments can induce the landlord of the inn to heat the *k'ang*, because the season for heating it has not arrived!

The reluctance of Chinese artificers to adopt new methods is sufficiently well known to all, but perhaps few even of these conservatives are more conservative than the head of the company of workmen employed to burn bricks in a kiln which, with all that appertained thereto, was the property of foreigners and not of those who worked it. As there was occasion to use a kind of square bricks larger than those which happened to be in fashion in that region, the foreigner ordered larger ones to be made. All that was necessary for this purpose was simply the preparation of a wooden tray, the size of the required brick, to be used as a mould. When the bricks were wanted they were not forthcoming, and the foreman, to whom the orders had been given, being called to account for his neglect, refused to be a party to any such innovation, adducing as his all-sufficient reason the affirmation that *under the whole heavens there is no such mould as this !*

The bearing of the subject of conservatism upon the relation of foreigners to China and the Chinese is not likely to be lost sight of for a moment by any one whose lot is cast in China, and who has the smallest interest in the future welfare of this mighty Empire. The last quarter of the nineteenth century seems destined to be a critical period in Chinese history. A great deal of very new wine is offered to the Chinese, who have no other provision for its reception than a varied assortment of very old wine-skins. Thanks to the instinctive conservatism of the Chinese nature, very little of the new wine has thus far been accepted, and, for that little, new bottles are in course of preparation.

The present attitude of China towards the lands of the West is an attitude of procrastination. There is on the one hand small desire for that which is new, and upon the other no desire at all, or even willingness, to give up the old. As we see ancient mud huts, that ought long ago to have reverted to their native earth, shored up with clumsy mud pillars which but postpone the inevitable fall, so we behold old customs, old superstitions, and old faiths now outworn, propped up and made to do the same duty as heretofore. "If the old does not go, the new does not come," we are told, and not without truth. The process of change from the one to the other may long be resisted, and may then come about suddenly.

At a time when it was first proposed to introduce telegraphs, the Governor-General of a maritime province reported to the Emperor that the hostility of the people to the innovation was so great that the wires could not be put up. But when war with France was imminent, and the construction of the line was placed upon an entirely different basis, the provincial authorities promptly set up the telegraph posts, and saw that they were respected.

Not many years ago the superstition of *fêng-shui* was believed by many to be an almost insuperable obstacle to the introduction of railways in China. The very first short line, constructed as an outlet for the K'ai-p'ing coal mines, passed through a large Chinese cemetery, the graves being removed to make way for it, as they would have been in England or in France. A single inspection of that bisected graveyard was sufficient to produce the conviction that *fêng-shui* could never stand before an engine, when the issue is narrowed down to a trial of strength between "wind-water" and steam. The

Engine Works and Yard at Hanyang.

experience gained in the subsequent extension of this initial line shows clearly that however financial considerations may delay the introduction of railways, geomantic superstitions are for this purpose quite inert.

The union of the conservative instinct with the capacity for invasion of precedents is visible in important Chinese affairs. In China no principle is better settled than that, when one of his parents dies, an official must retire from office. Yet against his repeated and "tearful" remonstrances, the most powerful subject in the Empire was commanded by the Throne to continue his attention to the intricate details of the most important plexus of duties to be found in the Empire, through all the years of what should have been mourning retirement after the death of his mother. No principle would seem to be more firmly established in China than that a father is the superior of his son, who must always do him reverence. Equally well established is the principle that the Emperor is superior to all his subjects, who must always do *him* reverence. When, therefore, as at the last change of rulers, it happens that from a collateral line is adopted a young Emperor whose father is still living, it would appear to be inevitable that the father must either commit suicide, or go into a permanent retirement. Such, it was supposed when Kuang Hsû ascended the throne, would actually be the end of Prince Ch'un. Yet during the illness of the latter, his son, the Emperor, made repeated calls upon his subordinate-superior, the father; and some *modus vivendi* was arrived at, since this same father until his death held important offices under his son.

As already remarked, the conservative instinct leads the Chinese to attach undue importance to precedent. But rightly understood and cautiously used, this is a great safeguard for foreigners in their dealings with so sensitive, so obstinate, and so conservative a people. It is only necessary to imitate the Chinese method, to take things for granted, to *assume* the existence of rights which have not been expressly withheld, to defend them warily when they are assailed, *and by all means to hold on.*   Thus, as in the case of the right of foreign residence in Peking, the right of foreign residence in the interior, and in many others, wise conservatism is the safest defence.   The threatening reef which seemed so insuperable a barrier to navigation, once penetrated, offers upon the inner side a lagoon of peace and tranquillity, safe from the storms and breakers which vainly beat against it.

CHAPTER XV.

INDIFFERENCE TO COMFORT AND CONVENIENCE.

IN what we have now to say, it must be premised at the outset that all that is affirmed of Chinese indifference to comfort and convenience respects not Oriental but Occidental standards, the principal object being to show how totally different those standards are.

Let us first direct our attention for a moment to the Chinese dress. In speaking of Chinese contempt for foreigners, we have already had occasion to mention that Western modes of apparel have very little which is attractive to the Chinese; we are now forced to admit that the converse is equally true. To us it certainly appears singular that a great nation should become reconciled to such an unnatural custom as shaving off the entire front part of the head, leaving that exposed which nature evidently intended should be protected. But since the Chinese were driven to adopt this custom at the point of the sword, and since, as already remarked, it has become a sign and a test of loyalty, it need be no further noticed in this connection than to call attention to the undoubted fact that the Chinese themselves do not recognise any discomfort from the practice, and would probably be exceedingly unwilling to revert to the Ming Dynasty tonsure.

The same considerations do not apply to the Chinese habit of going bareheaded at almost all seasons of the year, and especially in summer. The whole nation moves about in the blistering heats of the summer months holding one arm aloft.

with an open fan held at such an angle as to obstruct a portion of the rays of the sun. Those who at any part of their lives hold an umbrella in their hands to ward off heat, must constitute but a small part of the population. While men do often wear hats upon certain provocation, Chinese women, so far as we have observed, have no other kind of head-dress than that which, however great its failure viewed from the unsympathetic Western standpoint, is intended to be ornamental. One of the very few requisites for comfort, according to Chinese ideas, is a fan,—that is to say, in the season when it is possible to use such an accessory to comfort. It is not uncommon in the summer to see coolies, almost or quite devoid of clothing, struggling to track a heavy salt-junk up-stream, vigorously fanning themselves meanwhile. Even beggars frequently brandish broken fans.

It is one of the unaccountable phenomena of Chinese civilisation that this people, which is supposed to have been originally pastoral, and which certainly shows a high degree of ingenuity in making use of the gifts of nature, has never learned to weave wool in such a way as to employ it as clothing. The only exceptions to this general statement of which we are aware relate to the western parts of the Empire, where, to a certain extent, woollen fabrics are manufactured. But it is most extraordinary that the art of making such goods should not have become general, in view of the great numbers of sheep which are to be seen, especially in the mountainous regions.

It is believed that in ancient times, before cotton was introduced, garments were made of some other vegetable fibres, such as rushes. However this may be, it is certain that the nation as a whole is at present absolutely dependent upon cotton. In those parts of the Empire where the winter cold is severe, the people wear an amount of wadded clothing almost sufficient to double the bulk of their bodies. A child

A Middle Class Family in Winter Dress.

clad in this costume, if he happens to fall down, is often as utterly unable to rise as if he had been strapped into a cask. Of the discomfort of such clumsy dress we never hear the Chinese complain. The discomfort is in the want of it. It is certain, however, that no Anglo-Saxon would willingly tolerate the disabilities of such an attire, if he could by any possibility be relieved of it.

In connection with the heavy clothing of winter must be mentioned the total lack of any kind of underclothing. To us it seems difficult to support existence without woollen undergarments, frequently changed. The Chinese are conscious of no such need. Their burdensome wadded clothes hang around their bodies like so many bags, leaving yawning spaces through which the cold penetrates to the flesh, but they do not mind this circumstance, although ready to admit that it is not ideal. An old man of sixty-six, who complained that his circulation was torpid, was presented with a foreign undershirt, but told to keep it on every day, to avoid taking cold. A day or two later it was ascertained that he had taken it off, as he was "roasted to death."

Chinese shoes are made of cloth, and are always porous, absorbing moisture on the smallest provocation. Whenever the weather is cold this keeps the feet more or less chilled all the time. The Chinese have, indeed, a kind of oiled boots which are designed to keep out the dampness, but, like many other conveniences, on account of the expense, the use of them is restricted to a very few. The same is true of umbrellas as a protection against rain. They are luxuries, and are by no means regarded as necessities. Chinese who are obliged to be exposed to the weather do not as a rule think it important, certainly not necessary, to change their clothes when they have become thoroughly wet, and do not seem to find the inconvenience of allowing their garments to dry upon them at all a serious one. While the Chinese admire foreign gloves, they have none of their own, and while clumsy mittens are not unknown, even in the extreme north they are rarely seen.

One of the most annoying characteristics of Chinese costume, as seen from the foreign standpoint, is the absence of pockets. The average Westerner requires a great number of these to meet his needs. He demands breast-pockets in his coats for his memorandum books, pockets behind for his handkerchiefs, pockets in his vest for pencil, tooth-pick, etc., as well as for his watch, and in other accessible positions for the accommodation of his pocket-knife, his bunch of keys, and his wallet. If the foreigner is also provided with a pocket-comb, a folding foot-rule, a cork-screw, a boot-buttoner, a pair of tweezers, a minute compass, a folding pair of scissors, a pin-ball, a pocket mirror, and a fountain pen, it will not mark him out as a singular exception to his race. Having become accustomed to the constant use of these articles, he cannot dispense with them. The Chinese, on the other hand, has few or none of such things; if he were presented with them he would not know where to put them. If he has a handkerchief it is thrust into his bosom, and so also is a child which he may have to carry around. If he has a paper of some importance, he carefully unties the strap which confines his trousers to his ankle, inserts the paper, and goes on his way. If he wears outside drawers, he simply tucks in the paper without untying anything. In either case, if the band loosens without his knowledge, the paper is lost—a constant occurrence. Other depositaries of such articles are the folds of the long sleeves when turned back, the crown of a turned-up hat, or the space between the cap and the head. Many Chinese make a practice of ensuring a convenient, although a somewhat exiguous, supply of ready money, by always sticking a cash in one ear. The main dependence for security of articles carried, is the girdle, to which a small purse, the tobacco pouch and pipe, and similar objects, are attached. If the girdle should work loose, the articles are liable to be lost. Keys, moustache-combs, and a few ancient cash are attached to some prominent button of the jacket, and each removal of this garment involves care-taking to prevent the loss of the appendages.

If the daily dress of the ordinary Chinese seems to us objectionable, his nocturnal costume is at least free from criticism on the score of complexity, for he simply strips to the skin, wraps himself in his quilt, and sleeps the sleep of the just. Night-dress he or she has none. It is indeed recorded that Confucius "required his sleeping-dress to be half as long again as his body." It is supposed, however, that the reference in this passage is to a robe which the Master wore when he was fasting, and not to an ordinary night-dress; but it is at all events certain that modern Chinese do not imitate him in his night-robe, and do not fast if they can avoid it. Even new-born babes, whose skins are exceedingly sensitive to the least changes of temperature, are carelessly laid under the bedclothes, which are thrown back whenever the mother wishes to exhibit the infant to spectators. The sudden chill which this absurd practice occasions, is thought by competent judges to be quite sufficient to account for the very large number of Chinese infants who, before completing the first month of their existence, die in convulsions. When children have grown larger, instead of being provided with diapers, they are in some regions clad in a pair of bifurcated bags partly filled with sand or earth, the mere idea of which is sufficient to fill the breast of tender-hearted Western mothers with horror. Weighted with these strange equipments, the poor child is at first rooted to one spot like the frog which was "loaded" with buck-shot. In the particular districts where this custom prevails, it is common to speak of a person who exhibits small practical knowledge, as one who has not yet been taken out of his " earth-trousers "!

Chinese indifference to what we mean by comfort is exhibited as much in their houses as in their dress. In order to establish this proposition, it is necessary to take account not of the dwellings of the poor, who are forced to exist as they can, but rather of the habitations of those whose circumstances enable them to do as they please. The Chinese do not care for the shade of trees about their houses, but much prefer poles covered with mats. Those who are unable to afford such a luxury, however, and who might easily have a grateful shade-tree in their courtyard, do not plant anything of this sort, but content themselves with pomegranates or some other merely ornamental shrubs. When, owing to the fierce heat, the yard is intolerable, the occupants go and sit in the street, and when that is insufferable they retire to their houses again. Few houses have a north door opposite the main entrance on the south side. Such an arrangement would produce a draught, and somewhat diminish the miseries of the dog-days. When asked why such a convenience is not more common, the frequent reply is that "*We do not have north doors!*"

North of the thirty-seventh parallel of latitude, the common sleeping-place of the Chinese is the *k'ang*, a raised "brick-bed" composed of adobe bricks, and heated by the fire used for cooking. If there happens to be no fire, the cold earth appears to a foreigner the acme of discomfort. If the fire happens to be too great, he wakes in the latter part of the night, feeling that he is undergoing a process of roasting. In any event, the degree of heat will not be continuous throughout the night. The whole family is huddled together on this terrace. The material of which it is composed becomes infested with insects, and even if the adobe bricks are annually removed there is no way to secure immunity from these unwelcome guests, which are fixed occupants of the walls of all classes of dwellings.

Other universally prevalent animal infestations there are,

with which most Chinese are very familiar, but there are few who seem to regard parasites as a preventable evil, even if they are recognised as an evil at all. The nets which are used to keep winged torments at bay, are beyond the means of all but a small proportion even of the city population, and, so far as we know, are rarely heard of elsewhere. Sand-flies and mosquitoes are indeed felt to be a serious nuisance, and occasionally faint efforts are made to expel them by burning aromatic weeds, but such pests do not annoy the Chinese a thousandth part as much as they annoy us.

One of the typical instances of different standards of comfort is in the conception of what a pillow ought to be. In Western lands, a pillow is a bag of feathers adjusted to support the head. In China a pillow is a support for the neck, either a small stool of bamboo, a block of wood, or more commonly a brick. No Occidental could use a Chinese pillow in a Chinese way without torture, and it is not less certain that no Chinese would tolerate under his head for ten minutes the bags which we use for that purpose.

We have spoken of the singular fact that the Chinese do not to any extent weave wool. It is still more unaccountable that they take no apparent interest in the feathers which they pluck in such vast quantities from the fowls which they consume. It would be exceedingly easy to make up wadded bedding by employing feathers, and the cost of the feathers would be little or nothing, since they are allowed to blow away as beneath the notice even of the strict economy of the Chinese. Yet, aside from sale to foreigners, we do not know of any use to which such feathers are at present put, except that the larger ones are loosely tied to sticks to serve as dusters, and in western China, feathers are sometimes thickly sprinkled on growing wheat and beans, to prevent their being eaten by animals turned out to forage for themselves.

To an Occidental the ideal bed is at once elastic and firm.

The best example of such is perhaps that made from what is known as woven wire, which in recent years has come into such general use. But when one of the finest hospitals in China was furnished with these luxurious appliances, the kind-hearted physician who had planned for them was disgusted to find that, as soon as his back was turned, those patients who were strong enough to do so crawled from their elastic beds down upon the floor, where they felt at home!

Chinese houses are nearly always ill-lighted at night. The native vegetable oils are exceedingly disagreeable to the smell, and only afford sufficient illumination to make darkness visible. The great advantages of kerosene are indeed recognised, but in spite of them it is still true that throughout enormous areas the oil made from beans, cotton-seed, and peanuts continues to be used long after kerosene has been known, simply from the force of conservative *inertia*, backed by profound indifference to the greater comfort of being able to see clearly, as compared with being able to see scarcely at all.

Chinese furniture strikes a Westerner as being clumsy and uncomfortable. Instead of the broad benches on which our ancestors used to recline, the Chinese are generally content with very narrow ones, and it will not be surprising if some of the legs are loose, or are so placed as to tip off the unwary person who seats himself when there is no one at the other end. The Chinese are the only Asiatic nation using chairs, but according to our ideas Chinese chairs are models of discomfort. Some of them are made on a pattern which prevailed in England in the days of Queen Elizabeth or Queen Anne, tall, straight of back, and inordinately angular. The more common ones are shaped so as to accommodate persons who weigh about two hundred and fifty pounds, but the strength of the chairs is by no means proportioned to the magnitude, and they soon fall to pieces.

The greatest objections which Westerners have to Chinese

dwellings are undoubtedly the dampness and the cold. The radical error in the construction of buildings, is that which economises in the foundation. The inevitable and permanent result is dampness. Floors of earth or of imperfectly burned brick are to most foreigners not only sources of great discomfort, but are extremely prejudicial to health. Not less annoying are the loose doors, resting on pivots. The double leaves of these doors admit the cold air at each side at the top and at the bottom. Even if the cracks are pasted up with stout paper, a door is but an imperfect protection against the bitter winter weather, because it is almost impossible to teach Chinese to keep an outside door shut. The notice which a business man posted on his office door, "Everybody shuts the doors but you," would be a gross falsehood in China, where nobody shuts a door. The frames of doors, both to houses and to yards, are often made so low that a person of average stature must at each passage either bow his head or bump it.

Chinese paper windows will not keep out wind, rain, sun, heat, or dust. Window-shutters are not very common, and when they exist are often unused.

Most Chinese houses have only one cooking-boiler, a large concave iron bowl, with a capacity of several gallons. But one kind of food is generally cooked at a time, and when a meal is in preparation hot water is not to be had. The stalks and grass which are the fuel must be incessantly pushed under the low kettle by a person squatting or sprawling in front of the small flue. Almost all cooking is done in this way. Steam and often smoke fill the room to an extent adapted to blind and strangle a foreigner, but the Chinese seem to be indifferent to these evils, although aware that serious diseases of the eye are a common consequence.

A Chinese dwelling in winter always appears to a Westerner a thesaurus of discomfort, on account of the absence of artificial heat. The vast majority of the people, even where the winters are severe, have no other heat than that modicum obtained from the fuel burned in cooking, and conveyed to the *k'ang*. The Chinese so highly appreciate the comfort of a *k'ang* that the women sometimes speak of it as their "own mother." But while it is indeed the point of minimum discomfort in the establishment, to Occidentals who wish to feel positive heat from some source diffusing itself in grateful currents all over the body, a Chinese *k'ang* on a cold night is a very inadequate substitute for the "chimney-corner" or for the stove. In regions where coal is accessible, it is indeed employed as fuel, but as compared with the whole country these districts are very limited, and the smoke always escapes into the room, which becomes gradually filled with carbonic acid gas. Charcoal is very sparingly used even by those who are in good circumstances, and the danger from its incautious use, like that from the use of coal, is very great. The houses are so uncomfortable that even at home if the weather is cold the inmates often wear all the clothes they can put on. When abroad they have no more to add. "Are you cold ? " we ask them. "Of course," is the constant reply. They have never been artificially warmed, in an Occidental sense, during their whole lives. In the winter their blood seems to be like water in the rivers, congealed at the surface, and only moving with a sluggish current underneath. Considering these characteristics of Chinese dwellings, it is no wonder that a certain Taotai who had been abroad remarked that in the United States the prisoners in jail had quarters more comfortable than his *yamên*.

We have already had occasion to point out the Chinese indifference to crowding and noise. As soon as the weather becomes cold the Chinese huddle together as a matter of course, in order to keep warm. Even in the depth of the dog-days, it is not uncommon to see boats loaded with such numbers of passengers that there must be barely room to sit or to lie. No Westerners would tolerate such crowding, yet the Chinese do not appear to mind it. Occidentals like to have their dwellings at a little distance from those of the nearest neighbours, for ventilation and for privacy. The Chinese know nothing either of ventilation or of privacy, and they do not seem to appreciate these conditions when they are realised. Every little Chinese village is built on the plan of a city without any plan. In other words, the dwellings are huddled together as if land were excessively valuable. The inevitable effect is to raise the price of land, just as in a city, though for quite different reasons. Hence narrow courts, cramped accommodations, unhealthful overcrowding, even where there is abundant space to be had close at hand and at a moderate rate.

A Chinese guest at a Chinese inn enjoys the bustle which is concomitant upon the arrival of a long train of carts, and falls asleep as soon as he has bolted his evening meal. His fellow-traveller from Western climes lies awake half the night listening to the champing of three-score mules, varied by kicks and squeals that last as long as he keeps his consciousness. These sounds are alternated by the beating of a huge wooden rattle, and by the yelping of a large force of dogs. It is not uncommon to see as many as fifty donkeys in one inn-yard, and the pandemonium which they occasion at night can be but faintly imagined. The Chinese, as M. Huc has mentioned, are not unaware that the braying of this animal can be stopped by suspending a brick to its tail, but repeated inquiries fail to elicit information of a single instance in which the thing has been actually done. The explanation is simply that a Chinese does not particularly care whether fifty donkeys bray singly, simultaneously, or not at all. No Occidental would be likely to remain neutral on such a question. That this feeling is not confined to any particular stratum of the Chinese social scale might be inferred from the circumstance that the wife of the leading statesman of China had at one time in the vice-regal yamên about one hundred cats!

The Buddhist religion is responsible for the reluctance of the Chinese to put an end to the wretched existence of the pariah dogs with which all Chinese cities are infested, yet the trait of character thus exhibited is not so much Chinese as Oriental. Mr. J. Ross Browne, who was once Minister from the United States to China, published an entertaining volume of travels in the East, adorned with drawings of his own. One of these represented what appeared to be a congress of all varieties of lean and mangy dogs, which was offered as " a general view of Constantinople." The same cut would do good service as a sketch of many Chinese cities. The Chinese do not appear to experience any serious discomfort from the reckless and irrepressible barking of this vast army of curs, nor do they take much account of the really great dangers arising from mad dogs, which are not infrequently encountered. Under such circumstances, the remedy adopted is often that of binding some of the hair of the dog into the wound which it has caused, a curious analogy to the practice which must have originated our proverb that " the hair of the same dog will cure." The death of the dog does not seem to be any part of the object in view.

Most of the instances already adduced relate to Chinese indifference to comfort. It would not be difficult to cite as many more which bear upon disregard of convenience, but a few examples will be sufficient. The Chinese pride themselves upon being a literary nation ; in fact, *the* literary nation of the world. Pens, paper, ink, and ink-slabs are called the " four precious things," and their presence constitutes a " literary apartment." It is remarkable that not one of these four indispensable articles is carried about the person. They are by no means sure to be at hand when wanted, and all four of them are utterly useless without a fifth substance, to wit, water, which is required for rubbing up the ink. The pen cannot be used without considerable previous manipulation to soften its delicate hairs; it is very liable to be injured by inexpert handling, and lasts but a comparatively short time. The Chinese have no substitute for the pen, such as lead-pencils, nor if they had them would they be able to keep them in repair, since they have no penknives, and no pockets in which to carry them. We have previously endeavoured, in speaking of the economy of the Chinese, to do justice to their great skill in accomplishing excellent results with very inadequate means, but it is not the less true that such labour-saving devices as are so constantly met in Western lands are unknown in China. In a modern hotel in the Occident one has but to push something or to pull something and he gets whatever he wants—hot or cold water, lights, heat, service. But the finest hostelry in the Eighteen Provinces, like all inferior places of accommodation, obliges its guest, whenever he is conscious of an unsupplied need, to go to the outer door of his apartment and yell at the top of his voice, vainly hoping to be heard for his much speaking.

Many articles constantly required by the Chinese are not to be had on demand, but only when the dealer in the same happens to make his irregular appearance. At all other times one might as well find himself dropped in the interior of the Soudan, so far as the supply of current wants is concerned. In the city every one carries a lantern at night, yet in some cities, at least, lanterns are to be had only when the peddler brings them around, and those who want them buy at such times, as we do of a milkman or a dealer in fresh yeast. That percentage of the whole population which lives in Chinese cities cannot be a large one, and in the country this limitation of traffic is the rule and not the exception. In some districts, for example, it is customary to sell timber for house-building in the second moon, and the same logs are often dragged about the country from one large fair to another, till they are either sold, or taken back to their point of departure. But should any inexperienced person be so rash as to wish to buy timber in the fifth moon, he will soon ascertain why the wisest of Orientals remarked that "there is a time to every purpose under the heaven."

In speaking of economy we have mentioned that as most Chinese tools are not to be had in a completed state, the customer buys the parts and has them united to suit himself, which does not comport with our conception of convenience.

The writer once instructed a servant to buy a hatchet for splitting wood. There was none to be had, but he returned instead with fourteen large (imported) horse-shoes, which a blacksmith hammered into something resembling a miner's pick, to which a carpenter affixed a handle, the total cost being much greater than that of a good foreign axe!

Few inconveniences of the Celestial Empire make upon the Western mind a more speedy and a more indelible impression than the entire absence of "sanitation." Whenever there has been an attempt made to accomplish something in the way of drainage, as in Peking, the resultant evils are very much greater than those which they were designed to cure. No matter how long one has lived in China, he remains in a condition of mental suspense, unable to decide that most interesting question so often raised, Which is the filthiest city in the Empire? A visitor from one of the northern provinces boasted to a resident in Amoy that, in offensiveness to the senses, no city in south China could equal those of the north. With a view to decide this moot point, the city of Amoy was extensively traversed, and found to be unexpectedly clean— that is, for a Chinese city. Jealous for the pre-eminence of his adopted home, the Amoy resident claimed that he was taken at a disadvantage, as a heavy rain had recently done much to wash the streets! The traveller thinks he has found the worst Chinese city when he has inspected Foochow; he is certain of it when he visits Ningpo, and doubly sure on arriving in Tientsin. Yet, after all, it will not be strange if he heartily recants when he reviews with candour and impartiality the claims of Peking!

The three points upon which the Occidental mind is sure to lay principal stress when contemplating the inconveniences of Chinese civilisation, are the absence of postal facilities, the state of the roads, and the condition of the currency. Private companies do of course exist, by which letters and parcels may be transmitted from certain places in China to certain other places, but their functions are exceedingly limited, and compared with the whole Empire, the areas which they accommodate are but trifling. Of Chinese roads we have already spoken, when discussing the absence of public spirit. There is a road many miles in length cut through a mountain in Shantung, which is so narrow that carts cannot pass one another. Guards are stationed at each end, and traffic is only allowed in one direction in the forenoon, and in the other during the afternoon! It is because the Chinese costume—especially Chinese shoes—is what has been described, and because Chinese roads are what we know them to be, that whenever the weather is bad the Chinese confine themselves to their dwellings. In Western lands we speak of an unintelligent person as one who does not know enough to go in when it rains, but in China one should rather say of such a person that he does not know enough to stay in when it rains.

One of the most common characters in the Chinese language, used to denote *imperative necessity*, is composed of two parts, which signify " stopped by the rain." With the possible exception of official service, the idea that any human being has functions the discharge of which can be harmonised with the rapid precipitation of moisture in the outer atmosphere, is one that can only be introduced to most Chinese skulls by a process of trepanning. Not even public business is necessarily urgent, the proverb to the contrary notwithstanding. We have heard of a Chinese fort of undoubted strength, in a most important position, armed with the most elaborate muniments of war, such as Krupp guns, and provided with foreign drilled troops, where on occasion of a rain every one of the sentries judiciously retired to the guard-houses, leaving not a single man anywhere in sight. They were " stopped by the rain "! The Tientsin massacre of 1870 might have been quadrupled in atrocity, but for a timely rain which deterred the desperadoes already on their way to the Settlement. A portable shower would be one of the most perfect defences which a foreign traveller in the hostile parts of China could desire. We are confident that a steady stream of cold water delivered from a two-inch nozzle would, within five minutes of solar time, disperse the most violent mob ever seen by a foreigner in China. Grape-shot would be far less effectual, for many would stop to gather up the spent shot, while cold water is something for which every Chinese from the Han Dynasty downwards entertains the same aversion as does a cat. Externally or internally administered, he regards it as equally fatal.

The subject of Chinese currency demands not a brief paragraph, but a comprehensive essay, or rather a volume. Its chaotic eccentricities would drive any Occidental nation to madness in a single generation, or more probably such gigantic evils would speedily work their own cure. In speaking of the disregard of accuracy we have mentioned a few of the more prominent annoyances. A hundred cash are not a hundred, and a thousand cash are not a thousand, but some other and totally uncertain number, to be ascertained only by experience. In wide regions of the Empire one cash counts for two; that is, it does so in numbers above twenty, so that when one hears that he is to be paid five hundred cash he understands that he will receive two hundred and fifty pieces, less the local abatement, which perpetually shifts in different places. There is a constant intermixture of small or spurious cash, leading to inevitable disputes between dealers in any commodity. At irregular intervals the local magistrates become impressed with the evil of this debasement of the currency, and issue stern proclamations against it. This gives the swarm of underlings in the magistrate's yamên an opportunity to levy squeezes on all the cash-shops in the district, and to make the transaction of all business more or less difficult. Prices at once rise to meet the temporary necessity for pure cash. As soon as the paying ore in this vein is exhausted—and it is not worked to any extent—the bad cash returns, but prices do not fall. Thus the irrepressible law by which the worse currency drives out the better, is never for an instant suspended. The condition of the cash becomes worse and worse, until, as in some parts of the province of Honan, every one goes to market with two entirely distinct sets of cash, one of which is the ordinary mixture of good with bad, and the other is composed exclusively of counterfeit pieces. Certain articles are paid for with the spurious cash only. But in regard to other commodities, this is matter of special bargain, and accordingly there is for these articles a double market price.

Chinese cash is emphatically "filthy lucre." It cannot be handled without contamination. The strings, of five hundred or a thousand (nominal) pieces, are exceedingly liable to break, which involves great trouble in recounting and re-tying. There is no uniformity of weight in the current copper cash, but all is both bulky and heavy. Cash to the value of a Mexican dollar weigh not less than eight pounds avoirdupois. A few hundred cash are all that any one can carry about in the little bags which are suspended for this purpose from the girdle. If it is desired to use a larger sum than a few strings, the transportation becomes a serious matter. The losses on transactions in ingots of silver are always great, and the person who uses them is inevitably cheated both in buying and in selling. If he employs the bills of cash-shops, the difficulty is not greatly relieved, since those of one region are either wholly uncurrent in another region not far away, or will be taken only at a heavy discount, while the person who at last takes them to be redeemed has in prospect a certain battle with the harpies of the shop by which the bills were issued, as to the quality of the cash which is to be paid for them. Under these grave disabilities, the wonder is that the Chinese are able to do any business at all; and yet, as we daily perceive, they are so accustomed to these annoyances that their burden appears scarcely felt, and the only serious complaint on this score comes from foreigners.

It is very common for the traveller through a Chinese village to see a donkey lying at full length, and attached to a post by a strong strap passed about his neck. But instead of adjusting himself to the length of his strap, the beast frequently drags himself to the utmost limit of his tether, and reclines with his head at an angle of forty-five degrees, his neck stretched in such a way as to threaten the dislocation of the cervical vertebræ. We wonder why he does not break his neck, and still more what pleasure there can be in the apparent attempt to do so. No Occidental donkey would behave in such a way. The reader who has followed us thus far through these inadequate illustrations of our topic will bear in mind that the Chinese race, though apparently in a condition of semi-strangulation, seems to itself comparatively comfortable, which is but to say that the Chinese standard of comfort and convenience, and the standard to which we are accustomed, are widely variant, which is the proposition with which we began. The Chinese has learned to accommodate himself to his environment. To such inconveniences as he encounters, he submits with exemplary patience, well knowing them to be inevitable.

It is not unusual to hear persons who have considerable acquaintance with the Chinese and their ways, especially in the aspects to which our attention has just been drawn, affirm that the Chinese are not civilised. This very superficial and erroneous judgment is due to an unphilosophical confounding of civilisation and comfort. In considering the present condition of China, which is much what it was three centuries ago, it is well to look upon the changes through which we ourselves have passed, for thus only can we arrive at a just comparison. We cannot think of the England of Milton, Shakespeare, and Elizabeth as an uncivilised country, but nothing is more certain than that to the most of us it would now prove to be intolerable.

It is superfluous to allude to the manifold and complex causes which have brought about such astonishing changes in the British Islands within the past three centuries. Yet more wonderful is the radical revolution which within the last fifty years has taken place in the standard of comfort and convenience. If we were compelled to return to the crude ways of our great-grandfathers and grandfathers, it might be a question whether life for us would be worth living. Times have changed, and we have changed with them. In China, on the contrary, times have not changed, and neither have the people. The standard of comfort and convenience is the same now as it has been for centuries. When new conditions arise, these standards will inevitably alter. That they will ever be the same as those to which we have become accustomed is, however, to be neither expected nor desired.

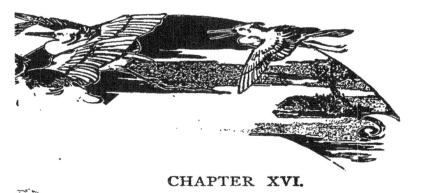

CHAPTER XVI.

THAT physical vitality which forms so important a background for other Chinese characteristics, deserves consideration by itself. It may be regarded in four aspects: the reproductive power of the Chinese race, its adaptation to different circumstances, its longevity, and its recuperative power.

The first impression which the traveller derives from the phenomena of Chinese life is that of redundance. China seems to be full of people. It seems to be so because it is so. Japan, too, appears to have a large population, but it does not take a very discriminating eye to perceive that the dense population of Japan bears no proportion to the dense population of China. In respect of relative and absolute density of population, China more nearly resembles India than any other country. But the people and the languages of India are many and various, while the people of China, with some exceptions not materially affecting the issue, are one and the same. This first impression of a redundant population is everywhere confirmed, no matter in what portion of this broad Empire we set our foot. Where the population is in reality sparse, this is generally found to be due to causes which are susceptible of easy explanation. The terrible inroads of the great T'aip'ing rebellion, followed by the only less destructive Mohammedan rebellion, and by the almost unparalleled famine of 1877—78, extending over five provinces, reduced the total population of China, perhaps by many scores of millions. The

144

devastations due to war are not·so soon repaired to the eye as they would be in Western lands, owing to the great reluctance of the Chinese to leave their ancestral homes and go into new regions. Nevertheless, it is not difficult to perceive that the forces of waste, no matter how devastating, are not so powerful as the forces of repair. With a few decades of peace and good crops, almost any part of China would, we think, recuperate from the disasters which during this century have come in such battalions. The provision for this recuperation is visible to every one, and forces itself upon his notice whether he does or does not desire to contemplate it. In any part of the Chinese Empire the most conspicuous objects in the towns and villages are the troops of Chinese children, with which, as Charles Lamb says in his deprecation of the pride of over-proud mothers, "every blind alley swarms." It is one of the standing marvels of Chinese society by what means such a vast army of little ones is fed and clothed, and it must be well borne in mind that many of them are not "fed and clothed" to any extent; in other words, that the most extreme poverty does not apparently tend to diminish Chinese population.

The only permanent and effective check upon the rapid increase of the Chinese population appears to be the confirmed use of opium, a foe to the Chinese race as deadly as war, famine, or pestilence. It is by no means necessary, in order to receive a high idea of the multiplying power of the Chinese, to assume the existence in China of a population far vaster in numbers than that of any other country. Even if we take the lowest estimate of about two hundred and fifty millions, the point is abundantly established, for the question is not one of the mere number of people, but of the rate of increase. In the absence of trustworthy statistics, we must be content to come at conclusions in a general and inexact way; but fortunately in this matter it is almost impossible to go wrong. The

Chinese marry at a very early age, and the desire for posterity is the one ruling passion in which, next to the love of money, the Chinese race is most agreed. Contrast the apparent growth of the Chinese at any point, with the condition of the population in France, where the rate of increase is the lowest in all Europe, and where the latest returns show an absolute decrease in the number of inhabitants. Such facts have excited the gravest fears as to the future of that great country. The Chinese, on the other hand, show no more signs of race decay than the Anglo-Saxons. The earliest recorded command given by God to mankind was that in which they were instructed to "be fruitful and multiply and replenish the earth." That command, as a learned professor once remarked, "has been obeyed, and it is the only command of God that has been obeyed," and of no country is this more true than of China.

The Chinese Empire, as we have already had occasion to remark, extends through a great area in latitude and longitude, and embraces within itself almost every variety of soil, climate, and production. So far as appears, the Chinese flourish equally in the subtropical region, the subarctic region, or anywhere between. Whatever differences are observed seem to be due to the character of the region itself and its capacity to sustain the population, rather than to any inherent difference in the capacity of the people to adapt themselves to one region rather than to another. The emigrating portions of the Chinese people come from a relatively minute area in the provinces of Kuangtung and Fukien, but wherever they go, to India, Burma, Siam, the East Indies, the Pacific Islands, Australasia, Mexico, the United States, the West Indies, Central America, or South America, we never hear that they fail to adapt themselves with wonderful and immediate success to their environment, whatever it may chance to be. What we do hear, however, is that their adaptation is so quick and so perfect, their industry and their economy so in excess of those of the natives of these lands, their solidarity and their power of mutual cohesion so phenomenal, that it is necessary for the security of the remainder of the human race that "the Chinese must go!" Under these circumstances, it is certainly most fortunate for the peace of mind of that portion of mankind which is not Chinese, that this people does not as a whole take to emigration on a large scale. If the eastern part of the Asiatic continent were now as full of irrepressible human beings, longing to turn their energies towards the rest of the planet, as was Central Asia in the middle ages, it is hard to see what would become either of us, or of our doctrine that the fittest only survive.

The utter absence of any kind of statistics renders it impossible to speak of the longevity of the Chinese people in any other than the most general way. Probably all observers would agree in the conclusion that there is no part of China in which old people are not exceedingly numerous. The aged are always treated with great respect, and old age is held to be an exceedingly great honour, and is reckoned as the foremost of the five varieties of felicity. The extreme care which is taken to preserve accurate records of the date of birth, down to the precise hour, tends to precision of statement when there is any occasion for such precision, albeit the ordinary method of counting, as has been mentioned, is so loose and inaccurate. The testimony of graveyard tablets is in favour of a considerable degree of longevity among the common people, but except in the vicinity of supplies of stone these tablets are found over only a few graves, so that, whatever inferences might otherwise be drawn from them as witnesses, the tablets are practically valueless.

It is not common to hear of Chinese who are more than a hundred years of age, but short of that limit the numbers of very aged who could anywhere be collected, if sufficient inducement were offered, we must consider as very large. Indeed, when the exceedingly imperfect nutrition of the poor, who constitute so large a part of the population of China, is taken into account, it becomes a wonder how such numbers of people survive to so great an age. It is well known that in all Western lands throughout the present century the average duration of life has been constantly rising. This is due to the increased attention paid to the laws of life, to improved means of preventing disease, and to better means of treating it. It must be remembered that in China, on the other hand, the conditions of life do not seem to vary greatly from what they were when Columbus discovered America. If social and medical science could do for China what has been done for England within the past fifty years, the number of very old people in the former country would certainly be very greatly increased.

The complete ignorance of the laws of hygiene which characterises almost all Chinese, and their apparent contempt for those laws even when apprehended, are well known to all foreigners who live in China. To a foreign observer it is a standing problem why the various diseases which this ignorance and defiance of natural laws invite, do not exterminate the Chinese altogether. While vast numbers of people do die every year in China of diseases which are entirely preventable, the fact that the number of such persons is not indefinitely greater argues on the part of the Chinese a marvellous capacity to resist disease and to recover from it. The readiness of Chinese to throw away their lives on very slight provocation is a characteristic as marked as the tenacity of their hold upon them.

In the total absence of those vital statistics to which we have already so often regretfully referred, we are obliged to depend upon the recorded observations of foreigners, which, owing to the constantly increasing number of foreign dispensaries and hospitals, are becoming year by year more numerous and more valuable.

To analyse and tabulate the medical reports issued even in a single year, with a view to illustrating the recuperative power of the Chinese, would be a most useful task, and the result would certainly present the object in a fresh and forcible manner. We must, however, be content with the mere statement of a few cases, by way of illustration, two of which occurred within the knowledge of the writer, while the third is taken from the published reports of a large hospital in Tientsin. The whole force of instances of this sort depends upon the undoubted fact that they are by no means isolated and altogether exceptional cases, but are such as could be matched by the observation of very many of our readers.

Several years ago, while living in a house with a Chinese family, the writer heard one afternoon the most dismal screams under the window, where was placed a large beehive, made of adobe bricks, and open at the bottom. A little boy fourteen months of age was playing in the yard, and seeing this opening into what looked like a convenient play-house, had injudiciously crawled in. The child's head was shaved perfectly bare, and was very red. The bees, either resenting the unusual intrusion, or mistaking the bald pate for a huge peony, promptly lit upon the head and began to sting. Before he could be removed the child had received more than thirty stings. The child cried but a few moments, and then, being laid on the *k'ang*, went to sleep. No medicine of any sort being at hand, nothing was applied to the skin. During the night the child was perfectly quiet, and the next day no trace of the swelling remained.

In the year 1878 a carter in the employ of a foreign family in Peking was taken with the prevalent typhus fever, of which so many died. On the thirteenth day, when the disease reached a crisis, the patient, who had been very ill indeed, became exceedingly violent, exhibiting the strength of several men. Three persons were deputed to watch him, all of whom were exhausted with their labours. During the night of this day the patient was tied to the bed to prevent his escape. While the watchers were all asleep he contrived to loosen the cords with which he was bound, and escaped from the house perfectly naked. He was missed at about 3 A.M., and the whole premises were searched, including the wells, into which it was feared he might have plunged. He was traced to the wall of the compound, which was nine or ten feet in height, and which he had scaled by climbing a tree. He leaped or fell to the ground on the outer side of this wall, and at once made his way to the moat just inside the great wall which separates the Tartar city of Peking from the Chinese city. Here he was found two hours later, his head wedged fast between the upright iron bars which prevent passage through the culvert under the wall. As he had passionately demanded to be taken to this place to cool his fever, it was evident that he had been in this situation for a great length of time. On being taken home, his fever was found to be thoroughly broken, and though troubled with rheumatism in the legs, he made a slow but sure recovery.

A Tientsin man, about thirty years of age, had been in the habit of making a living by collecting spent shells around the ground where Chinese troops were engaged in artillery practice. On one occasion he secured a shell, when, on attempting to break it open, it exploded and blew off his left leg. He was admitted to the hospital, and an amputation was performed below the knee. Instead of being cured of this dangerous mode of getting a precarious living, the man returned to it again as soon as possible, and about six months later, under similar circumstances, another explosion took place, which blew off his left hand about two inches above the wrist, leaving a ragged wound. The upper portion of the right arm was severely singed by powder. Deep lacerations took place over the bridge of the nose and on the upper lip; punctured wounds, the result of exploding pieces of shell, were made on the right cheek, on the right upper eyelid, on the posterior edge of the frontal bone, and on the right wrist. There was also a deep cut over the right tibia, exposing the bone. On receiving these severe injuries the man lay in a semi-unconscious and helpless condition for four hours, exposed to the heat of the sun. A mandarin happening to see him, ordered some coolies to carry him to the hospital, himself accompanying them for two miles. The bearers apparently became tired of their burden, and as soon as the mandarin was gone, threw the poor wretch into a ditch to die. Though much exhausted by the hæmorrhage, he managed to crawl out and hop for five hundred yards to a grain-shop, where he found a large basket of meal, which he overturned with his sound arm and coiled himself inside. To get rid of him the owners of the shop carried him in the basket to the hospital gates, where he was left outside to die. Although in a condition of extreme collapse, and with a feeble pulse, due to the loss of so much blood, the patient had no mental impairment and was able to converse intelligibly. He had been addicted to opium smoking, a circumstance which could not have been favourable to recovery. Yet with the exception of diarrhœa on the fifth and sixth days, and slight attacks of malaria, the patient had throughout no bad symptoms, and left the hospital with a wooden leg four weeks after his admission.

If a people with such physical endowments as the Chinese were to be preserved from the effects of war, famines, pestilence, and opium, and if they were to pay some attention to the laws of physiology and of hygiene, and to be uniformly nourished with suitable food, there is reason to think that they alone would be adequate to occupy the principal part of the planet and more.

CHAPTER XVII.

THE term "patience" embraces three quite different mean-- ings. It is the act or quality of expecting long, without complaint, anger, or discontent. It is the power or the act of suffering or bearing quietly or with equanimity any evil—calm endurance. It is also employed as a synonym of persever- ance. That the group of qualities to which reference is here made has a very important bearing on the life of the people to whom they belong, is obvious at a glance. The disadvan- tage arising from a separate and a distinct examination of individual Chinese characteristics is nowhere more obvious than in the consideration of the qualities of patience and per- severance. These characteristics of the Chinese are insep- arably connected with their comparative "absence of nerves," with their "disregard of time," and especially with that quality of "industry" by which the national patience and persever- ance are most conspicuously and most effectively illustrated. What has been already said upon these topics will have served to suggest one of the chief virtues in the Chinese character, but the necessarily desultory treatment involved in such inci- dental mention deserves to be supplemented by a more com- prehensive presentation.

Among a dense population like that of the Chinese Empire, life is often reduced to its very lowest terms, and those terms are literally a "struggle for existence." In order to live, it is necessary to have the means of living, and those means each must obtain for himself as best he can. The Chinese have been well said to "reduce poverty to a science." Deep poverty and a hard struggle for the means of existence will of themselves never make any human being industrious; but if a man or a race is endowed with the instinct of industry, these are the conditions which will tend most effectually to develop industry. The same conditions will also tend to the development of economy, which, as we have seen, is a prominent Chinese quality. These conditions also develop patience and perseverance. The hunter and the fisherman, who know that their livelihood depends upon the stealth and wariness of their movements, and the patience with which they wait for their opportunity, will be stealthy, wary, and patient, no matter whether they happen to belong to the races of mankind classed as "civilised," to those called "semi-civilised," or to those known as "savage." The Chinese have for ages been hunting for a living under conditions frequently the most adverse, and they have thus learned to combine the active industry of the most civilised peoples with the passive patience of the North American Indian.

The Chinese are willing to labour a very long time for very small rewards, because small rewards are much better than none. Ages of experience have taught them that it is very difficult to make industry a stepping-stone to those wider opportunities which we of the West have come to look upon as its natural results. They are "natural" results only in the sense that when appropriate conditions are found these results will follow. A population of five hundred to the square mile. it is scarcely necessary to observe, is not one of the conditions adapted to lead to practical verification of the adage that industry and economy are the two hands of fortune. But the Chinese is content to toil on for such rewards as he may be able to get, and in this contentment he illustrates his virtue of patience.

It is related of the late General Grant, that on his return from his trip around the globe, he was asked what was the most remarkable thing that he saw. He replied at once that the most extraordinary sight which he anywhere beheld was the spectacle of a petty Chinese dealer by his keen competition driving out a Jew. There was great significance in the observation. The qualities of Jewish people are by this time well known, and have led to most surprising results, but the Jews are after all but a small part of the human race. The Chinese, on the other hand, are a considerable percentage of the whole population of the planet. The Jew who was driven out by the Chinese did not presumptively differ in any essential respect from any other Jew. The result of the competition would probably have been the same though the competitors had been different in their identity, for it is morally certain that the successful Chinese did not differ in any essential particular from millions of other Chinese who might have chanced to be in his situation.

It is in his *staying qualities* that the Chinese excels the world. Of that quiet persistence which impels a Chinese student to keep on year after year attending the examinations, until he either takes his degree at the age of ninety or dies in the effort, mention has been already made. No rewards that are likely to ensue, nor any that are possible, will of themselves account for this extraordinary perseverance. It is a part of that innate endowment with which the Chinese are equipped, and is analogous to the fleetness of the deer or the keen sight of the eagle. A similar quality is observed in the meanest beggar at a shop door. He is not a welcome visitor, albeit so frequent in his appearances. But his patience is unfailing, and his perseverance invariably wins its modest reward, a single brass cash.

There is a story of an Arab whose turban was stolen by some unknown person, upon which the loser of this important article of apparel promptly betook himself to the tribal burial-place and seated himself at the entrance. Upon being asked his reason for this strange behaviour, and why he did not pursue the thief, he made the calm and characteristically Oriental reply, " He must come here at last! " One is not infrequently reminded of this exaggeration of passive persistence, not only in the behaviour of individual Chinese, but in the acts of the government as well. The long and splendid reign of the Emperor K'ang Hsi, lasting from 1662 until 1723, made his name more celebrated than that of any other Asiatic monarch. Yet it was in the reign of this greatest of Chinese rulers that the Chinese patriotic pirate, known under the name of Koxinga, ravaged the coasts of the provinces of Kuangtung and Fukien to such a degree that the government junks were totally unable to cope with him. Under these circumstances, K'ang Hsi hit upon the happy expedient of ordering all the people inhabiting this extended coast line to retire into the interior to a distance of thirty *li*, or about nine miles, at which point they were inaccessible even to such stout attacks as this adherent of the old order of things was able to make. This strange command was generally obeyed, and was quite successful in accomplishing its design. Koxinga retired, baffled in his plans, and contented himself with driving the Dutch out of Formosa, and was eventually ennobled under the title of the " Sea-quelling Duke," by which means he was at once pacified and extinguished. Every foreigner reading this singular account is impelled to assent to the comment of the author of the " Middle Kingdom," that a government which was strong enough to compel such a number of maritime subjects to leave their towns and villages, and to retire at such great loss into the interior, ought to have been strong enough to equip a fleet and to put an end to the attacks upon these desolated homes.

Another example of the persistence of the Chinese government is not less remarkable, and is still fresh in the minds of foreign residents in China. In the year 1873 the Chinese General Tso Tsung-tang established himself in Barkoul and Hami, having been sent by the government to endeavour to put a stop to the great Mohammedan rebellion, which, beginning with a mere spark, had spread like wildfire all over western China and through Central Asia. The difficulties to be overcome were so great as to appear almost insuperable. It was then common to meet with articles in the foreign press in China ridiculing both the undertaking of Tso and the fatuity of the government in endeavouring to raise money by loans, in order to pay the heavy war expenses thus incurred. Within a year of his arrival in the rebellious districts, Tso's army was marching on either side of the lofty T'ien-shan in parallel columns, driving the rebels before them. When they reached a country in which the supplies were insufficient, the army was turned into a farming colony and set to cultivating the soil with a view to raising crops for their future support. Thus alternately planting and marching, the "agricultural army" of Tso thoroughly accomplished its work, an achievement which has been thought to be among "the most remarkable in the annals of any modern country."

That quality of Chinese patience which to us seems the most noteworthy of all, is its capacity to wait without complaint and to bear with calm endurance. It has been said that the true way to test the real disposition of a human being is to study his behaviour when he is cold, wet, and hungry. If that is satisfactory, take the individual in question, " warm him, dry him, and fill him up, and you have an angel." There is a conviction which often finds utterance in current literature, that it is as dangerous to meet an Englishman deprived of his dinner as a she-bear robbed of her cubs, and it is not easy to perceive why the truth which underlies this statement is not as applicable to all Anglo-Saxons as to the inhabitants of the British Isles. With all our boasted civilisa-tion we are under bondage to our stomachs.

The writer once saw about one hundred and fifty Chinese, most of whom had come several miles in order to be present at a feast, meet a cruel disappointment. Instead of being able, as was expected, to sit down at about ten o'clock to the feast, which was for many of them the first meal of the day, owing to a combination of unforeseen circumstances they were compelled to stand aside and act as waiters on about as many more individuals. The latter ate with relish and that deliberation which is a trait of Chinese civilisation in which it is far in advance of our own. Before the meal for which they had so long and so patiently waited could be served, an-other delay became necessary, as unforeseen as the first, and far more exasperating. What did these hundred and fifty outraged persons do? If they had been inhabitants of the British Isles, or even of some other portions of "nominally Christian lands," we know very well what they would have done. They would have worn looks of sour discontent, and would have spent the entire day until three o'clock in the afternoon, when it was at last possible to sit down, in growl-ing at their luck, and in snarling at their environment generally. They would have passed fiery resolutions, and have "written a letter with five 'Now, Sirs,' to the London *Times*." The hundred and fifty Chinese did nothing whatever of the sort, and were not only good-tempered all day, but repeatedly observed to their hosts with evident sincerity and with true politeness that it was of no consequence whatever that they had to wait, and that one time was to them exactly as good as another! Does the reader happen to know of any form of Occidental civilisation which would have stood such a sudden and severe strain as that?

That Chinese nerves are totally different from those with which we are endowed has been already shown, but that does not prove that the "obtuse-nerved Turanian" is a stoic like the North American Indian. The Chinese bear their ills not only with fortitude, but, what is often far more difficult, with patience. A Chinese who had lost the use of both eyes applied to a foreign physician to know if the sight could be restored, adding simply that if it could not be restored he should stop being anxious about it. The physician told him that nothing could be done, upon which the man remarked, "Then my heart is at ease." His was not what we call resignation, much less the indifference of despair, but merely the quality which enables us to "bear the ills we have." We have come to recognise worry as the bane in our modern life, the rust which corrodes the blade far more than the hardest use can destroy it. It is well for the Chinese that they are gifted with the capacity not to worry, for taking the race as a whole, there are comparatively few who do not have some very practical reason for deep anxiety. Vast districts of this fertile Empire are periodically subject to drought, flood, and, in consequence, to famine. Social calamities, such as lawsuits, and disasters even more dreaded because indefinite, overhang the head of thousands, but this fact would never be discovered by the observer. We have often asked a Chinese whose possession of his land, his house, and sometimes of his wife, was disputed, what the outcome would be. "There will never be any peace," is a common reply. "And when will the matter come to a head?" "Who knows?" is the frequent answer; "it may be early or it may be late, but there is sure to be trouble in plenty." For life under such conditions what can be a better outfit than an infinite capacity for patience?

The exhibition of Chinese patience which is likely to make the strongest impression upon a foreigner, is that which is unfortunately so often to be seen in all parts of the Empire, when the calamities to which reference has just been made have been realised upon an enormous scale. The provinces of China with which foreigners are most familiar are seldom altogether free from disasters due to flood, drought, and resultant famine. The recollection of the terrible sufferings in the famine of 1877–78, which involved untold millions of people, will not soon fade from the memories of those who were witnesses of that distress. Since then the woes inflicted upon extensive regions by the overflows of the Yellow River, and by its sudden change of channel, have been past all computation or comprehension. Some of the finest parts of several different provinces have been devastated, and fertile soil has been buried a fathom deep in blighting sands of desolation. Thousands of villages have been annihilated, and the wretched inhabitants who have escaped death by flood have been driven forth as wanderers on the face of the earth, without homes and without hope. Great masses of human beings, suddenly ruined and reduced to desperation by no fault of their own, are not agreeable objects of contemplation to any government. Self-preservation is the first law of nature, and what is more natural than that those who, through no preventable causes, have been suddenly brought to starvation, should combine to compel those who have food to share with those who have none?

While it is true that relief is extended in a certain way in some large cities, and where the poor sufferers are most congregated, it is also true that this relief is limited in quantity, brief in duration, and does not provide the smallest remedy for more than a minute percentage of even the worst distress. Towards the prolongation of the lives of those who suffer from great calamities, the government feels itself able to do but a trifle. Towards the reclamation of their land, the reconstruction of their houses, and the resumption of life under new conditions, the government does nothing whatever. It does all that the people expect if it remits its taxes, and it frequently does not remit them until it has been again and again demonstrated to the district magistrate that out of nothing nothing comes. To a foreigner from the lands of the West, where the revolutionary cry of " Bread, bread, or blood! " has become familiar, it is hard to understand why the hordes of homeless, famishing, and desperate refugees, who roam over the provinces blighted by flood or famine, do not precipitate themselves in a mass upon the district magistrate of the region where they have been ruined, and demand some form of succour. It is true that the magistrate would be quite powerless to give them what they demand, but he would be forced to do something, and this would be a precedent for something more. If he failed to " tranquillise " the people he would be removed, and some other official put in his place. To repeated and pressing inquiries put to the Chinese in the great famine as to the reasons why some such plan was not taken, the invariable answer was in the words, " Not dare." It is vain to argue, in reply to this statement, that one might as well be killed for rebellion, albeit unjustly, as to starve to death—nay, much better. The answer is still the same, " Not dare, not dare."

There seem to be two reasons why the Chinese do not adopt some such course. They are a most practical people, and by a kind of instinct the futility of the plan is recognised, and hence it would be next to impossible to effect the needed combination. But we must believe that the principal reason is the unlimited capacity of the Chinese for patient endurance. This it is which brings about one of the most melancholy spectacles to be seen in China, that of thousands of persons quietly starving to death within easy reach of overflowing abundance. The Chinese are so accustomed to this strange sight that they are hardened to it, as old veterans disregard the horrors of battle. Those who suffer these evils have been all their lives confronted by them, although at a little distance. When the disaster comes it is therefore accepted as alike inevitable and remediless. If those who are overtaken by it can trundle their families on wheelbarrows off to some region where a bare subsistence can be begged, they will do that. If the family cannot be kept together, they will disperse, picking up what they can, and reuniting if they succeed in pulling through the distress. If no relief is to be had near at hand, whole caravans will beg their way a journey of a thousand miles in mid-winter to some province where they hope to find that the crops have been better, that labour is more in demand, and that the chances of survival are greater. If the floods have abated, the mendicant farmer returns to his home long enough to scratch a crack in the mud while it is still too soft to bear the weight of an animal for ploughing, and in this tiny rift he deftly drops a little seed wheat, and again goes his devious way, begging a subsistence until his small harvest shall be ripe. If Providence favours him he becomes once more a farmer, and no longer a beggar, but with the distinctly recognised possibility of ruin and starvation never far away.

It has always been thought to be a powerful argument for the immortality of the soul, that its finest powers often find in this life no fit opportunity for expansion. If this be a valid argument, is there not reason to infer that the unequalled patient endurance of the Chinese race must have been designed for some nobler purpose than merely to enable them to bear with fortitude the ordinary ills of life and the miseries of gradual starvation? If it be the teaching of history that the fittest survive, then surely a race with such a gift, backed by a splendid vitality, must have before it a great future.

CHAPTER XVIII.

WE have already seen that the capacity of the Chinese to bear the ills they have, is a wonderful, and to us in most cases an incomprehensible talent, which has well been called a psychological paradox. Notwithstanding their apparently hopeless condition, they do not appear to lose hope, or rather, they seem to struggle on without it and often against it. We do not perceive among them that restlessness which characterises the people of most other nations, especially towards the close of the nineteenth century. They do not cherish plans which seem to them to lead ultimately to "a good time coming," and they do not appear to suppose that there is any such time to be expected.

But the terms "patience" and "perseverance" by no means cover the whole field of the Chinese virtues in this direction. We must also take account of their quietness of mind in conditions often very unfavourable to it, and of that chronic state of good spirits which we designate by the term "cheerfulness." Our main object is to call attention to the existence of such virtues; yet we may perhaps be able incidentally to suggest certain considerations which in part help to account for them.

By the term "contentedness" we do not mean to imply that any individual in China is satisfied with what he possesses in such a way and to such a degree that he does not wish to better his condition. The contentedness of the Chinese, as we have seen in speaking of their conservatism, is most conspicuously seen when we consider the system under which they live. That system they do not wish to change. That this is the temper of the great mass of the Chinese, we have no doubt whatever. It is a mode of viewing the phenomena of life which we designate by the general name "conservative," and of this the Chinese are as conspicuous examples as any people of whom we have any record. It must be evident that such conceptions of Chinese society, permeating the whole mass of the people and inherited from distant ages, powerfully tend to repress any practical exhibitions of discontent with the allotments of fortune. Evils of course they feel, but these are considered to be inevitable. Persons who seriously and uniformly take this view are not the ones who are likely to endeavour to upset the established order of things simply because the pressure upon themselves is severe. In no country is the educated class more really a leader of thought and action than in China. But the educated class is firmly persuaded that for China and the Chinese the present system is the best obtainable. Their vast and varied experience in the long reach of Chinese history has taught the Chinese by convincing object-lessons that solid, practical improvements in their system are not to be got for the trying. Their adamantine conservatism is the slow outgrowth of this experience.

Without being fully aware of the fact, the Chinese are a nation of fatalists. There is a great deal in the Classics about the "decrees of heaven." There is a great deal in popular speech about "heaven's will." Expressions of this sort often bear a close analogy to the manner in which we speak of Providence. But there is this radical distinction in the underlying thought: to us "Providence" signifies the care and forethought of a Being who is in distinct relations to all creatures that on earth do dwell, all of whom are included in His thought and forethought; to the Chinese, whose practical conception of "heaven" is an altogether impersonal one and utterly vague, whatever the mode of expression, the practical aspect of the matter is simply that of fate. "Good fate" and "bad fate" are phrases which have to the Chinese a meaning similar to that conveyed by the expressions in children's story-books, "good fairy" and "bad fairy." By means of these mysterious agencies anything whatever can be done, anything whatever can be undone.

The whole complicated theory and practice of Chinese geomancy, necromancy, and fortune-telling, are based upon the play and interplay of forces which are visibly expressed by means of straight lines. The number of Chinese who make a living out of these theories of the universe practically applied, is past all estimation. While the extent to which such superstitions influence the daily life of the people varies greatly in different parts of the Empire, they are everywhere real and living factors in the minds of the masses. Nothing is more common than to hear an especially unfortunate Chinese man or woman remark, "It is my fate." The natural outcome of such a creed would be to cause despair, or if the hopefulness with which mankind, and especially the Chinese, are mercifully endowed come to the rescue, to urge them to a patient biding till their time shall come, and fate shall again favour them. Perhaps the Chinese are not as consistent fatalists as the Turks, and perhaps the "fate" of the Chinese is not identical with "Kismet"; but it is evident that a people so persuaded of the existence of fate as are the Chinese, must be indisposed for violent struggles against what they believe to be, in the nature of things, unavoidable.

It is a venerable observation of the Greeks that history is philosophy teaching by examples. As we have just seen, their own history has been the teacher of the Chinese, and the lessons which they have drawn are all of a conservative character. But no nation is educated by simply knowing its own annals, as no man can be said to know anything who knows only what has happened to himself. It is at this point that Chinese knowledge is fatally defective. Of those great episodes in modern history which we denote by the expressions the Renaissance, the Reformation, the discovery of America, and the birth of modern science, the Chinese know nothing. By those influences which brought nations into a more intimate contact than ever before, and which have slowly developed a conception of the rights of man, the Chinese as a people have been totally unaffected.

The improvement of the condition of the people is not a living issue to those who exist and have all their being in the extinct dynasties of the past. The application of the great laws of political economy to the advantage of all departments of the state, has no attractions to those who know no more of political economy than our ancestors at the time of the crusades, and who would not care for it if they did know of it. The first impulse to improvement comes from seeing the superior condition of others. The vast mass of the Chinese people do not see any evidence of such a better condition elsewhere, because they know nothing whatever about other countries. Those, on the other hand, who do know something of such countries, and who might know much more, are chained by fetters of conservatism. Nothing really beneficial to the masses can be done, except upon a large scale, and no body of persons in China capable of working upon a large scale wishes anything done in these lines. While this does not of itself promote content among the masses, it strangles any effective manifestation of discontent before it can find expression. Thus, viewed from the social standpoint, Chinese contentedness is the antithesis of progress, and interdicts it.

We have already spoken of the fact that Chinese experience is against the practicability of any amelioration of the condition of the people by means which are at hand. To the foreigner, acquainted with the experience of other lands in modern times, the simple, obvious, indispensable recipe for the relief of many of the ills to which the Chinese are subject, is emigration. This we know from induction to be the remedy which the Chinese could adopt most easily, and with the greatest assurance of success. But this is an expedient which the Chinese themselves will never adopt, for the reason that it will take them away from the home of their fathers and from the graves of their ancestors, to which, by the theory of Confucianism, they are inexorably linked. Generally speaking, no Chinese will leave his home to seek his fortune at a distance, unless he is in some way driven to do so. His ideal of life is to be

> " Fixed like a plant on his peculiar spot,
>   To draw nutrition, propagate, and rot."

Generally speaking, no Chinese leaves his home not intending to return. His hope is always to come back rich, to die and be buried where his ancestors are buried. As long as this fatal "thirst for decomposing under the immediate feet of their posterity" continues to be the principal passion of the Chinese, so long will they be debarred from the one obvious method by which their ills might be effectually lightened. Real amelioration of the condition of the mass of the Chinese people where they are, we believe to be well-nigh impossible, and transplantation on any adequate scale they would not tolerate except as a decree of "fate." An unconscious consciousness of this state of things checks the expression of a discontent which has abundant cause to make itself heard.

But what we have thus far said in elucidation of the peculiar Chinese faculty of being contented, to which we in Western lands have nothing corresponding, fails after all to go to the root of the matter. The truth seems to be that the Chinese is a being formed for contentment, as the fin of the fish is formed for the water, or the wing of the bird for the air. He is what he calls "heaven-endowed" with a talent for industry, for peace, and for social order. He is gifted with a matchless patience, and with unparalleled forbearance under ills the causes of which are perceived to be beyond his reach. As a rule, he has a happy temperament, no nervous system to speak of, and a digestion like that of the ostrich. For these reasons, and others which we have imperfectly expressed, instead of spending his energies in butting against stone walls, which he has found to be more or less unyielding, he simply submits for the most part without serious complaint to what he cannot help. He acts in the spirit of the old adage, "What can't be cured must be endured." In short, a Chinese knows how to abound, and he knows how to want, and, what is of capital importance, he knows how to be contented in either condition.

The cheerfulness of the Chinese, which we must regard as a national characteristic, is intimately connected with their contentedness of mind. To be happy is more than they expect, but, unlike us, they are generally willing to be as happy as they can. Inordinate fastidiousness is not a common Chinese failing. They are generally model guests. Any place will do, any food is good enough for them. Even the multitudes who are insufficiently clothed and inadequately fed, preserve their serenity of spirit in a way which to us appears marvellous.

An almost universal illustration of Chinese cheerfulness is to be found in their sociability, in striking contrast to the glum exclusiveness so often characteristic of the Anglo-Saxon. One of the main enjoyments of the Chinese seems to be chatting with one another, and whether they are old friends or perfect strangers makes very little difference. That this appreciation of human society is a great alleviation of many of the miseries which the Chinese suffer, cannot be doubted.

It is also to be noted that many Chinese have the happy art

of adorning their very humble surroundings with plants and flowers, of which they are extremely fond.   This is but an in-articulate way of saying, " We have not much, but we make the most of what we have."

Many as are the criticisms which we perhaps justly make upon our Chinese servants, it is only fair to mention that they will frequently submit to serious inconveniences, and will do extra work for many persons for a great length of time, not only without complaint, but often with an apparent uncon-sciousness that there is anything to complain of.

The Chinese who is in the service of others and is in the habit of bewailing his hard fate, is often laughed at by his companions, and sometimes he becomes a by-word and a proverb.   Of the tireless industry of the Chinese we have already spoken, but it is noteworthy that those whose spindle is heard till after midnight, working it may be in the dark in order to save a farthing's worth of oil, are not the ones whose mouths are filled with bitter plaints.   They rise early and toil late, and they do so as a matter of course.   Some of those whose labour is most exhausting, as coolies, boat-trackers, and wheelbarrow men, not only are not heard to murmur at the unequal distribution of this world's goods, but when they have opportunities of resting do so in excellent spirits, and with an evident enjoyment of their humble fare.   Discerning travellers have often called attention to this very significant trait of the Chinese workman.   In Mr. Hosie's " Three Years in Western China," he says, speaking of the upper Yang-tze : " The trackers, too, deserve a word of mention.   They were, with the exception of the musician and the diver, almost all lithe young fellows, always willing to jump on shore, never spending more than a quarter of an hour over their rice and vegetables, and never out of temper."   Mr. Archibald Little, in his " Through the Yang-tze Gorges " bears a similar testimony: " Our five trackers clung on their hands and feet to the jagged rocks, as they pulled the boat up inch by inch. I cannot sufficiently admire the pluck and endurance of these poor coolies, earning but two dollars in cash for the two months' voyage, and getting three meals of coarse rice, fla- voured with a little fried cabbage, for their sustenance, upon which they are called to put forth their strength from dawn to dark daily."

The writer is acquainted with a Chinese who was employed by a foreigner in pushing a heavy barrow, on journeys often months in duration. Upon these trips it was necessary to start early, to travel late, to transport heavy loads over steep and rugged mountains, in all seasons and in all weathers, fording chilling rivers with bare feet and legs, and at the end of every stage to prepare his master's food and lodging. All this labo- rious work was done for a very moderate compensation, and always without complaint, and at the end of several years of this service his master testified that he had never once seen this servant out of temper! Is there any reader of these lines of whom, *mutatis mutandis*, the same statement could be truth- fully made?

Perhaps it is in time of sickness that the innate cheerful- ness of the Chinese disposition shows to most advantage. As a rule, they take the most optimistic view, or, at all events, wish to seem to do so, both of their own condition and of that of others. Their cheery hopefulness often does not forsake them even in physical weakness and in extreme pain. We have known multitudes of cases where Chinese patients, suffering from every variety of disease, frequently in deep poverty, not always adequately nourished, at a distance from their homes, sometimes neglected or even abandoned by their relatives, and with no ray of hope for the future visible, yet maintained a cheerful equanimity of temper, which was a constant albeit an unintentional rebuke to the nervous impatience which, under like circumstances, would be sure to characterise the Anglo-Saxon.

Chinese endued with this happy temperament we believe to be by no means rare. Every one of much experience in China has met them. We repeat that if the teaching of history as to what happens to " the fittest " is to be trusted, there is a magnificent future for the Chinese race.

Interior of a Mohammedan Mosque.

CHAPTER XIX.

FILIAL PIETY.

TO discuss the characteristics of the Chinese without men-
tioning filial piety, is out of the question. But the filial
piety of the Chinese is not an easy subject to treat. These
words, like many others which we are obliged to employ, have
among the Chinese a sense very different from that which we
are accustomed to attach to them, and a sense of which no
English expression is an exact translation. This is also true
of a great variety of terms used in Chinese, and of no one
more than of the word ordinarily rendered "ceremony" (*li*),
with which filial piety is intimately connected. To illustrate
this, and at the same time to furnish a background for what
we have to say of the characteristic under discussion, we cannot do better than to cite a passage from M. Callery (quoted
in the "Middle Kingdom"): "Ceremony epitomises the entire
Chinese mind; and in my opinion, the Book of Rites is *per se*
the most exact and complete monograph that China has been
able to give of herself to other nations. Its affections, if it
has any, are satisfied by ceremony; its duties are fulfilled by
ceremony; its virtues and vices are referred to ceremony; the
natural relations of created beings essentially link themselves
in ceremonial—in a word, to that people ceremonial is man
as a moral, political, and religious being, in his multiplied
relations with family, society, and religion." Every one must
agree in Dr. Williams's comment upon this passage, that it
shows how "meagre a rendering is 'ceremony' for the Chinese idea of *li*, for it includes not only the external conduct,

but involves the right principles from which all true etiquette and politeness spring."

One of the most satisfactory methods to ascertain the Chinese view of filial piety would be to trace the instruction which is contained on this subject in the Four Books, and in the other Classics, especially in the " Filial Piety Classic." Our present object is merely to direct attention to the doctrine as put into practice by the Chinese, of whom filial piety, in the sense in which they understand it, is not merely a characteristic but a peculiarity. It must be remembered that Chinese filial piety is many-sided, and the same things are not to be seen in all situations or by all observers.

At the Missionary Conference held in Shanghai in the year 1877, a paper was read by Dr. Yates on "Ancestral Worship," in which he embodied the results of his thirty years' experience in China. In one of the opening sentences of this elaborate essay, the author, after speaking of ancestral worship considered merely as a manifestation of filial piety, continues: " The term ' filial ' is misleading, and we should guard against being deceived by it. Of all the people of whom we have any knowledge, the sons of the Chinese are most unfilial, disobedient to parents, and pertinacious in having their own way from the time they are able to make known their wants." Dr. Legge, the distinguished translator of the Chinese Classics, who retired from China after thirty-three years' experience, has quoted this passage from Dr. Yates, for the purpose of most emphatically dissenting from it, declaring that his experience of the Chinese has been totally different. This merely illustrates the familiar truth that there is room for honest difference of opinion among men, as among thermometers, and that a correct view can only be reached by combining results that appear to be absolutely inharmonious into a whole that shall be even more comprehensive than either of its parts.

That Chinese children have no proper discipline, that they are not taught to obey their parents, and that as a rule they have no idea of prompt obedience as we understand it, is a most indubitable fact attested by wide experience. But that the later years of these ungoverned or half-governed children generally do not exhibit such results as we should have expected, appears to be not less a truth. The Chinese think and say that "the crooked tree, when it is large, will straighten itself," by which metaphor is figured the belief that children when grown will do the things which they ought to do. However it may be in regard to other duties, there really appears to be some foundation for this theory in the matter of filial behaviour. The occasion of this phenomenon seems to lie in the nature of the Chinese doctrine of filial piety, the manner in which it is taught, and the prominence which is everywhere given to it. It is said in the "Filial Piety Classic" that: "There are three thousand crimes to which one or the other of the five kinds of punishment is attached as a penalty, and of these no one is greater than disobedience to parents." One of the many sayings in common circulation runs as follows: "Of the hundred virtues filial conduct is the chief, but it must be judged by the intentions, not by acts; for, judged by acts, there would not be a filial son in the world." The Chinese are expressly taught that a defect of any virtue, when traced to its root, is a lack of filial piety. He who violates propriety is deficient in filial conduct. He who serves his prince but is not loyal lacks filial piety. He who is a magistrate without due respect for its duties is lacking in filial piety. He who does not show proper sincerity towards his friends lacks filial piety. He who fails to exhibit courage in battle lacks filial piety. Thus the doctrine of filial conduct is seen to embrace much more than mere acts, and descends into the motives, taking cognisance of the whole moral being.

In the popular apprehension, the real basis of the virtue of filial conduct is felt to be gratitude. This is emphasised in the " Filial Piety Classic," and in the chapter of the Sacred Edicts on the subject. The justification of the period of three years' mourning is found, according to Confucius, in the undoubted social fact that " for the first three years of its existence the child is not allowed to leave the arms of its parents," as if the one term were in some way an offset for the other. The young lamb is proverbially a type of filial behaviour, for it has the grace to kneel when sucking its dam. Filial piety demands that we should preserve the bodies which our parents gave us, otherwise we seem to slight their kindness. Filial piety requires that we should serve our parents while they live, and worship them when dead. Filial piety requires that a son should follow in the steps of his father. " If for the three years he does not alter from the way of his father," says Confucius, " he may be called filial." But if the parents are manifestly in the wrong, filial piety does not forbid an attempt at their reformation, as witness the following, quoted by Dr. Williams from the Book of Rites: " When his parents are in error, the son, with a humble spirit, pleasing countenance, and gentle tones, must point it out to them. If they do not receive his reproof, he must strive more and more to be dutiful and respectful to them till they are pleased, and then he must again point out their error. But if he does not succeed in pleasing them, it is better that he should continue to reiterate reproof than permit them to do injury to the whole department, district, village, or neighbourhood. And if the parents, irritated and displeased, chastise their son till the blood flows from him, even then he must not dare to harbour the least resentment ; but on the contrary, should treat them with increased respect and dutifulness." It is to be feared that in most Western lands the admonition of parents upon these terms would be allowed to fall into desuetude, and it is not to be wondered that we do not hear much of it even in China!

In the second book of the " Confucian Analects " we find record of several different answers which Confucius gave as to the nature of filial piety, his replies being varied according to the circumstances of the questioners. The first answer which is mentioned is that to an officer of the State of Lu, and is comprised in the compendious expression " wu-wei," which he apparently left in the mind of the querist as a kind of seed to be developed by time and reflection. The words " wu-wei " simply mean " not disobedient," and it is natural that Mang I, the officer who had inquired, so understood them. But Confucius, like the rest of his countrymen since, had a " talent for indirection," and instead of explaining himself to Mang I, he waited until some time later when one of Confucius' disciples was driving him out, when the Master repeated the question of Mang I to this disciple, and also the reply. The disciple, whose name was Fan Ch'ih, on hearing the words " wu-wei," very naturally asked, " What did you mean ? " which gave the Master the requisite opportunity to tell what he really meant, in the following words: " That parents when alive should be served according to propriety, that when dead they should be buried according to propriety, and that they should be sacrificed to according to propriety." The conversation between Confucius and Fan Ch'ih was intended by the former to lead the latter to report it to Mang I, who would thus discover what was meant to be inferred from the words " wu-wei "! In other answers of the Master to the question, What is denoted by filial piety? Confucius laid stress upon the requirement that parents should be treated with reverence, adding that when they are not so treated, mere physical care for them is on a plane with the care bestowed upon dogs and horses.

These passages have been quoted in this connection, to show that the notion that filial piety consists largely in compliance with the wishes of parents, and in furnishing them what they need and what they want, is a very ancient idea in China. Confucius expressly says: "The filial piety of the present time means (only) the support of one's parents," implying that in ancient times, of which he was so fond, and which he wished to revive, it was otherwise. Many ages have elapsed since these conversations of the Master took place, and his doctrine has had time to penetrate the marrow of the Chinese people, as indeed it has done. But if Confucius were alive to-day, there is good reason to think that he would affirm more emphatically than ever, "The filial piety of the present time means only the support of one's parents." That the popular conscience responds to the statement of the claims of filial piety, as to no other duty, has been already observed, but in the same connection it ought to be clearly understood what this filial piety is supposed to connote. If ten uneducated persons, taken at random, were to be asked what they mean by being "filial," it is altogether probable that nine of them would reply, "Not letting one's parents get angry," that is, because they are not properly served. Or, in a more condensed form, filial piety is "wu-wei," "not disobedient," which is what the Master said it is, albeit he used the words in "a Pickwickian sense."

If any of our readers wish to see this theory in a practical form, let them consider the four-and-twenty ensamples of filial piety, immortalised in the familiar little book called by that name. In one of these cases, a boy who lived in the "After Han Dynasty," at the age of six paid a visit to a friend, by whom he was entertained with oranges. The precocious youth on this occasion executed the common Chinese feat of stealing two oranges, and thrusting them up his sleeve. But as he was making his parting bows the fruit rolled out, and left the lad in an embarrassing situation, to which, however, he was equal. Kneeling down before his host, he made the memorable observation which has rendered his name illustrious for nearly two millenniums: "My mother loves oranges very much, and I wanted them for her." As this lad's father was an officer of high rank, it would seem to an Occidental critic that the boy might have enjoyed other opportunities for gratifying her desire for oranges, but to the Chinese the lad is a classic instance of filial devotion, because at this early age he was thoughtful for his mother, or perhaps so quick at inventing an excuse. Another lad, of the Chin Dynasty, whose parents had no mosquito nets, at the age of eight hit upon the happy expedient of going to bed very early, lying perfectly quiet all night, not even brandishing a fan, in order that the family mosquitoes might gorge themselves upon him alone, and allow his parents to sleep in peace! Another lad of the same dynasty lived with a stepmother who disliked him, but as she was very fond of carp, which were not to be obtained during the winter, he adopted the injudicious plan of taking off his clothes and lying on the ice, which so impressed a brace of carp who had observed the proceeding from the under side that they made a hole in the ice and leaped forth in order to be cooked for the benefit of the irascible stepmother!

According to the Chinese teaching, one of the instances of unfilial conduct is found in "selfish attachment to wife and children." In the chapter of the Sacred Edict already quoted, this behaviour is mentioned in the same connection with gambling, and the exhortations against each are of the same kind. The typical instance of true filial devotion among the twenty-four just mentioned, is a man who lived in the Han Dynasty, and who, being very poor, found that he had not sufficient food to nourish both his mother and his child, three years of age. "We are so poor," he said to his wife, "that we cannot even support mother. Moreover, the little one shares mother's food. Why not bury the child? We may have another, but if mother should die we cannot obtain her again." His wife dared not oppose him, and accordingly a hole was dug more than two feet deep, when a vase of gold was found with a suitable inscription, stating that Heaven bestowed this reward on a filial son. If the golden vase had not emerged, the child would have been buried alive, and according to the doctrine of filial piety, as commonly understood, rightly so. " Selfish attachment to wife and children " must not hinder the murder of a child to prolong the life of its grandparent.

The Chinese believe that there are cases of obstinate illness of parents, which can only be cured by the offering of a portion of the flesh of a son or a daughter, which must be cooked and eaten by the unconscious parent. While the favourable results are not certain, they are very probable. The Peking *Gazette* frequently contains references to cases of this sort. The writer is personally acquainted with a young man who cut off a slice of his leg to cure his mother, and who exhibited the scar with the pardonable pride of an old soldier. While such cases are doubtless not very common, they are probably not excessively rare.

The most important aspect of Chinese filial piety is indicated in a saying of Mencius, that: " There are three things which are unfilial, and to have no posterity is the greatest of them." The necessity for posterity arises from the necessity for continuing the sacrifices for ancestors, which is thus made the most important duty in life. It is for this reason that every son must be married at as early an age as possible. It is by no means uncommon to find a Chinese a grandfather by the time he is thirty-six. An acquaintance of the writer's accused himself upon his death-bed of having been unfilial in two particulars: first, that he had not survived long enough to bury his old mother; and second, that he had neglected to arrange for the marriage of his son, a child of about ten years of age. This view of filial piety would doubtless commend itself to the average Chinese.

The failure to have male children is mentioned first among the seven causes for the divorce of a wife. The necessity for male children has led to the system of concubinage, with all its attendant miseries. It furnishes a ground, eminently rational to the Chinese mind, for the greatest delight at the birth of sons, and a corresponding depression on occasion of the birth of daughters. It is this aspect of the Chinese doctrine which is responsible for a large proportion of the enormous infanticide which is known to exist in China. This crime is much more common in the south of China than in the north, where it often seems to be wholly unknown. But it must be remembered that it is the most difficult of all subjects upon which to secure exact information, just in proportion to the public sentiment against it. The number of illegitimate children can never be small, and there is everywhere the strongest motive to destroy all such, whatever the sex. Even if direct testimony to the destruction of the life of female infants in any region were much less than it is, it would be a moral certainty that a people among whom the burial alive of a child of three in order to facilitate the support of its grandmother is held to be an act of filial devotion, could not possibly be free from the guilt of destroying the lives of unwelcome female infants.

Reference has already been made to the theory of Chinese mourning for parents, which is supposed to consume three full years, but which in practice is mercifully shortened to twenty-seven months. In the seventeenth book of the " Confucian Analects " we read of one of the disciples of the Master, who argued stoutly against three years as a period for mourning, maintaining that one year was enough. To this the Master conclusively replied that the superior man could not be happy during the whole three years of mourning, but that if this particular disciple thought he could be happy by shortening it a year, he might do so, but the Master plainly regarded him as " no gentleman."

The observance of this mourning takes precedence of all other duties whatsoever, and amounts to an excision of so much of the lifetime of the sons, if they happen to be in government employ. There are instances in which extreme filial devotion is exhibited by the son's building a hut near the grave of the mother or father, and going there to live during the whole time of the mourning. The most common way in which this is done is to spend the night only at the grave, while during the day the ordinary occupations are followed as usual. But there are some sons who will be content with nothing less than the whole ceremonial, and accordingly exile themselves for the full period, engaging in no occupation whatever, but being absorbed by grief. The writer is acquainted with a man of this class, whose extreme devotion to his parents' grave for so long a time unsettled his mind and made him a useless burden to his family. To the Chinese such an act is highly commendable, irrespective of its consequences, which are not considered at all. The ceremonial duty is held to be absolute and not relative.

It is not uncommon to meet with cases of persons who have sold their land to the last fraction of an acre, and even pulled down the house and disposed of the timbers, in order to provide money for a suitable funeral for one or both of the parents. That such conduct is a social wrong, few Chinese can be brought to understand, and no Chinese can be brought to realise. It is accordant with Chinese instinct. It is accordant with *li*, or propriety, and therefore it was unquestionably the thing to be done.

The Abbé Huc gives from his own experience an excellent example of that ceremonial, filial conduct, which to the Chinese is so dear. While the Abbé was living in the south of China, during the first year of his residence in this Empire, he had occasion to send a messenger to Peking, and he bethought him that perhaps a Chinese schoolmaster in his employ, whose home was in Peking, would like to embrace the rare opportunity to send a message to his old mother, from whom he had not heard for four years, and who did not know of her son's whereabouts. Hearing that the courier was to leave soon, the teacher called to one of his pupils, who was singing off his lesson in the next room, " Here, take this paper, and write me a letter to my mother. Lose no time, for the courier is going at once." This proceeding struck M. Huc as singular, and he inquired if the lad was acquainted with the teacher's mother, and was informed that the boy did not even know that there was such a person. " How then was he to know what to say, not having been told?" To this the schoolmaster made the conclusive reply: "Don't he know quite well what to say? For more than a year he has been studying literary composition, and he is acquainted with a number of elegant formulas. Do you think he does not know perfectly well how a son ought to write to a mother?" The pupil soon returned with the letter not only all written, but sealed up, the teacher merely adding the superscription with his own hand. The letter would have answered equally well for any other mother in the Empire, and any other would have been equally pleased to receive it.

The amount of filial conduct on the part of Chinese children to their parents will vary in any two places. Doubtless both extremes are to be found everywhere. Parricides are not common, and such persons are usually insane, though that makes no difference in the cruel punishment which they suffer. But among the common people, groaning in deepest poverty, some harsh treatment of parents is inevitable. On the other hand, voluntary substitutions of a son for the father, in cases of capital punishment, are known to occur, and such instances speak forcibly for the sincerity and power of the instinct of filial devotion to a parent, though this parent may be a deeply dyed criminal.

To the Occidental, fresh from the somewhat too loose bonds of family life which not infrequently prevail in lands nominally Christian, the theory of Chinese filial conduct presents some very attractive features. The respect for age which it involves is most beneficial, and might profitably be cultivated by Anglo-Saxons generally. In Western countries, when a son becomes of age he goes where he likes, and does what he chooses. He has no necessary connection with his parents, nor they with him. To the Chinese such customs must appear like the behaviour of a well-grown calf or colt to the cow and the mare, suitable enough for animals, but by no means conformable to *li* as applied to human beings. An attentive consideration of the matter from the Chinese standpoint will show that there is abundant room in our own social practice for improvement, and that most of us really live in glass houses, and would do well not to throw stones recklessly. Yet, on the other hand, it is idle to discuss the filial piety of the Chinese without making most emphatic its fatal defects in several particulars.

This doctrine seems to have five radical faults, two of them negative and three of them positive. It has volumes on the duty of children towards parents, but no word on the duty of parents to children. China is not a country in which advice of this kind is superfluous. Such advice is everywhere most needed, and always has been so. It was an inspired wisdom which led the Apostle Paul to combine in a few brief sentences addressed to his Colossian church the four pillars of the ideal home : " Husbands, love your wives, and be not bitter against them." " Wives, submit yourselves unto your own husbands, as it is fit in the Lord." " Children, obey your parents in all things, for this is well pleasing unto the Lord." "Fathers, provoke not your children to anger, lest they be discouraged." What is there in all Confucian morality which for practical wisdom can for a moment be put into competition with these far-reaching principles? The Chinese doctrine has nothing to say on behalf of its daughters, but everything on behalf of its sons. If the Chinese eye had not for ages been colour-blind on this subject, this gross outrage on human nature could not have failed of detection. By the accident of sex the infant is a family divinity. By the accident of sex she is a dreaded burden, liable to be destroyed, and certain to be despised.

The Chinese doctrine of filial piety puts the wife on an inferior plane. Confucius has nothing to say of the duties of wives to husbands or of husbands to wives. Christianity requires a man to leave his father and mother, and cleave to his wife. Confucianism requires a man to cleave to his father and mother, and to compel his wife to do the same. If the relation between the husband and his parents conflicts with that between the husband and his wife, the latter, as the lesser and inferior, is the relation which must yield. The whole structure of Chinese society, which is modelled upon the patriarchal plan, has grave evils. It encourages the suppression of some of the natural instincts of the heart that other instincts may be cultivated to an extreme degree. It results in the almost entire subordination of the younger during the whole life of those who are older. It cramps the minds of those who are subjected to its iron pressure, preventing development and healthful change.

That tenet of the Chinese doctrine which makes filial conduct consist in leaving posterity is responsible for a long train of ills. It compels the adoption of children, whether there is or is not any adequate provision for their support. It leads to early marriages, and brings into existence millions of human beings, who, by reason of the excessive pinch of poverty, can barely keep soul and body together. It is the efficient cause of polygamy and concubinage, always and inevitably a curse. It is expressed and epitomised in the worship of ancestors, which is the real religion of the Chinese race. This system of ancestral worship, when rightly understood in its true significance, is one of the heaviest yokes which ever a people was compelled to bear. As pointed out by Dr. Yates in the essay to which reference has been already made, the hundreds of millions of living Chinese are under the most galling subjection to the countless thousands of millions of the dead. "The generation of to-day is chained to the generations of the past." Ancestral worship is the best type and guarantee of that leaden conservatism to which attention has already been directed. Until that conservatism shall have received some mortal wound, how is it possible for China to adjust herself to the wholly new conditions under which she finds herself in this last quarter of the century? And while the generations of those who have passed from the stage continue to be regarded as the true divinities by the Chinese people, how is it possible that China should take a single real step forward?

The true root of the Chinese practice of filial piety we believe to be a mixture of fear and self-love, two of the most powerful motives which can act on the human soul. The spirits must be worshipped on account of the power which they have for evil. From the Confucian point of view, it was a sagacious maxim of the Master, that "to respect spiritual beings, but to keep aloof from them, may be called wisdom." If the sacrifices are neglected the spirits will be angry. If the spirits are angry they will take revenge. It is better to worship the spirits by way of insurance. This appears to be a condensed statement of the Chinese theory of all forms of worship of the dead. As between the living, the process of reasoning is equally simple. Every son has performed his filial duties to his father, and demands the same from his own son. That is what children are for. Upon this point the popular mind is explicit. "Trees are raised for shade, children are reared for old age." Neither parents nor children are under any illusions upon this subject. "If you have no children to foul the bed, you will have no one to burn paper at the grave." Each generation pays the debt which is exacted of it by the generation which preceded it, and in turn requires from the generation which comes after, full payment to the uttermost farthing. Thus is filial piety perpetuated from generation to generation, and from age to age.

It is a melancholy comment upon the exaggerated Chinese doctrine of piety that it not only embodies no reference to a Supreme Being, but that it does not in any way lead up to a recognition of His existence. Ancestral worship, which is the most complete and the ultimate expression of this filial piety, is perfectly consistent with polytheism, with agnosticism, and with atheism. It makes dead men into gods, and its only gods are dead men. Its love, its gratitude, and its fears are for earthly parents only. It has no conception of a Heavenly Father, and feels no interest in such a being when He is made known. Either Christianity will never be introduced into China, or ancestral worship will be given up, for they are contradictories. In the death struggle between them the fittest only will survive.

CHAPTER XX.

THE Chinese have placed the term "benevolence" at the head of their list of the Five Constant Virtues. The character which denotes it, is composed of the symbols for "man" and "two," by which is supposed to be shadowed forth the view that benevolence is something which ought to be developed by the contact of any two human beings with each other. It is unnecessary to remark that the theory which the form of the character seems to favour, is not at all substantiated by the facts of life among the Chinese, as those facts are to be read by the intelligent and attentive observer. Nevertheless, it is far from being true, as a superficial examination would seem to indicate, that there is among the Chinese no benevolence, though this has been often predicated by those who ought to have known the truth. "The feeling of pity," as Mencius reminds us, "is common to all men," widely as they differ in its expression. The mild and in some respects really benevolent teachings of the Buddhist religion have not been without a visible effect upon the Chinese people. There is, moreover, among the Chinese a strong practical instinct in every direction, and when the attention has once been directed towards the "practice of virtue," there is a great variety of forms in which there is certain to be abundant scope for the exercise of benevolence.

Among the kinds of benevolence which have commended themselves to the Chinese may be named the establishment of foundling hospitals, refuges for lepers and for the aged, and free schools. As China is a land which for most practical purposes is quite free from a census, it is impossible to ascertain to what extent these forms of benevolent action are to be found. Rev. David Hill, who has investigated the charities of central China, reports thirty benevolent institutions in the city of Hankow, expending annually some eight thousand pounds sterling. But it is hazarding little to say that such establishments must be relatively rare; that is to say, as regards the enormous population, and the enormous aggregation of that population in huge hives, where the needs are greatest.

The vast soup-kitchens which are set up anywhere and everywhere when some great flood or famine calls for them are familiar phenomena, as well as the donation of winter clothing to those who are destitute. It is not the government only which engages in these enterprises, but the people also co-operate in a highly creditable manner, and instances are not uncommon in which large sums have been thus judiciously expended. The ordinary streams of refugees which swarm over the country in a bad year are also allowed to camp down in cart-sheds, empty rooms, etc., but this is to a considerable extent a necessity. When such refugees come in extensive bands, and meet in all quarters with repulses, they are certain to be provoked into some form of reprisal. Common prudence dictates some concessions to those in such circumstances.

We do not reckon among the benevolences of the Chinese such associations as the provincial clubs for the care of those who may be destitute at a distance from home, and who without this help could not return, or who, having died, could not otherwise be taken home and buried. This is an ordinary business transaction of the nature of insurance, and is probably so regarded by the Chinese themselves.

In some of the books which have for their express object exhortations to " virtue," an account is opened, in which the

individual charges himself with every bad act which he can
remember, and credits himself with every good act. The
balance between the two exhibits his standing at any particular time in the account books of the Chinese Rhadamanthus.
This system of retributive bookkeeping exhibits clearly the
practical character of the Chinese, already remarked, as well
as their constant and irrepressible tendency to consider the
next life, if there be one, as only an extension and an amplifi-
cation of the present state of existence. The apparent motive
for a large percentage of Chinese benevolence is therefore the
reflex benefit which such acts are expected to insure to the
man who indulges his benevolent impulses. The open avowal
of a selfish motive in all acts of merit sometimes leads to
curious results. In the month of April, 1889, the prefect of
Hangchow attempted to raise funds for the sufferers from the
Yellow River floods, by levying a tax on each cup of tea sold
in the tea-houses of that great city. To the people of that
ancient capital this assessment presented itself in a light similar to that in which the Bostonians of 1773 regarded the tea
tax of their day. The prefect endeavoured to win the people
over by a proclamation, in which they were informed that
" happiness was sure to be their reward, if they cheerfully contributed to so excellent a cause." The people, however, boy-
cotted the tea-shops, and were in the end entirely victorious.
It is not every day that we are treated to the spectacle of a
cityful of people banded together to resist compulsory " happiness "!

Among the acts by which merit is to be accumulated may
be named the providing of coffins for those too poor to buy
them; the gathering of human bones which have become exposed, and their reburial in a suitable manner; the collection
of written or printed paper that it may be burned to save it
from desecration; and the purchase of live birds and fish,
that they may be restored to their native element. In some

places plasters of a mysterious nature are also given to all applicants, free vaccination is (theoretically) furnished, and "virtue books" are provided for sale at a price below cost, or are even given away. While such works of merit occupy a very prominent place in Chinese benevolence, so far as our observation goes, acts of kindly good-will to men and women occupy a very subordinate place. When such acts occur they are almost sure to be on some stereotyped pattern, involving a minimum of trouble and thought on the part of the doer. It is much easier to stand on the brink of a river, watch a fisherman lower his net, pay for his entire catch, and throw it back again into the water, than to look into the cases of the needy at one's doors, and give help in a judicious manner.

Moreover, to the mind of the practical Chinese there is a very important difference. As soon as the fish touches the water or the bird skims the air they are on a wholly self-supporting basis, and that is the end of the work. They will not expect the man who has released them to provide them and their numerous families with means of subsistence. For the man it only remains to register his virtuous act and go about his business, sure of no disagreeable consequences. But in China "virtue's door is hard to open," and it is still harder to shut. No one can possibly foresee all the remote consequences of some well-meant act of kindness, and knowing the danger of incurring responsibility, the prudent will be wary what they undertake. A missionary living in an interior province was asked by some native gentlemen to do a kind act for a poor beggar who was totally blind, and restore to him his sight. It proved to be a case of cataract, and excellent vision was secured. When the result became certain, the missionary was waited upon by the same gentlemen, and told that as he had destroyed the only means by which the blind man could get a living, that is, by begging, it was the duty of the missionary to make it up to him by taking him into employ as a gatekeeper! Sometimes a benevolent old lady who is limited in the sphere of her activity makes a practice of entertaining other old ladies who seem to be deserving, but who are victims of cruel fate. We have heard of one case of this sort—and of one only—and they may not be so rare as is supposed. But after all abatements, it must be admitted that "real kindness kindly expressed" is not often to be met in Chinese life.

When a vast calamity occurs, like the great famine, or the outburst of the Yellow River, the government, local or general, often comes to the front with a greater or less degree of promptness, and attempts to help the victims. But instead of doing this on any uniform and extensive scale, such as the perpetual recurrence of the necessity might seem to suggest, it is done in a makeshift way, as if the occasion had never before arisen and might never arise again. The care of the refugees is moreover usually abandoned at the very time when they most need help, namely, in the early spring, when, having been weakened by their long suffering and by atrocious overcrowding, they are most liable to disease. It is then that they are sent away with a little ready money, to make the best of their way home, and to get back into their normal state of life as best they can. The excuses for this are apparent: the funds are usually exhausted; there is work to be done on the farms, if the workers can but get food till wheat harvest. The government knows that they will die of pestilence if they remain till warm weather where they are, and destruction in detail seems to the officials to be a less, because a less conspicuous, evil than death in masses.

The same spirit is evinced in the curious ebullition of charitableness, which is known as the "twelve eight gruel." This performance may be regarded as a typical case of the most superficial form of Chinese benevolence. On the eighth day of the twelfth moon it is the custom for every one who

has accumulated a quantity of benevolent impulses, which
have had no opportunity for their gratification, to make the
most liberal donations to all comers, of the very cheapest and
poorest quality of soup, during about twelve hours of solar
time. This is called "practising virtue," and is considered to
be a means of laying up merit. If the year happens to be
one in which the harvest is bountiful, those who live in the
country have perhaps no applicants for their coarse provender,
as even the poorest people have as good or better at home.
This circumstance does not, however, lead to the pretermis-
sion of the offer, much less to the substitution of anything of
a better quality. On the contrary, the donors advertise their
intentions with the same alacrity as in other years, not to say
with greater, and when the day passes, and no one has asked
for a single bowl of the rich gruel designed for them, it is
merely put into the broken jars out of which the pigs are fed,
and the wealthy man of practical benevolence retires to rest
with the proud satisfaction that however it may be with the
poor wretches who would not come to his feast, he at least
has done his duty for another year, and can in good conscience
pose as a man of benevolence and virtue. But if, on the
other hand, the year should be a bad one, and grain rises to
a fabulous price, then this same man of means and of virtue
fails to send out any notices of the "practice of virtue" for
this particular year, for the reason that he "cannot afford it"!

We have already referred to the gifts to beggars, of whom
one almost everywhere sees a swarm. This donation also is
of the nature of an insurance. In the cities the beggars are,
as is well known, organised into guilds of a very powerful
sort, more powerful by far than any with which they can have
to contend, for the reason that the beggars have nothing to
lose and nothing to fear, in which respects they stand alone.
The shopkeeper who should refuse a donation to a stalwart
beggar, after the latter has waited for a reasonable length

of time, and has besought with what the Geneva arbitrators styled "due diligence," would be liable to an invasion of a horde of famished wretches, who would render the existence even of a stolid Chinese a burden, and who would utterly prevent the transaction of any business until their continually rising demands should be met. Both the shopkeepers and the beggars understand this perfectly well, and it is for this reason that benevolences of this nature flow in a steady, be it a tiny rill.

The same principle, with obvious modifications, applies to the small donations to the incessant stream of refugees to be seen so often in so many places. In all these cases it will be observed that the object in view is by no means the benefit of the person upon whom the "benevolence" terminates, but the extraction from the benefit conferred of a return benefit for the giver. Every such object of Chinese charity is regarded as a "little Jo," and the main aim of those who have anything to do with him is to make it reasonably certain that he will "move on."

To the other disabilities of Chinese benevolence must be added this capital one, that it is almost impossible for any enterprise, however good or however urgent, to escape the withering effects of the Chinese system of squeezes, which is as well organised as any other part of the scheme of Chinese government. It is not easy to possess one's self of full details of the working of any regular Chinese charity, but enough has been observed during such a special crisis as the great famine, to make it certain that the deepest distress of the people is no barrier whatever to the most shameful peculation on the part of officials entrusted with the disbursement of funds for relief. And if such scandals take place under these circumstances, when public attention is most fixed on the distress and its relief, it is not difficult to conjecture what happens when there is no outside knowledge either of the funds contributed or of their use.

When the Chinese come to know mcre of thaι Occidental civilisation of which too often only the worst side obtrudes itself upon them, it will certainly seem to them not a little remarkable that all Christendom is dotted with institutions such as have no parallel out of Christendom, and then it will perhaps occur to them to inquire into the *rationale* of so significant a fact. They may be led to notice the suggestive circumstance that the Chinese character for benevolence, unlike most of those which relate to the emotions, which generally have the heart radical, is written *without the heart.* The virtue for which it stands is also too often practised without heart, with the general results which we have noticed. That state of mind in which practical philanthropy becomes an instinct, demanding opportunity to exhibit its workings whenever the need of it is clearly perceived, may be said to be almost wholly wanting among the Chinese. It is not, indeed, a human development. If it is to be created among the Chinese, it must be by the same process which has made it an integral constituent of life in the lands of the West.

CHAPTER XXI.

THE ABSENCE OF SYMPATHY.

ATTENTION has been directed to that aspect of Chinese life which is represented by the term "benevolence," the very first of the so-called Constant Virtues. Benevolence is well-wishing. Sympathy is fellow-feeling. Our present object, having premised that the Chinese do practise a certain amount of benevolence, is to illustrate the proposition that they are conspicuous for a deficiency of sympathy.

It must ever be borne in mind that the population of China is dense. The disasters of flood and famine are of periodical occurrence in almost all parts of the Empire. The Chinese desire for posterity is so overmastering a passion that circumstances which ought to operate as an effectual check upon population, and which in many other countries would do so, appear to be in China relatively inefficient for that purpose. The very poorest people continue to marry their children at an early age, and these children bring up large families, just as if there were any provision for their maintenance. The result of these and other causes is that a large proportion of the population lives, in the most literal sense, from hand to mouth. This may be said to be the universal condition of day-labourers, and it is a condition from which there appears to be no possibility of escape. No foreigner can long deal with the ordinary Chinese whom he everywhere meets, without at once becoming aware of the fact that hardly any one has any ready money. The moment that anything whatever is

to be done, the first demand is for cash, that those who are to do it may get something to eat, the presumption being that as yet they have had nothing. It is often very hard even for well-to-do people to raise the most moderate sums of money when it suddenly becomes necessary to do so. There is a most significant expression commonly employed on such occasions, which speaks of a man who is obliged to collect a sum with which to prosecute a lawsuit, to arrange for a funeral, and the like, as " putting through a famine," that is, acting like a starving person, in the urgency and persistency of his demands for help. None but those who are well off ever expect to be able to manage affairs of this sort without assistance. Hopeless poverty is the most prominent fact in the Chinese Empire, and the bearing of this fact upon the relations of the people to one another must be evident to the most careless observer. The result of the pressure for the means of subsistence, and of the habits which this pressure cultivates and fixes, even after the immediate demand is no longer urgent, is to bring life down to a hard materialistic basis, in which there are but two prominent facts. Money and food are twin foci of the Chinese ellipse, and it is about them as centres that the whole social life of the people revolves.

The deep poverty of the masses of the people of the Chinese Empire, and the terrible struggle constantly going on to secure even the barest subsistence, have familiarised them with the most pitiable exhibitions of suffering of every conceivable variety. Whatever might be the benevolent impulses of any Chinese, he is from the nature of the case wholly helpless to relieve even a thousandth part of the misery which he sees about him all the time—misery multiplied many times in any year of special distress. A thoughtful Chinese must recognise the utter futility of the means which are employed to alleviate distress, whether by individual kindness or by government interference. All these methods, even when taken at their best,

amount simply to a treatment of the symptoms, and do absolutely nothing towards removing disease.   Their operation is
akin to that of societies which should distribute small pieces of
ice among the victims of typhoid fever—so many ounces to
each patient, with no hospitals, no dieting, no medicine, and
no nursing.   It is not, therefore, strange that the Chinese are
not in practical ways more benevolent, but rather that, with
the total lack of system, of prevision, and of supervision, benevolence continues at all.   We are familiar with the phenomenon of the effect, upon the most cultivated persons, of constant contact with misery which they have no power either to
hinder or to help, for this is illustrated in every modern war.
The first sight of blood causes a sinking of the epigastric nerves,
and makes an indelible impression; but this soon wears away,
and is succeeded by a comparative callousness, which, even
to him who experiences it, is a perpetual surprise.   In China
there is always a social war, and every one is too accustomed
to its sickening effects to give them more than a momentary
attention.

One of the manifestations of Chinese lack of sympathy is
their attitude towards those who are in any way physically de-
formed.   According to the popular belief, the lame, the blind,
especially those who are blind of but one eye, the deaf, the
bald, the cross-eyed, are all persons to be avoided.   It appears
to be the assumption that since the physical nature is defective,
the moral nature must be so likewise.   So far as our observation extends, such persons are not treated with cruelty, but
they excite very little of that sympathy which in Western lands
is so freely and so spontaneously extended.   They are looked
upon as having been overtaken by a punishment for some
secret sin, a theory exactly accordant with that of the ancient
Jews.

The person who is so unfortunate as to be branded with
some natural defect or some acquired blemish will not go long

without being reminded of the fact. One of the mildest forms of this practice is that in which the peculiarity is employed as a description in such a way as to attract to it public attention. " Great elder brother with the pockmarks," says an attendant in a dispensary to a patient, " from what village do you come? " It will not be singular if the man whose eyes are afflicted with strabismus hears an observation to the effect that " when the eyes look asquint, the heart is askew " ; or if the man who has no hair is reminded that " out of ten bald men, nine are deceitful, and the other would be so also, were he not dumb." Such freaks of nature as albinos form an unceasing butt for a species of cheap wit, which appears never for an instant to be intermitted. The unfortunate possessor of peculiarities like this must resign himself (or herself) to a lifetime of this treatment, and happy will he be if his temperament admits of his listening to such talk in perpetual reiteration without becoming by turns furious and sullen.

The same excess of frankness is displayed towards those who exhibit any mental defects. " This boy," remarks a bystander, " is idiotic." The lad is probably not at all " idiotic," but his undeveloped mind may easily become blighted by the constant repetition in his presence of the proposition that he has no mind at all. This is the universal method of treating all patients afflicted with nervous diseases, or indeed with any other. All their peculiarities, the details of their behaviour, the method in which the disease is supposed to have originated, the symptoms which attend its exacerbations, are all public property, and are all detailed in the presence of the patient, who must be thoroughly accustomed to hearing himself described as " crazy," " half-witted," " besotted in his intellect," etc., etc.

Among a people to whom the birth of male children is so vital a matter, it is not surprising that the fact of childlessness is a constant occasion of reproach and taunts, just as in the ancient days, when it was said of the mother of the prophet Samuel that "her adversary also provoked her sore, for to make her fret." If it is supposed for any reason, or without reason, that a mother has quietly smothered one of her children, it will not be strange if the announcement of the same is publicly made to a stranger.

One of the most characteristic methods in which the Chinese lack of sympathy is manifested is in the treatment which brides receive on their wedding-day. They are often very young, are always timid, and are naturally terror-stricken at being suddenly thrust among strangers. Customs vary widely, but there seems to be a general indifference to the feelings of the poor child thus exposed to the public gaze. In some places it is allowable for any one who chooses to turn back the curtains of the chair and stare at her. In other regions, the unmarried girls find it a source of keen enjoyment to post themselves at a convenient position as the bride passes, to throw upon her handfuls of hay-seed or chaff, which will obstinately adhere to her carefully oiled hair for a long time. Upon her emergence from the chair at the house of her new parents, she is subjected to the same kind of criticism as a newly bought horse, with what feelings on her part it is not difficult to imagine.

Side by side with the punctilious ceremony which is so dear to the Chinese heart is the apparent inability to perceive that some things must be disagreeable to other persons, and should for that reason be avoided. A Chinese friend, who had not the smallest idea of saying what would be deficient in politeness, remarked to the writer that when he first saw foreigners it seemed most extraordinary that they should have beards that reached all round their faces *just like those of monkeys,* but he added, reassuringly, "I am quite used to it now!" The teacher who is asked in the presence of his pupils as to their capacity, replies before them all that the one nearest the door is much the brightest, and will be a graduate by the time he is twenty years of age, but the two at the next table are certainly the stupidest children he ever saw. That such observations have any reflex effect upon the pupils, never for a moment enters into the thought of any one.

The whole family life of the Chinese illustrates their lack of sympathy. While there are great differences in different households, and while from the nature of the case generalisation is precarious, it is easy to see that most Chinese homes which are seen at all are by no means happy homes. It is impossible that they should be so, for they are deficient in that unity of feeling which to us seems so essential to real home life. A Chinese family is generally an association of individuals who are indissolubly tied together, having many of their interests the same, and many of them very different. The result is not our idea of a home, and it is not sympathy.

Daughters in China are from the beginning of their existence more or less unwelcome. This fact has a most important bearing on their whole subsequent career, and furnishes many significant illustrations of the absence of sympathy.

Mothers and daughters who pass their days in the narrow confinement of a Chinese court under the conditions of Chinese life, are not likely to lack topics of disagreement, in which abusive language is indulged in with a freedom which the unconstraint of everyday life tends to promote. It is a popular saying, full of significance to those who know Chinese homes, that a mother cannot by reviling her own daughter make her cease to be her own daughter! When a daughter is once married she is regarded as having no more relations with her family than those which are inseparable from community of origin. There is a deep-seated reason for omitting daughters from all family registers. She is no longer our daughter, but the daughter-in-law of some one else. Human nature will assert itself in requiring visits to the mother's home, at more or less frequent intervals, according to the local usage. In some districts these visits are very numerous and very prolonged, while in others the custom seems to be to make them as few as possible, and liable to almost complete suspension for long periods in case of a death in the family. But whatever the details of usage, the principle holds good that the daughter-in-law belongs to the family of which she has become a part. When she goes to her mother's home, she goes on a strictly business basis. She takes with her it may be a quantity of sewing for her husband's family, which the wife's family must help her get through with. She is accompanied on each of these visits by as many of her children as possible, both to have her take care of them and to have them out of the way when she is not at hand to look after them, and most especially to have them fed at the expense of the family of the maternal grandmother for as long a time as possible. In regions where visits of this sort are frequent, and where there are many daughters in a family, their constant raids on the old home are a source of perpetual terror to the whole family, and a serious tax on the common resources. For this reason these visits are often discouraged by the fathers and the brothers, while secretly favoured by the mothers. But as local custom fixes for them certain epochs, such as a definite date after the New-Year, special feast-days, etc., the visits cannot be interdicted.

When the daughter-in-law returns to her mother-in-law, it is true of her, as the adage says of a thief, that she never comes back empty-handed. She must take a present of some sort for her mother-in-law, generally food. Neglect of this established rite, or inability to comply with it, will soon result in dramatic scenes. If the daughter is married into a family which is poor, or which has become so, and if she has brothers who are married, she will find that her visits to her mother are, in the language of the physicians, "contra-indicated."

Native Women Sewing and Weaving Lace.

There is war between the daughters-in-law of a family and the married sisters of the same family, like that between the Philistines and the children of Israel, each regarding the territory as peculiarly its own, and the other party as interlopers. If the daughters-in-law are strong enough to do so, they will, like the Philistines, levy a tax upon the enemy whom they cannot altogether exterminate or drive out. A daughter-in-law is regarded as a servant for the whole family, which is precisely her position, and in getting a servant it is obviously desirable to get one who is strong and well grown, and who has already been taught the domestic accomplishments of cooking, sewing, and whatever industries may be the means of livelihood in that particular region, rather than a child who has little strength or capacity. Thus we have known of a case where a buxom young woman of twenty was married to a slip of a boy literally only half her age, and in the early years of their wedded life she had the pleasure of nursing him through the smallpox, which is considered as a disease of infancy.

The woes of daughters-in-law in China should form the subject rather for a chapter than for a brief paragraph. When it is remembered that all Chinese women marry, and generally marry young, being for a considerable part of their lives under the absolute control of a mother-in-law, some faint conception may be gained of the intolerable miseries of those daughters-in-law who live in families where they are abused. Parents can do absolutely nothing to protect their married daughters, other than remonstrating with the families into which they have married, and exacting an expensive funeral if the daughters should be actually driven to suicide. If a husband should seriously injure or even kill his wife, he might escape all legal consequences by representing that she was " unfilial " to his parents. Suicides of young wives are, we must repeat, excessively frequent, and in some regions scarcely a group of villages can be found where they have not recently taken place. What can be more pitiful than a mother's reproaches to a married daughter who has attempted suicide and been rescued: " Why didn't you die when you had a chance? "

The Governor of Honan, in a memorial published in the Peking *Gazette* a few years ago, showed incidentally that while there is responsibility in the eye of the law for the murder of a child by a parent, this is rendered nugatory by the provision that even if a married woman should wilfully and maliciously murder her young daughter-in-law, the murderess may ransom herself by a money payment. The case reported was that in which a woman had burned the girl who was reared to become her son's wife with incense sticks, then roasted her cheeks with red-hot pincers, and finally boiled her to death with kettlefuls of scalding water. Other similar instances are referred to in the same memorial, the source of which places its authenticity beyond doubt. Such extreme barbarities are probably rare, but the cases of cruel treatment which are so aggravated as to lead to suicide, or to an attempt at suicide, are so frequent as to excite little more than passing comment. The writer is personally acquainted with many families in which these occurrences have taken place.

The lot of Chinese concubines is one of exceeding bitterness. The homes in which they are to be found—happily relatively few in number—are the scenes of incessant bickerings and open warfare. " The magistrate of the city in which I live," writes a resident of China of long experience, " was a wealthy man, a great scholar, a doctor of literature, an able administrator, well acquainted with the good teachings of the Classics; but he would lie and curse and rob, and torture people to any extent to gratify his evil passions. One of his concubines ran away; she was captured, brought back, stripped, hung up to a beam by her feet, and cruelly and severely beaten."

In a country like China the poor have no time to be sick. Ailments of women and children are apt to be treated by the men of the family as of no consequence, and are constantly allowed to run into incurable maladies, because there was no time to attend to them, or because the man "could not afford it."

As we have noticed in speaking of filial piety, it is a constituent part of the theory that the younger are relatively of little account. They are valued principally for what they may become, and not for what they are. Thus the practice of most Western lands is in China reversed. The youngest of three travellers is proverbially made to take the brunt of all hardships. The youngest servant is uniformly the common drudge of the rest. In the grinding poverty of the mass of the people, it is not strange that the spirit even of a Chinese boy often rebels against the sharp limitations to which he finds himself pinned, and that he not infrequently runs away. The boy who has made up his mind to go will seldom fail to find some slight thread by which he may attach himself to some one else. The causes for this behaviour on the part of boys are various, but so far as we have observed, the harsh treatment of others is by far the most common. In a case of this sort, a boy recently recovered from a run of typhus fever, being possessed by the hearty appetite common to such patients, and finding the coarse black bread of the family fare hard eating, went to a local market and indulged in the luxury of expending cash to the value of about twenty cents. For this he was severely reproved by his father, upon which the lad ran away to Manchuria, an unfailing resort of lads all over the northeastern provinces, and was never heard of again.

It was a saying of George D. Prentice, that man was the principal object in creation, woman being merely "a side issue." The phrase is a literal expression of the position of a wife in a Chinese family. The object had in view in matrimony by the family of the girl is to get rid of supporting her.   The object on the part of the husband's family is to propagate that family. These objects are not in themselves open to criticism, except on the ground of a too complete occupation of the field of human motives.   But in China no one indulges in any illusions on the subject.

That which is true of the marriages of those in the ordinary walks of life is pre-eminently true of the poorer classes.   It is a common observation in regard to a widow who has re-married, that " now she will not starve."   It is a popular proverb that a second husband and a second wife are husband and wife only as long as there is anything to eat; when the food-supply fails each shifts for himself.   In times of famine relief cases have often been observed where the husband simply abandons the wife and the children, leaving them to pick up a wretched subsistence or to starve.   In many instances daughters-in-law were sent back to their mothers' family to be supported or starved as the event might be.   " She is your daughter, take care of her yourself."   In other cases where special food was given by distributers of famine relief to women who were nursing small infants, it was sometimes found that this allowance had been taken from the women and devoured by the men, although these instances were probably exceptional.

While it would be obviously unfair to judge a people only by the phenomena of such years as those of great famine, there is an important sense in which such occasions are a species of touchstone by which the underlying principles of social life may be ascertained with more accuracy and certainty than on ordinary occasions.   The sale of wives and of children in China is a practice not confined to years of peculiar distress, but during those years it is carried on to an extent which throws all ordinary transactions of this nature into insignificance.   It is perfectly well known to those acquainted with the facts, that during several recent years in many districts stricken with famine, the sale of women and children was conducted as openly as that of mules and donkeys, the only essential difference being that the former were not driven to market. During the great famine of 1878, which extended over nearly all parts of the three most northern provinces, as well as further south, so extensive a traffic sprung up in women and girls who were exported to the central provinces that in some places it was difficult to hire a cart, as they had all been engaged in the transportation of the newly purchased females to the regions where they were to be disposed of. In these cases young women were taken from a region where they were in a condition of starvation, and where the population was too redundant, to a region which had been depopulated by rebels, and where for many years wives had been hard to procure. It is one of the most melancholy features of this strange state of affairs, that the enforced sales of members of Chinese families to distant provinces was probably the best thing for all parties, and perhaps the only way in which the lives, both of those who were sold as well as the lives of those who sold them, could be preserved.

We have referred to the common neglect of sickness in the family because the victims are " only women and children." Smallpox, which in Western lands we regard as a terrible scourge, is so constant a visitor in China that the people never expect to be free from its ravages. But it is not much thought of, because its victims are mainly children! It is exceedingly common to meet with persons who have lost the sight of both eyes in consequence of this disease. The comparative disregard of the value of infant life is displayed in ways which we should by no means have expected from the Chinese, who object so strongly to the mutilation of the human body. Young children are often either not buried at all, an ordinary expression for their death being the phrase " thrown out," or if rolled in a mat, they are so loosely covered that they soon fall a prey to dogs. In some places the horrible custom prevails of crushing the body of a deceased infant into an indistinguishable mass, in order to prevent the " devil " which inhabited it from returning to vex the family!

While the Chinese are so indifferent to smallpox, our fear of which they fail to appreciate, they have a similar dread of typhus and typhoid fevers, which are regarded much as we regard the scarlet fever. It is very difficult to get proper attention, or any attention at all, if one happens to be taken with either of these diseases when away from home. To all appeals for help it is a conclusive reply, " That disease is contagious." While this is true to some extent of many fevers, it is perhaps most conspicuous in a terrible scourge found in some of the valleys of Yunnan, and described by Mr. Baber:*
" The sufferer is soon seized with extreme weakness, followed in a few hours by agonising aches in every part of the body; delirium shortly ensues, and in nine cases out of ten the result is fatal." According to the native accounts: " All parts of the sick-room are occupied by devils; even the tables and mattresses writhe about and utter voices, and offer intelligible replies to all who question them. Few, however, venture into the chamber. The missionary assured me that the patient is, in most cases, deserted like a leper, for fear of contagion. If an elder member of the family is attacked, the best attention he receives is to be placed in a solitary room with a vessel of water by his side. The door is secured, and a pole laid near it, with which twice a day the anxious relatives, cautiously peering in, poke and prod the sick person to discover if he retains any symptoms of life."

Among a people of so mild a disposition as the Chinese there must be a great deal of domestic kindness of which nothing is seen or heard. Sickness and trouble are peculiarly

* " Travels and Researches in Western China."

adapted to call out the best side of human nature, and in a foreign hospital for Chinese we have witnessed many instances of devotion not merely on the part of parents towards children, or children towards parents, but of wives towards husbands and also of husbands towards wives. The same thing is even more common among strangers towards one another. Many a Chinese mother nursing an infant will give of her overflowing abundance to a motherless child which else might starve.

Unwillingness to give help to others, unless there is some special reason for doing so, is a trait that runs through Chinese social relations in multifold manifestations. It is a common and in many cases a perfectly valid excuse which is made when a bright boy is advised to try to learn to read a little, although he has no opportunity to go to school, that no one will tell him the characters, although there may be plenty of reading men within reach who have abundant leisure. The very mention of such an ambition is certain to excite unmeasured ridicule on the part of those who have had the longest experience of Chinese schools, as if they were saying: "By what right does this fellow think to take a short cut, and pick up in a few months what cost us years of toil, and then was forgotten in half the time which we took to get it? Let him hire a teacher for himself as we did." It is very rare indeed to meet with a genuine case of one who has anything which can be called a knowledge of characters, even of the most elementary description, which he has "picked up" for himself, though such cases do occasionally occur.

The general omission to do anything for the relief of the drowning strikes every foreigner in China. A few years ago a foreign steamship was burned in the Yang-tze River, and the crowds of Chinese who gathered to witness the event did little or nothing to rescue the passengers and crew. As fast as they made their way to the shore many of them were robbed even of the clothing which they had on, and some were murdered outright.   Yet it should be remarked in connection with such atrocities as this, that it is not so very long ago that wrecking was a profession in England.   On the other hand, in the autumn of 1892 a large British steamer went ashore on the China coast, and both the local fishermen and the officials did everything in their power to rescue and relieve the survivors. It remains true, however, that there is in China a general callousness to the many cases of distress which are to be seen almost everywhere, especially along lines of travel.   It is a common proverb that to be poor at home is not to be counted as poverty, but to be poor when on the high-road, away from home, will cost a man his life.

It is in travelling in China that the absence of helpful kindness on the part of the people towards strangers is perhaps most conspicuous.   When the summer rains have made all land travel almost impossible, he whose circumstances make travel a necessity will find that " heaven, earth, and man " are a threefold harmony in combination against him.   No one will inform him that the road which he has taken will presently end in a quagmire.   If you choose to drive into a morass, it is no business of the contiguous tax-payers.   We have spoken of the neglect of Chinese highways.   When the traveller has been plunged into one of the sloughs with which all such roads at certain seasons abound, and finds it impossible to extricate himself, a great crowd of persons will rapidly gather from somewhere, " their hands in their sleeves, and idly gazing," as the saying goes.   It is not until a definite bargain has been made with them that any one of these bystanders, no matter how numerous, will lift a finger to help one in any particular.   Not only so, but it is a constant practice on such occasions for the local rustics to dig deep pits in difficult places, with the express purpose of trapping the traveller, that he may be obliged to employ these same rustics to help the traveller out!   When there is any doubt as to the road in such places, one might as well plunge forward, disregarding the cautions of those native to the spot, since one can never be sure that the directions given are not designed to hinder rather than help.

We have heard of one instance in which a foreign family, moving into an interior city of China, was welcomed with apparent cordiality by the people, the neighbours even volunteering to lend them articles for housekeeping until such time as they might be able to procure an outfit of their own. Other examples there doubtless are, but it is well known that these are wholly exceptional. By far the most usual reception is total indifference on the part of the people, except so far as curiosity is excited to see what the new-comers are like; a spirit of cupidity to make the most of the fat geese whom fate has sent thither to be plucked; and sullen hostility. In the case of foreigners who may have been reduced to distress, we have never heard of any assistance voluntarily given by Chinese, though of course there may have been such cases. We have known of instances in which sailors have attempted the journey overland from Tientsin to Chefoo, and from Canton to Swatow, and during the whole time of their travel they were never once given a lodging or a mouthful of food.

It is often difficult, and frequently impossible, for those who are taking a dead body home to secure admission to an inn. We have known a case of this sort where the brother of the deceased was obliged to stand guard all night in the street, because the landlord would not allow the coffin to come within the gate. An extortionate price is exacted for ferrying a corpse over a river, and we have been cognisant of several instances in which a dead body has been doubled up into a parcel and tied with mat wrappings, to make it appear like merchandise, to avoid suspicion. It was reported during a recent severe winter in Shantung, that the keeper of an inn in the city of Wei Hsien refused to allow several travellers who were half dead with cold to enter his inn, lest they should die there, but turned them into the street, where they all froze to death!

There are some crimes committed in China for which the perpetrators are often not prosecuted before a magistrate, partly on account of the difficulty and expense of securing a conviction, and partly because of the shame of publicity. Many cases of adultery are thus dealt with by the law of private revenge. The offender is attacked by a large band of men, on the familiar Chinese principle that "where there are many persons, their prestige is great." Sometimes the man's legs are broken, sometimes his arms, and very often his eyes are destroyed by rubbing into them quicklime. The writer has known several instances of this sort, and they are certainly not uncommon. A very intelligent Chinese, himself not unfamiliar with Occidental ways of thought, upon hearing a foreigner remonstrate against this practice as a refinement of cruelty, expressed unfeigned surprise, and remarked that in China such a mode of dealing with a criminal is thought to be "extremely mild," as he is thus merely maimed for life, when he really ought to be killed!

"What do you keep coming here to eat for?" said a sister-in-law to her husband's brother, who had been away for several years, and having got into trouble had had his eyes rubbed out with quicklime. "We have no place for you. If you want something hard, here is a knife; and if you want something soft, there is a rope; so get along with you." This conversation was mentioned incidentally by an incurably blind man, as an explanation of his desire to get a little sight if that were possible, but if not, he intimated that either the "hard" or the "soft" could be made to adjust his difficulties. It is rare to hear of any instances in which the victim of such outrages succeeds in getting a complaint heard before a magistrate. The evidence against him would be overwhelming, and nine officials out of ten would probably consider that the man who had been thus dealt with deserved it all, and more. Even if the man were to win his case, he would be no better off than before, but rather the worse, as the irritation of his neighbours would only be increased, and his life would not be safe.

It must be understood that despite the sacredness of human life in China, there are circumstances in which it is worth very little. One of the crimes which are most exasperating to the Chinese is theft. In a crowded population always on the edge of ruin, this is regarded as a menace to society only less serious than murder. In a time of famine relief one of the distributers found an insane woman, who had become a kleptomaniac, chained to a huge mill-stone as if she were a mad dog. If a person becomes known as a thief or in other ways is a public nuisance, he is in danger of being made away with by a summary process, not differing essentially from the vigilance committees of the early days of California. Sometimes this is done by stabbing, but the method most frequently adopted is burying alive. Doubtless there are those who suppose this expression to be a mere figure of speech, as when (according to some) one is said "to swallow gold." It is, on the contrary, a very serious reality. The writer is acquainted with four persons who were threatened with death in this form. In two instances they were bound as a preliminary, and in one case the pit was actually dug, and in all cases the burial was only prevented by the intervention of some older member of the attacking party. In another instance, occurring in a village where the writer is well acquainted, a young man who was known to be insane was an incorrigible thief. A party of the villagers belonging to his own family only "consulted" (!) with his mother, and as the result of their deliberations he was bound, a hole made in the ice covering the river flowing near the village, and the youth was dropped in.

During the years in which the refluent waves of the great T'ai-p'ing rebellion overspread so large a part of China, the excitement was everywhere intense. At such times a stranger had but to be suspected to be seized, and subjected to a rigorous examination. If he could give no account of himself which was satisfactory to his captors, it went hard with him. Within a few hundred yards of the spot at which these lines are written two such tragedies occurred, little more than twenty years ago. The magistrates found themselves almost powerless to enforce the laws, and issued semi-official notifications to the people to seize all suspicious characters. The villagers saw a man coming on a horse, who looked as if he were a native of another province, and who failed to give adequate explanations of his antecedents. His bedding being found to be full of articles of jewellery, which he had evidently plundered from somewhere, the man was tied up, a pit was dug, and the victim tumbled into it. While this was going on another was seen racing across the fields in a terrified manner, and it needed but the suggestion of some bystander that he was probably an accomplice, to secure for the second victim the same fate as the first. In some cases the strangers were compelled to dig their own graves. Any native of the provinces of China principally affected by the lawlessness of those lawless times, old enough to recollect the circumstances, will testify that instances of this sort were too numerous to be remembered or counted. In the epoch of terror caused by a mysterious cutting off of cues, in the year 1877, an intense panic seemed to pervade a large part of the Empire, and there can be no doubt that many persons who were suspected were made away with in this manner. Such periods of panic, however, under certain conditions, are common to all races, and must not be laid to the charge of the Chinese as a unique phenomenon.

One of the most striking of all the many exhibitions of the

Chinese lack of sympathy is to be found in their cruelty. It is popularly believed by the Chinese that the Mohammedans in China are more cruel than the Chinese themselves. However this may be, there can be no doubt in the mind of any one who knows the Chinese that they display an indifference to the sufferings of others which is probably not to be matched in any other civilised country. Though children at home are almost wholly ungoverned, yet the moment their career of education is begun the reign of mildness ceases. The "Trimetrical Classic," the most general of the minor text-books of the Empire, contains a line to the effect that to teach without severity is a fault in a teacher. While this motto is very variously acted upon, according to the temperament of the pedagogue and the obtuseness of his pupils, great harshness is certainly common. We have seen a scholar fresh from a preceptor who was struggling to induct his pupils into the mysteries of examination essays, when the former presented the appearance of having been through a street fight, his head covered with wounds and streaming with blood. It is not rare that pupils are thrown into fits from the abuse which they receive from angry teachers. On the other hand, it is not unusual for mothers whose children are so unfortunate as to be subject to fits, to beat them in those paroxysms, as an expression of the extreme disgust which such inconvenient attacks excite. It is not difficult to perceive that mothers who can beat children because they fall into convulsions will treat any of their children with cruelty when irritated by special provocation.

Another example of "absence of sympathy" on the part of the Chinese is their system of punishments. It is not easy, from an examination of the legal code of the Empire, to ascertain what is and what is not in accordance with law, for custom seems to have sanctioned many deviations from the letter of the statutes. One of the most significant of these is the enormous number of blows with the bamboo which are constantly resorted to, often ten times the number named in the law, and sometimes one hundred times as many. We have no space even to mention the dreadful tortures which are inflicted upon Chinese prisoners in the name of justice. They may be found enumerated in any good work on China, such as "The Middle Kingdom," or "Huc's Travels." The latter author mentions seeing prisoners on the way to the yamên, with their hands nailed to the cart in which they were conveyed, because the constables had forgotten to bring fetters. Nothing so illustrates the proposition that though the Chinese have "bowels," they certainly have no "mercies," as the deliberate, routine cruelty with which all Chinese prisoners are treated who cannot pay for their exemption. A few years ago the press of Shanghai chronicled the infliction upon two old prisoners in the yamên of the District Magistrate of that city of a sentence for levying blackmail on a new prisoner. They received between two thousand and three thousand blows with the bamboo, and had their ankles broken with an iron hammer. Is it strange that the Chinese adage advises the dead to keep out of hell and the living to keep out of yamêns ? *

Since the preceding paragraphs were written an unexpected confirmation of some of the statements made has appeared

* A Chinese who is practising law in the United States, Mr. Hang Yen-chang, in an article on the administration of the law in China, published in a leading religious journal, quotes what has been hereinbefore said of the Chinese " absence of nerves," remarking that the punishments of the Chinese are not regarded by themselves as cruel. While we are unable to agree with this view, it must not be forgotten that the Chinese being what they are, their laws and their customs being as they are, it would probably be wholly impracticable to introduce any essential amelioration of their punishments without a thoroughgoing reformation of the Chinese people as individuals. Physical force cannot safely be abandoned until some moral force is at hand adequate to take its place.

from a most unimpeachable source. The following is an extract from a translation of the Peking *Gazette* of February 7, 1888:

"The Governor of Yunnan states that in some of the country districts of that province the villagers have a horrible custom of burning to death any man caught stealing corn or fruits in the fields. They at the same time compel the man's relations to sign a document, giving their consent to what is done, and then make them light the fire with their own hands, so as to deter them from lodging a complaint afterwards. Sometimes the horrible penalty is exacted for the breaking of a single branch or stalk, or even false accusations are made, and men put to death out of spite. This terrible practice, which seems incredible when heard, came into use during the time of the Yunnan rebellion; and the constant efforts of the authorities have not succeeded in extirpating it since."

Native Chinese newspapers have within a few years contained detailed accounts of an enforced suttee practised in a district near Foochow. Widows are compelled to strangle themselves, and their bodies are then burned, after which ornamental portals are erected to their virtuous memory! Magistrates have in vain endeavoured to stop this cruel custom, but their success has been only local and temporary.

China has many needs, among which her leading statesmen place armies, navies, and arsenals. To her foreign wellwishers it is plain that she needs a currency, railways, and scientific instruction. But does not a deeper diagnosis of the conditions of the Empire indicate that one of her profoundest needs is more human sympathy? She needs to feel with childhood that sympathy which for eighteen centuries has been one of the choicest possessions of races and peoples which once knew it not. She needs to feel sympathy for wives and for mothers, a sympathy which eighteen centuries have done so much to develop and to deepen. She needs to feel sympathy for man as man, to learn that quality of mercy which droppeth as the gentle rain from heaven, twice blest in blessing him that gives and him that takes—that divine compassion which Seneca declared to be "a vice of the mind," but which the influence of Christianity has cultivated until it has become the fairest plant that ever bloomed upon the earth, the virtue in the exercise of which man most resembles God.

FOUR GENERATIONS.

CHAPTER XXII.

SOCIAL TYPHOONS.

AMONG a population of such unexampled density as in China, where families often of great size are crowded together in narrow quarters, it is impossible that occasions for quarrels should not be all-pervasive. " How many are there in your family?" you inquire of your neighbour. " Between ten and twenty mouths," he replies. "And do you have everything in common?" you ask. " Yes," is the most common reply. Here, then, are fifteen or twenty human beings, probably representing three, if not four, generations, who live from the income of the same business or farm, an income which is all put into a common stock; and the wants of all the members of the family are to be met solely from this common property. The brothers each contribute their time and strength to the common fund, but the sisters-in-law are an element of capital importance, and very difficult it is to harmonise them. The elder sister-in-law enjoys tyrannising somewhat over the younger, and the younger ones are naturally jealous of the prerogatives of the elder. Each strives to make her husband feel that in this community of property he is the one who is worsted.

The younger generation of children furnish a prolific source of domestic unpleasantness. Where is the society capable of withstanding the strain to which it must be subjected under conditions such as these? Troubles of this nature are far from being uncommon in well-ordered homes in Western lands ; how much more in the complex and compact life of the Chinese ! The occasions for differences are as numerous as the objects and interests with which human beings have to do. Money, food, clothes, children and their squabbles, a dog, a chicken, anything or nothing, will serve as the first loop on which will be knit a complicated tangle of quarrel.

One of the most enigmatical characters in the Chinese language is that which is used to denote the rise of passion, and which has been euphemistically translated "wrath-matter." The word *"ch'i"* is a most important one in all kinds of Chinese philosophy and in practical life. *Ch'i* is generated when a man becomes very angry, and the Chinese believe that there is some deadly connection between this developed "wrath-matter" and the human system generally, so that a violent passion is constantly named as the exciting cause of all varieties of diseases and ailments, such as blindness, failure of the heart, etc. One of the first questions which a Chinese doctor asks his patient is, "What was it that threw you into a passion?" Foreign physicians in China of wide experience are ready to believe that Chinese *ch'i* is capable of producing all that is claimed for it by the Chinese themselves. Of this the following case is a striking illustration : A man living in the mountains in central Shantung had a wife and several children, two of them of tender age. In October, 1889, the wife died. This made the husband very angry, not, as he explained, in answer to a question, because he was specially attached to his wife, but because he could not see how he was to manage the small children. In a paroxysm of fury he seized a Chinese razor, and made three deep cuts in his abdomen. Some of his friends afterwards sewed up the wound with cotton thread. Six days later the man had another accession of *ch'i*, and ripped open the wound. On each occasion he was afterwards unable to remember what he had done.

From these fearful injuries he nevertheless recovered, to such an extent that six months later he was able to walk several hundred miles to a foreign hospital for treatment. The abdominal wound had partly closed, leaving only a small fistula, but the normal action of the bowels was interrupted. He is a striking exemplification of that physical vitality to which attention has been already directed.

The habit of yelling to enforce command or criticism is ingrained in the Chinese, and appears to be ineradicable. To expostulate with another in an ordinary tone of voice, pausing at times to listen to his opponent's reply, is to a Chinese almost a psychological impossibility. He *must* shout, he *must* interrupt, by a necessity as inexorable as that which leads a dog labouring under great excitement to bark.

The Chinese have carried to a degree of perfection known only among Orientals the art of reviling. The moment that a quarrel begins abusive words of this sort are poured forth in a filthy stream to which nothing in the English language offers any parallel, and with a virulence and pertinacity suggestive of the fish-women of Billingsgate. The merest contact is often sufficient to elicit a torrent of this invective, as a touch induces the electric spark, and it is in constant and almost universal use by all classes and both sexes, always and everywhere. It is a common complaint that women use even viler language than men, and that they continue it longer, justifying the aphorism that what Chinese women have lost in the compression of their feet seems to have been made up in the volubility of their tongues. Children just beginning to talk learn this abusive dialect from their parents and often employ it towards them, which is regarded as extremely amusing. The use of this language has become to the Chinese a kind of second nature. It is confined to no class of society. Literary graduates and officials of all ranks up to the very highest, when provoked, employ it as freely as their coolies. It is even used by common people on the street as a kind of bantering salutation, and as such is returned in kind.

Occidental curses are sometimes not loud but deep, but Chinese maledictions are nothing if not loud. An English oath is a winged bullet; Chinese abuse is a ball of filth. Much of this abusive language is regarded as a sort of spell or curse. A man who has had the heads removed from his field of millet stands at the entrance of the alley which leads to his dwelling, and pours forth volleys of abuse upon the unknown (though often not unsuspected) offender. This proceeding is regarded as having a double value: first, as a means of notifying the public of his loss and of his consequent fury, thus freeing his mind; and second, as a prophylactic, tending to secure him against the repetition of the offence. The culprit is (theoretically) in ambush, listening with something like awe to the frightful imprecations levelled at him. He cannot, of course, be sure that he is not detected, which is often the case. Perhaps the loser knows perfectly well who it was who stole his goods, but contents himself with a public reviling, as a formal notice that the culprit is either known or suspected, and will do well to avoid the repetition of his act. If provoked too far the loser will, it is thus tacitly proclaimed, retaliate. This is the Chinese theory of public reviling. They frankly admit that it not only does not stop theft, but that it has no necessary tendency to prevent its repetition, since among a large population the thief or other offender is by no means certain to know that he has been reviled.

The practice of "reviling the street" is often indulged in by women, who mount the flat roof of the house and shriek away for hours at a time, or until their voices fail. A respectable family would not allow such a performance if they could prevent it, but in China, as elsewhere, an enraged woman is a being difficult to restrain. Abuse delivered in this way, on general principles, attracts little or no attention, and one sometimes comes upon a man at the head of an alley, or a woman on the roof, screeching themselves red in the face, with not a single auditor in sight. If the day is a hot one the reviler bawls as long as he (or she) has breath, then proceeds to refresh himself by a season of fanning, and afterwards returns to the attack with renewed fury.

If a Chinese quarrel be at all violent, it is next to impossible that it should be concluded without more or less personal vilification. English travellers in the south of Europe have noted the astonishment of the Latin races at the invariable habit of the inhabitant of the British Isles to strike out from the shoulder if he gets into a fight. The Chinese, like the Italians, have seldom learned to box, or if they have learned it is not scientific boxing. The first and chief resource of Chinese when matters come to extremities is to seize the cue of their opponent, endeavouring to pull out as much hair as possible. In nine fights out of ten, where only two parties are concerned, and where neither party can lay hold of any weapon, the "fight" resolves itself simply into a hair-pulling match.

A Chinese quarrel is also a reviling match, low language and high words. But an infinitesimal fraction of the participants in Chinese fights is seriously disabled in other respects than that by incessant bawling they have become hoarse. We should be surprised to hear that any one ever saw a Chinese crowd egg on combatants. What we have seen, what we always expect to see, is the instant and spontaneous appearance on the scene of the peace-maker. He is double, perhaps quadruple. Each of the peace-makers seizes a roaring belligerent, and tranquillises him with good advice. As soon as he finds himself safely in charge of the peace-maker, the principal in the fight becomes doubly furious. He has judiciously postponed losing control of himself until there is some one else ready to take that control, and then he gives way to spasms of apparent fury, unquestionably innocuous both to himself and to others. In his most furious moments a Chinese is amenable to "reason," for which he has not only a theoretical, but a very practical, respect. Who ever saw a belligerent turn and rend the officious peace-maker, who is holding him from flying at his foe ? This is the crucial point in the struggle. Even in his fury the Chinese recognises the desirableness of peace—in the abstract—only he thinks that in his concrete case peace is inapplicable. The peace-maker judges differently, and nearly always drags away the bellicose reviler, who yells back to his opponent malignant defiance as he goes.

It is a curious feature of the universal Chinese practice of reviling that it is not considered " good form " in hurling this abuse at another to touch upon his actual faults, but rather to impute to him the most ignoble origin, and to heap contempt upon his ancestors. The employment of this language towards another is justly regarded as a great indignity and a grave offence, but the point of the insult consists not in the use of such language in the presence of another, nor even principally in its application to him, but in the loss of " face " which this application of such terms implies. The proper apology for the commission of this offence is not that the person who has been guilty of it has demeaned himself, and has done a disgraceful act, but that he was wrong in applying those terms to that person at that time.

It is fortunate for the Chinese that they have not the habit of carrying weapons about them, for if they had revolvers or swords, like the former *samurai* class of Japan, it would not be possible to predict the amount of mischief which the daily evolution of *ch'i* would produce.

When any Chinese is once seized of the idea that he has been deeply wronged, there is no power on earth which can prevent the sudden and often utterly ungovernable development of a certain amount of *ch'i*, or rather of a very uncertain amount of it. We have heard of a man who applied for baptism to an old and experienced missionary and was very properly refused, whereupon he got a knife and threatened to attack the missionary to prove by ordeal of battle the claim to the rite of initiation. Happily this method of taking the kingdom of heaven by violence does not commend itself to most novitiates, but the underlying principle is one that is constantly acted upon in all varieties of Chinese social life. An old woman who will not take "no" for an answer asks for financial assistance, and throws herself on the ground in front of your carter's mules. If she is run over so much the better for her, for she is thus reasonably sure of a support for an indefinite period. An old vixen living in the same village as the writer was constantly threatening to commit suicide, but though all her neighbours were willing to lend their aid, she never seemed to accomplish her purpose. At last she threw herself into one of the village mudholes with intent to drown, but found to her disgust that the water was only up to her neck. She lacked that versatility of invention which would have enabled her to put her head under water and hold it there, but contented herself with reviling the whole village at the top of her voice for her *contretemps*. The next time she was more successful.

If a wrong has been committed for which there is no legal redress, such as abuse of a married daughter beyond the point which custom warrants, a party of the injured friends will visit the house of the mother-in-law, and if they are resisted, will engage in a pitched battle. If they are not resisted, and the offending persons have fled, the assailants will proceed to smash all the crockery in the house, the mirrors, the water-jars, and whatever else is frangible, and having thus allowed their *ch'i* to escape, they depart. If their coming is known in advance, the very first step is to remove all these articles to the house of some neighbour. One of the Chinese newspapers mentioned a case which occurred in Peking, where a man had arranged for a wedding with a beautiful woman, who turned out to be ugly, bald-headed, and elderly. The disappointed bridegroom became greatly enraged, struck the go-betweens, reviled the whole company, and smashed the bride's wedding-outfit. Any Chinese would have acted in the same way, if he was in such relations to his environment that he dared to do so.* It is after the preliminary paroxysms of *ch'i* have had opportunity to subside, that the work of the "peace-talker" —that useful factor in Chinese social life—is accomplished. Sometimes these most essential individuals are so deeply impressed with the necessity of peace, that even when the matter is not one which concerns them personally, they are willing to go from one to the other making prostrations now to this side and now to that, in the interests of harmony.

Whenever social storms prove incapable of adjustment by the ordinary processes—in other words, when there is such a preponderance of *ch'i* that it cannot be dispersed without an explosion—there is the beginning of the lawsuit, a term in China of fateful significance. The same blind rage which leads a person to lose all control of himself in a quarrel leads him, after the first stages of the outbreak have passed, to determine to take the offender before a magistrate, in order "to have the law on him." This proceeding in Western lands is generally injudicious, but in China it is sheer madness. There is sound sense in the proverb which praises the man who will suffer himself to be imposed upon to the death before he will

---

* It was reported in Peking that the present Emperor was not pleased with the choice of a wife which was made for him. He had been so often crossed in his wishes by the Empress Dowager that any selection which was made by her would have been distasteful. It was also whispered that scenes occurred in the palace not remotely unlike those mentioned as taking place at the wedding of one of his subjects. "When those above act, those below will imitate."

go to the law, which will often be worse than death. We smile at the fury of the immigrant whose dog had been shot by a neighbour, and who was remonstrated with by a friend when the resolution to go to law was declared. "What was the value of the dog?" "Ze dog vas vort nottings, but since he vas so mean as to kill him, he shall pay ze full value of him." In an Occidental land such a suit would be dismissed with costs, and there it would end. In China it might go on to the ruin of both parties, and be a cause of feud for generations yet to come. But generally speaking, every Chinese lawsuit calls out upon each side the omnipresent peace-talker, whose services are invaluable. Millions of lawsuits are thus strangled before they reach the fatal stage. In a village numbering a thousand families, the writer was informed that for more than a generation there had not been a single lawsuit, owing to the restraining influence of a leading man who had a position in the yamên of the District Magistrate.

A social machinery so complicated as that of China must often creak, and sometimes under extreme pressure bend, yet it seldom actually breaks beneath the strain, for, like the human body, the Chinese body politic is provided, as we see, with little sacs of lubricating fluid, distilled, a drop at a time, exactly when and where they are most needed. It is the peaceable quality of the Chinese which makes him a valuable social unit. He loves order and respects law, even when it is not in itself respectable. Of all Asiatic peoples, the Chinese are probably most easily governed, when governed on lines to which they are accustomed. Doubtless there are other forms of civilisation which are in many or in most respects superior to that of China, but perhaps there are few which would sustain the tension to which Chinese society has for ages been subject, and it may be that there is none better entitled to claim the benediction once pronounced upon the peace-makers.

CHAPTER XXIII.

MUTUAL RESPONSIBILITY AND RESPECT FOR LAW.

ONE of the most distinctive features of Chinese society is that which is epitomised in the word "responsibility," a word which carries with it a significance and embraces a wealth of meaning to which Western lands are total strangers. In those lands, as we well know, the individual is the unit and the nation is a large collection of individuals. In China the unit of social life is found in the family, the village, or the clan, and these are often convertible terms. Thousands of Chinese villages comprise exclusively persons having the same surname and the same ancestors. The inhabitants have lived in the same spot ever since they began to live at all, and trace an unbroken descent for many hundred years back to the last great political upheaval, such as the overthrow of the Ming Dynasty or its establishment. In such a village there can be no relationship laterally more distant than "cousin," and every male member of an older generation is either a father, an uncle, or some kind of a "grandfather." Sometimes eleven generations are represented in the same small hamlet. This does not imply, as might be supposed, extreme old age on the part of any representative of the older generations. The Chinese marry young, marry repeatedly, often late in life, and constantly adopt children. The result is such a tangle among relatives that without special inquiry and minute attention to the particular characters which are employed in writing the names of all who belong to the same "generation," it is im-

226

possible to determine who constitute " the rising generation,"
and who form the generation which rose long ago. An old
man nearly seventy years of age affirms that a young man of
thirty is his " grandfather." All the numerous " cousins " of
the same generation are termed "brothers," and if the per-
plexed foreigner insists upon accuracy, and inquires whether
they are " own brothers," he will not infrequently be enlight-
enéd with the reply that they are " own brother-cousins." The
writer once proposed a question of this sort, and after some
little hesitation the person addressed replied, " Why, yes, you
might call them own brothers."

These items are but particulars under the general head of
the social solidarity of the Chinese. It is this solidarity which
forms the substratum upon which rests Chinese responsibility.
The father is responsible for his son, not merely until the latter
attains to " years of discretion," but as long as life lasts, and
the son is responsible for his father's debts. The elder brother
has a definite responsibility for the younger brother, and the
" head of the family "—usually the oldest representative of the
oldest generation—has his responsibility for the whole family
or clan. What these responsibilities actually are will depend,
however, upon circumstances.

Customs vary widely, and the "personal equation " is a
most important factor, of which mere theory takes no account. Thus in a large and influential family, embracing
many literary men, some of whom are local magnates and
perhaps graduates, the " head of the clan " may be an addle-
headed old man who can neither read nor write, and who has
never in his life been ten miles from home.

The influence of an elder brother over a younger, or indeed
of any older member over a younger member of the same
family, is of the most direct and positive sort, and is entirely
irreconcilable with what we mean by personal liberty. The
younger brother is employed as a servant and would like to

give up his place, but his elder brother will not let him do so. The younger brother wishes to buy a winter garment, but his elder brother thinks the cost is too great, and will not allow him to incur the expense. Even while these remarks are committed to paper, a case is reported in which a Chinese has a number of rare old coins, which a foreigner desires to purchase. Lest the owner should refuse to sell—as is the Chinese way when one happens to have what another wants—the middleman who made the discovery proposes to the foreigner that he should send to *the uncle* of the owner of the coins a present of foreign candy and other trifles, by which oblique means such pressure will be brought to bear upon the owner of the coins that he will be obliged to give them up!

There is a burlesque tale which relates that a traveller in a Western land once came upon a very old man with a long white beard, who was crying bitterly. Struck with the singularity of this spectacle, the stranger halted and asked the old man what he was crying about, and was surprised to be told that it was because his father had just whipped him! " Where is your father ? " " Over there," was the reply. Riding in the direction named, the traveller found a much older man, with a beard much longer and whiter than the other. " Is that your son? " asked the traveller. " Yes, it is." " Did you whip him? " " Yes, I did." " Why? " " Because he was saucy to his grandfather, and if he does it again I will whip him some more! " Translated into the conditions of Chinese life the burlesque disappears.

Next in order to the responsibility of members of a family for one another comes the mutual responsibility of neighbours for neighbours. Whether these " neighbours " are or are not related makes no difference in their responsibility, which depends solely upon proximity. This responsibility is based upon the theory that virtue and vice are contagious. Good neighbours will make good neighbours, and bad neighbours will make others like them.   The mother of Mencius removed three times in order to reach a desirable neighbourhood.   To an Occidental, fresh from the republican ideas which dominate the Anglo-Saxons, it seems a matter of little or no consequence who his neighbours are, and if he be a resident of a city he may occupy a dwelling for a year in ignorance even of the name of the family next door.   But in China it is otherwise. If a crime takes place the neighbours are held guilty of something analogous to what English law calls "misprision of treason," in that when they knew of a criminal intention they did not report it.   It is vain to reply " I did not know."   You are a " neighbour," and therefore you must have known.

The proceedings which are taken when the crime of killing a parent has been committed, furnish a striking illustration of the Chinese theory of responsibility.   As has been already mentioned in speaking of filial piety, in such instances the criminal is often alleged to be insane, as indeed one must be who voluntarily subjects himself to death by the slicing process when he might escape it by suicide.   In a memorial published in the Peking *Gazette* a few years since, the Governor of one of the central provinces reported in regard to a case of parricide that he had had the houses of all the neighbours pulled down, on the ground of their gross dereliction of duty in not exerting a good moral and reformatory influence over the criminal!   Such a proceeding would probably strike an average Chinese as eminently reasonable.   In some instances when this crime has occurred in a district, in addition to all the punishments of persons, the city wall itself is pulled down in parts, or modified in shape, a round corner substituted for a square one, or a gate removed to a new situation, or even closed up altogether.   If the crime should be repeated several times in the same district, it is said that the whole city would be razed to the ground, and a new one founded elsewhere, but of this we have met with no certain examples.

Next above the neighbours comes the village constable or bailiff, whose functions are of a most miscellaneous nature, sometimes confined to a single village, and sometimes extending to many. In either case he is the medium of communication between the local magistrate and the people, and is always liable to get into trouble from any one of innumerable causes, and may be beaten to a jelly by a captious official for not reporting what he could not possibly have known.

At a vast elevation above the village constables stand the District Magistrates, who, so far as the people are concerned, are by far the most important officers in China. As regards the people below them they are tigers. As regards the officials above them they are mice. A single local magistrate combines functions which ought to be distributed among at least six different officers. A man who is at once the civil and the criminal judge, the sheriff, the coroner, the treasurer, and the tax-commissioner for a large and populous district, cannot attend to the details of all his work. This vicious agglomeration of duties in one office renders it both a physical and a moral impossibility that these duties should be properly discharged. Many magistrates have no interest whatever in the business which they despatch, except to extract from it all that it can be made to yield, and, from the nature of their miscellaneous and incongruous duties, they are largely dependent upon their secretaries and other subordinates. Having so much to do, even with the best intentions these officials cannot fail to make numerous mistakes, and many things must go wrong, for which they will be held responsible. The District Magistrate, like all Chinese officials, is supposed to have an exhaustive acquaintance with everything within his jurisdiction which is an object of knowledge, and an unlimited capacity to prevent what ought to be prevented. To facilitate this knowledge and that of the local constables, each city and village is divided into compound atoms composed of ten families each.

At every door hangs a placard or tablet upon which is inscribed the name of the head of the family, and the number of individuals which it comprises. This system of registration, analogous to the old Saxon tithings and hundreds, makes it easy to fix local responsibility. The moment a suspicious stranger appears in the district comprised in a tithing, he is promptly reported to the head of the tithing by whoever sees him first. By the head of the tithing he is immediately reported to the local constable, and by the local constable to the District Magistrate, who at once takes steps "rigorously to seize and severely to punish." By the same simple process all local crimes, not due to "suspicious-looking strangers" but to permanent residents, are instantly detected before they have hatched into overt acts, and thus the pure morals of the people are preserved from age to age.

It is evident that such regulations as these can be efficient only in a state of society where fixity of residence is the rule. It is also evident that even in China, where the most extreme form of permanence of abode is found, the system of tithing is to a large extent a mere legal fiction. Sometimes a city, where no one remembers to have seen them before, suddenly blossoms out with ten-family tablets on every door-post, which indicates the arrival of a District Magistrate who intends to enforce the regulations. In some places these tablets are observable in the winter season only, for this is the time when bad characters are most numerous and most dangerous. But so far as our knowledge extends, the system as such is little more than a theoretical reminiscence, and even when observed it is probably merely a form. Practically, it is not generally observed, and in some provinces at least one may travel for a thousand miles, and for months together, and not find ten-family tablets posted in more than one per cent. of the cities and villages along the route.

It may be mentioned in passing that the Chinese tithing

system is intimately connected with the so-called census. If each doorway exhibits an accurate list, constantly corrected, of the number of persons in each family; if each local constable has accurate copies of the lists of all the tithings within his territory; if each District Magistrate has at his disposal accurate summaries of all these items—it is as easy to secure a complete and accurate census of the Empire as to do a long sum in addition, for the whole is equal to the aggregate of all its parts. But these are large *ifs*, and, as a matter of fact, none of the conditions are realised. The tablets are non-existent, and when the local magistrate is occasionally called upon for the totals which should represent them, neither he nor the numerous constables upon whom he is entirely dependent has the least interest in securing accuracy, which indeed from the nature of the case is difficult. There is no " squeeze " to be got from a census, and for this reason alone a really accurate Chinese census is a mere figment of the imagination. Even in the most enlightened Western lands the notion that a census means taxation appears to be ineradicable, but in China the suspicion which it excites is so strong, that for this reason alone, unless the tithing system were carried out with uniform faithfulness in all places and at all times, an accurate enumeration would be impossible.

For a local magistrate to be guilty of all kinds of misdemeanours for which he gets into no trouble whatever, or getting into it, escapes scot-free by means of influential friends or by a judicious expenditure of silver, and yet after all to lose his post on account of something that happened within his jurisdiction but which he could not have prevented, is a constant occurrence.

How the system of responsibility operates in the domain of all the successive grades of officials, it is unnecessary to illustrate in detail. Multiplied examples are found in almost every copy of the translations from the Peking *Gazette*. A case was mentioned a few years ago, where a soldier on guard had stolen some thirty boxes of bullets placed in his care, and sold them to a tinner, who supposed them to be condemned and surplus stores. The soldier was beaten one hundred blows, and banished to the frontiers of the Empire in penal servitude. A petty officer whose duty it was to inspect the stores was condemned to eighty blows and dismissed from the service, though allowed to commute his punishment for a money payment. The purchasers of the material were considered innocent of any blame, but on general principles were beaten forty blows of the light bamboo. The lieutenant in charge was cashiered in order to be put upon trial for his " connivance " in the theft, but he judiciously disappeared. The Board to which the memorial was addressed was requested to determine the penalty to be inflicted upon the general in command, for his share in the matter. Thus each individual is a link in the chain which is followed up to the very end, and no link can escape by pleading ignorance or inability to prevent the crime.

Still more characteristic examples of Chinese responsibility are furnished by the memorials annually appearing in the Peking *Gazette*, reporting the outbreak of some irrepressible river. In the case of a flood in the Yung-ting River in the province of Chihli during the summer of 1888, the waters came down from the mountains with the velocity of a mill-race. The officials seem to have been promptly on hand, and to have risked their lives in struggling to do what was utterly beyond the powers of man. They were helpless as ants under a rain-spout during a summer torrent. But this did not prevent Li Hung-chang from requesting that they should be immediately stripped of their buttons, or deprived of their rank without being removed from their posts (a favourite mode of expressing Imperial dissatisfaction), and the Governor-General consistently concludes his memorial with the usual request that his own name should be sent to the Board of Punishments for the determination of a penalty to be inflicted upon him for his complicity in the affair. Similar floods have occurred several times since, and upon each occasion a similar memorial has been presented. The Emperor always instructs the proper Board to "take note." In like manner the failure of the embankments built a few years ago to bring back the Yellow River into its old channel was the signal for the degradation and banishment of a great number of officers, from the Governor of the province of Honan downwards.

The theory of responsibility is carried upwards with unflinching consistency to the Son of Heaven himself. It is no unusual thing for the Emperor in published edicts to confess to Heaven his shortcomings, taking upon himself the blame of floods, famines, and revolutionary outbreaks, for which he begs Heaven's forgiveness. His responsibility to Heaven is as real as that of his officers to himself. If the Emperor loses his throne, it is because he has already lost "Heaven's decree," which is presumptively transferred to whoever can hold the Empire.

That aspect of the Chinese doctrine of responsibility which is the most repellent to Western standards of thought, is found in the Oriental practice of extinguishing an entire family for the crime of one of its members. Many instances of this sort were reported in connection with the T'aip'ing rebellion, and more recently the family of the chieftain Yakub Beg, who led the Mohammedan rebellion in Turkestan, furnished another. These atrocities are not, however, limited to cases of overt rebellion. In the year 1873 "a Chinese was accused and convicted of having broken open the grave of a relative of the Imperial family, in order to rob the coffin of certain gold, silver, and jade ornaments which had been buried in it. The entire family of the criminal, consisting of four generations, from a man more than ninety years of age to a female infant only a few months old, was exterminated. Thus eleven persons suffered death for the offence of one. And there was no evidence to show that any of them were parties to, or were even aware of, his crime."

The Chinese theory and practice of responsibility has been often cited as one of the causes of the perpetuity of Chinese institutions. It forges around every member of Chinese society iron fetters from which it is impossible that he should break loose. It constantly violates every principle of justice by punishing all grades of officers, as well as private individuals, for occurrences in which they had no part, and of which, as in the example just cited, they were not improbably utterly ignorant. It is the direct cause of deliberate and systematic falsification in all ranks of officials, from the very lowest to the very highest. If an officer is responsible for the existence of crimes which he does not find it easy to control, or of which he is ignorant till it is too late to prevent them, he will inevitably conceal the facts so as to screen himself. This is what constantly happens in all departments of the government, to the complete subversion of justice, for it is not in human nature to give truthful reports of events when, in consequence of such reports, the person who makes them may be severely and unjustly punished. The abuse of this principle alone would suffice to account for a large part of the maladministration of justice in China, to which our attention is so often called.

An additional evil connected with the official system has been noticed by every writer on China. It is the absence of independent salaries for the officers, whose allowances are so absurdly small that often they would not pay the expenses of the yamên for a day. Besides this, the officials are subject to so many forfeitures that it is said that they rarely draw their nominal allowances at all, as it would be necessary to pay them all back again in fines. The absolute necessity for levying squeezes and taking bribes arises from the fact that there is no other way by which a magistrate can exist.

Still, while we are impressed with flagrant violations of justice which the Chinese theory of responsibility involves, it is impossible to be blind to its excellences.

In Western lands, where every one is supposed to be innocent until he is proved to be guilty, it is exceedingly difficult to fix responsibility upon any particular person. A bridge breaks down with a heavy train of cars loaded with passengers, and an investigation fails to find any one in fault. A lofty building falls and crushes scores of people, and while the architect is criticised, he shows that he did the best he could with the means at his disposal, and no one ever hears of his being punished. If an ironclad capsize, or a military campaign is ruined because the proper preparations were not made, or not made in time, eloquent speeches set forth the defects of the system which renders such events possible, but no one is punished. The Chinese are far behind us in their conceptions of public justice, but might we not wisely learn again from them the ancient lesson that every one should be held rigidly responsible for his own acts, in order to the security of the body politic?

The relation of the Chinese theory of responsibility to foreigners in China is one of great importance. The " Boy," into whose hands everything is committed, and who must produce every spoon, fork, or curio ; the steward, who takes general charge of your affairs, suffering no one but himself to cheat you ; the compradore, who wields vast powers but who is individually responsible for every piece of property and for every one of hundreds of coolies—these types of character we still have with us, and shall always have, as long as we have anything to do with the Chinese. Innkeepers in China are not noted for flagrant virtues of any kind, especially for consideration towards foreign travellers. Yet we have known of a Chinese innkeeper who ran half a mile after a foreigner, bringing an empty sardine-tin which he supposed to be a forgotten valuable. He knew that he was responsible, unlike American hotel-keepers, who coolly notify their guests that "the proprietor is not responsible for boots left in the hall to be blacked."

Responsibility for the character, behaviour, and debts of those whom they recommend or introduce, is a social obligation of recognised force, and one which it behoves foreigners dealing with Chinese to emphasise. The fact that a headman, whatever his position, is "responsible " for any and every act of omission or commission of all his subordinates, exerts over the whole series of links in the chain a peculiar influence, which has been instinctively appreciated by foreigners in all the long history of their dealings with Chinese. There is a tradition of a head compradore in a bank, who in the "more former days " was called to account because the "Boy " had allowed a mosquito to insinuate itself within the mosquito-net of the bank manager! If the Chinese perceive that a foreigner is ignorant of the responsibility of his employés, or disregards it, it will not take them long to act upon this discovery in extremely disagreeable ways.

One of the many admirable qualities of the Chinese is their innate respect for law. Whether this element in their character is the effect of their institutions, or the cause of them, we do not know. But what we do know is that the Chinese are by nature and by education a law-abiding people. Reference has been already made to this trait in speaking of the national virtue of patience, but it deserves special notice in connection with Chinese theories of mutual responsibility. In China every man, woman, and child is directly responsible to some one else, and of this important fact no one for a moment loses sight. Though one should "go far and fly high " he cannot escape, and this he well knows. Even if he should himself escape, his family cannot escape. The certainty of this does not indeed make a bad man good, but it frequently prevents him from becoming tenfold worse.

It is an illustration of Chinese respect for law, and all that appertains thereto, that it often happens that men of literary rank are so terrified in the presence of a District Magistrate that they dare not open their mouths unless compelled to do so, although the case may not in any way concern themselves. We have indeed known of one instance where a man of this class appeared to be thrown into a condition resembling epilepsy by sheer fright in giving evidence. He was taken home in a fit, and soon after died.

Contrast the Chinese inherent respect for law with the spirit often manifested where republican institutions flourish most, and manifested, it must be said, by those whose antecedents would least lead us to expect it. College laws, municipal ordinances, state and national enactments, are quietly defied, as if the assertion of personal liberty were one of the greatest needs, instead of one of the principal dangers of the time. It is rightly regarded as one of the most serious indictments against the transaction of Chinese public business of all kinds, that every one not only connives at acts of dishonesty which it is his duty to prevent and to expose, but that such is the constitution of public and private society that every one must connive at such acts. But is it less disgraceful that in Christian countries men of education and refinement, as well as the uncultivated, quietly ignore or deliberately disregard the laws of the land as if by common consent, and as if it were now a well-ascertained fact that a law is more honoured in the breach than in the observance ? How shall we explain or defend the existence upon our statute-books of multitudinous laws which are neither repealed nor enforced—laws which by their anomalous non-existent existence tend to bring all legislation into a common contempt? By what means shall we explain the alarming increase of crime in many Western lands during the last thirty years? How shall we explain that conspicuous indifference to the sacredness of human life which is unquestionably a characteristic of some Western lands? It is vain to dogmatise in regard to matters which from the nature of the case are beyond the reach of statistics. Still we must confess to a decided conviction that human life is safer in a Chinese city than in an American city—safer in Peking than in New York. We believe it to be safer for a foreigner to traverse the interior of China than for a Chinese to traverse the interior of the United States. It must be remembered that the Chinese as a whole are quite as ignorant as any body of immigrants in the United States, and not less prejudiced. They are, as we constantly see, ideal material for mobs. The wonder is not that such outbreaks take place, but that they have not occurred more frequently, and have not been more fatal to the lives of foreigners.

It is a Chinese tenet that Heaven is influenced by the acts and by the spirit of human beings. Upon this principle depends the efficacy of the self-mutilation on behalf of parents, to which reference was made in speaking of filial piety. That this is a correct theory we are not prepared to maintain, yet certain facts deserve mention which might seem to support it. The geographical situation and extent of the Eighteen Provinces of China bear a marked resemblance to that part of the United States of America east of the Rocky Mountains. The erratic eccentricities of the climate of the United States are, as little Marjorie Fleming remarked of the multiplication table, "more than human nature can bear." It was Hawthorne who observed of New England that it has "no climate, but only samples." Contrast the weather in Boston, New York, or Chicago with that of places in the same latitude in China. It is not that China is not, as the geographies used to affirm of the United States, " subject to extremes of heat and cold," for in the latitude of Peking the thermometer ranges through about one hundred degrees Fahrenheit, which ought to afford sufficient variety of temperature to any mortal.

But in China these alternations of heat and cold do not follow one another with that reckless and incalculable lawlessness witnessed in the great republic, but with an even and unruffled sequence suited to an ancient and a patriarchal system.   The Imperial almanac is the authorised exponent of the threefold harmony subsisting in China between heaven, earth, and man.   Whether the Imperial almanac is equally trustworthy in all parts of the Emperor's broad domain we do not know, but in those regions with which we happen to be familiar the almanac is itself a signal-service.   At the point marked for the " establishment of spring," spring appears.   In several different years we have remarked that the day on which the " establishment of autumn " fell was distinguished by a marked change in the weather, after which the blistering heats of summer returned no more.   Instead of allowing the frost to make irregular and devastating irruptions in every month of the year —as is too often the case in lands where democracy rules— the Chinese calendar fixes one of its four-and-twenty " terms " as " frost-fall."   A few years ago this " term " fell on the 23d of October.   Up to that day no lightest frost had been seen. On the morning of that day the ground was covered with white frost, and continued to be so covered every morning thereafter.   We have noted these correspondences for some years, and have seldom observed a variation of more than the usual three days of grace.

It is not inanimate nature only which in China is amenable to reason and to law, but animated nature as well.   For some years we have noticed that on a particular day in early spring the window-frames were adorned with several flies, where for many months no flies had been seen, and on each occasion we have turned to the Imperial almanac with a confidence justified by the event, and ascertained that this particular day was the one assigned for the "stirring of insects"!

It has been remarked that there is in the blood of the English-speaking race a certain lawlessness, which makes us intolerant of rules and restless under restraints. "Our sturdy English ancestors," says Blackstone, "held it beneath the condition of a freeman to appear, or to do any other act, at the precise time appointed." But for this trait of our doughty forefathers the doctrine of personal liberty and the rights of man might have waited long for assertion.

But now that these rights are tolerably well established, might we not judiciously lay somewhat more emphasis upon the importance of subordinating the individual will to the public good, and upon the majesty of law? And in these directions have we not something to learn from the Chinese?

CHAPTER XXIV.

MUTUAL SUSPICION.

IT is an indisputable truth that without a certain amount of mutual confidence it is impossible for mankind to exist in an organised society, especially in a society so highly organised and so complex as that of China. Assuming this as an axiom, it is not the less necessary to direct our attention to a series of phenomena, which, however inharmonious they may appear with our theory, are sufficiently real to those who are acquainted with China. Much of what we shall have to say of the mutual suspicion of the Chinese is by no means peculiar to this people; it is rather a trait which they share in common with all Orientals, the manifestations of which are doubtless much modified by the genius of Chinese institutions. The whole subject is intimately connected with that of mutual responsibility, already discussed. Nothing is more likely to excite the suspicion not of the Chinese only but of any human being, than the danger that he may be held to account for something which has no concern whatever with himself, but the consequences of which may be most serious.

The first manifestation which attracts a stranger's attention of the chronic suspicion prevailing in China is the existence in all parts of the Empire of lofty walls which enclose all cities. The fact that the word for city is in Chinese the equivalent for a walled city, is as significant as the fact that in the Latin language the word which denoted army also meant drill or practice. The laws of the Empire require that every city

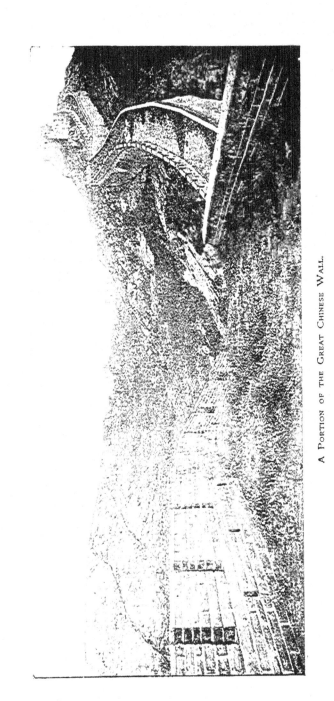

A Portion of the Great Chinese Wall.

shall be enclosed by a wall of a specified height. Like other laws this statute is much neglected in the letter, for there are many cities the walls of which are allowed to crumble into such decay that they are no protection whatever, and we know of one district city invested by the T'ai-p'ing rebels and occupied by them for many months, the walls of which, although utterly destroyed, were not restored at all for more than a decade afterwards. Many cities have only a feeble mud rampart, quite inadequate to keep out even the native dogs, which climb over it at will. But in all these cases the occasion of these lapses from the ideal state of things is simply the poverty of the country. Whenever there is an alarm of trouble, the first step is to repair the walls. The execution of such repairs affords a convenient way in which to fine officials or others who have made themselves too rich in too short a time.

The firm foundation on which rest all the many city walls in China is the *distrust* which the government entertains of the people. However the Emperor may be in theory the father of his people, and his subordinates called "father and mother officials," all parties understand perfectly that these are purely technical terms, like *plus* and *minus*, and that the real relation between the people and their rulers is that between children and a stepfather. The whole history of China appears to be dotted with rebellions, most of which might apparently have been prevented by proper action on the part of the general government if taken in time. The government does not expect to act in time. Perhaps it does not wish to do so, or perhaps it is prevented from doing so. Meantime, the people slowly rise, as the government knew they would, and the officials promptly retire within these ready-made fortifications, like a turtle into its shell or a hedgehog within its ball of quills, and the disturbance is left to the slow adjustment of the troops.

The lofty walls which enclose all premises in Chinese, as in other Oriental cities and towns, are another exemplification of the same traits of suspicion.   If it is embarrassing for a foreigner to know how to speak to a Chinese of such places as London or New York, without unintentionally conveying the notion that they are "walled cities," it is not less difficult to make Chinese who may be interested in Western lands understand how it can be that in those countries people often have about their premises no enclosures whatever.   The immediate, although unwarranted, inference on the part of the Chinese is that in such countries there must be no bad characters of any kind.

The almost universal massing of the rural Chinese population in villages, which are in reality miniature cities, is another illustration of mutual suspicion.   The object is protection, not from a foreign enemy, but from one another.   The only exceptions to this agglomeration of Chinese dwellings with which we are acquainted, is in the case of some mountainous regions where the land is so barren that it is incapable of supporting more than one or two families, the people being so poor that they have no dread of thieves, and the province of Szechuan, in which, as Mr. Baber mentions, "the farmer and his work-people live, it may be said, invariably in farm-houses on their land, and the tendency is to the separation rather than to the congregation of dwellings."   If this exception to the general rule was made because the expectation of peace in that remote province was thought to be greater than in others, as Baron von Richthofen suggested, it has proved, as Mr. Baber remarks, an expectation which has suffered many and grievous disappointments, especially—although after a long-previous peace—in the days of the T'ai-p'ing rebels.

A most significant illustration of the Chinese—and also Oriental—suspicion found in social life is to be seen in the theory and practice in regard to woman.   What that theory is is sufficiently well known.   An entire chapter would scarcely do justice to this branch of the subject. As soon as they come to the age of puberty, girls are proverbially a commodity as "dangerous as smuggled salt." When once they are betrothed they are kept far more secluded than before. The smallest and most innocent circumstance is sufficient to start vicious and malevolent gossip, and it is a social axiom that scandals cluster about a widow's door. While Chinese women have incomparably more liberty than their sisters in Turkey or in India,* Chinese respect for women cannot be rated as high. Universal ignorance on the part of women, universal subordination, the existence of polygamy and concubinage—these are not good preparations for that respect for womanhood which is one of the fairest characteristics of Western civilisation. It would be easy to cite popular expressions in illustration of the views which the Chinese hold of women in general, and which may be regarded as the generalisations of long experience. She is spoken of as if it were her nature to be mean, short-sighted, and not to be trusted—she is considered to be an incarnation of jealousy, as in the phrase, "it is impossible to be more jealous than a woman," where the word "jealous" suggests, and is intended to suggest, another word with the same sound, but meaning "poisonous." This theory is well embodied in a verse of ancient Chinese poetry, of which the following lines are a translation :

> "The serpent's mouth in the green bamboo,
> The yellow hornet's caudal dart ;
> Little the injury these can do ;
> More venomous far is a woman's heart."

* The existence of this liberty, is not, however, to be judged of by superficial indications. A lady who resided for some years in the Indian city of Delhi, and subsequently at the capital of the province of Shansi, remarked that fewer Chinese women were ordinarily to be seen upon the streets of the latter city, than Indian women upon the streets of the former one. Yet this circumstance does not at all conflict with the truth of the statement to which this note is appended.

These views are incidentally exemplified with a fine and unconscious impartiality in the very structure of the Chinese language, in a manner to which attention has been often directed. An excellent scholar in Chinese, in response to a request from the writer, examined with care a list of one hundred and thirty-five of the more common characters which are written with the radical denoting woman, and found that fourteen of them conveyed a meaning which might be classed as good, such as the words " good," " skilful," and the like ; of the remainder, thirty-five are bad, and eighty-six indifferent in meaning. But those classed as bad contain some of the most disreputable words in the whole language. The radical for woman combined with that denoting shield signifies " deceitful, fraudulent, villainous, traitorous, selfish " ; while three women in combination convey the ideas of " fornication, adultery, seduction, to intrigue."

There are said to be two reasons why people do not trust one another : first, because they do not know one another, and second, because they do. The Chinese think that they have each of these reasons for mistrust, and they act accordingly. While the Chinese are gifted with a capacity for combination which at times seems to suggest the union of chemical atoms, it is easy to ascertain by careful inquiry at the proper sources and at the proper times, that the Chinese do not by any means trust one another in the implicit way which the external phenomena might imply. Members of the same family are constantly the victims of mutual suspicion, which is fanned by the women who have married into the family, and who as sisters-in-law are able to do much, and who frequently do what they can, to foment jealousy between their husbands in regard to the division of the proceeds of the common labour.

Not to enlarge upon this aspect of domestic life, which by itself might occupy a chapter, we pass to the notice of the same general state of things among those who are not united by the complex ties of Chinese family life. A company of servants in a family often stand to one another in a relation of what may be called armed neutrality, that is, if they have not been introduced by some one who is responsible for them all. If anything comes out to the disadvantage of any one of them, his first question to himself is not, "How did the master find that out?" but "Who told him of me?" Even if the servant is well aware that his guilt has been proved, his first thought will be to show that some other servant had a grudge against him. We have known a Chinese woman to change colour and leave a room in great dudgeon on hearing loud voices in the yard, because she supposed that as there was an angry discussion, it *must* be about her, whereas the matter was in relation to a pile of millet stalks bought for fuel, for which a dealer demanded too high a price.

It is this kind of suspicion which fans the fires of dissension that are almost sure to arise when a servant has been unexpectedly discharged. He suspects every one but himself, is certain that some one has been speaking ill of him, insists upon being told the allegations against him, although he knows that there are half a score of reasons, any of which would justify his immediate dismissal. His "face" must be secured, and his suspicious nature must be gratified. These occurrences take place in Chinese families as well as in foreign families with Chinese servants, but not in the same degree, because a Chinese servant has learned how far he can impose upon the good-nature of the foreigner, as he would never think of doing in the case of a Chinese master. It is for this reason that so many foreigners have in their employ Chinese servants whom they ought to have discharged long ago, and would have discharged if they had dared. They know that the mere proposal of such a thing will be the stirring up of a hornet's nest, the central figure of which will be the accused and "disgraced" servant, and they have not the courage to make a strike for liberty, lest in the case of failure their condition should be worse than before.

There is a story of an Austrian city which was besieged by the Turks in the middle ages, and which was just on the point of capture. At a critical moment an Austrian girl bethought herself of a number of bee-hives, which she at once brought and tumbled over the wall on the Turks, now almost up to the parapet. The result was a speedy descent on the part of the Turks, and the saving of the city. The tactics of a Chinese often resemble that of the Austrian maiden, and his success is frequently as signal, for this kind of a disturbance is such that, as a Latin professor said of a storm, one would much rather " face it *per alium* " than " face it *per se.*" No wonder that the adage runs, " If you employ one, do not suspect him ; if you suspect him, do not employ him." The Chinese way in such cases is simply to close one's eyes and to pretend that one does not see, but for a foreigner this may not be so simple and easy to achieve.

We find it necessary to impress upon our children, when they come to be of an age to mingle in the world on their own account, that it is well not to be too confiding in strangers. This kind of caution does not need to be conveyed to the Chinese in their early years, for it is taken in with their mother's milk. It is a proverb that one man should not enter a temple, and that two men should not look together into a well. And why, we inquire in surprise, should one man not enter a temple court alone? Because the priest may take advantage of the opportunity to make away with him! Two men should not gaze into a well, for if one of them is in debt to the other, or has in his possession something which the other wants, that other may seize the occasion to push his companion into the well!

Another class of examples of mutual suspicion are those

arising in the ordinary affairs of everyday life. There is a freedom and an absence of constraint in Western lands which in China is conspicuously absent. To us it seems a matter of course that the simplest way to do a thing is for that reason the best. But in China there are different and quite other factors of which account must be taken. While this is true in regard to everything, it is most felt in regard to two matters which form the warp and woof of the lives of most Chinese— money and food. It is very difficult to convince a Chinese that a sum of money, which may have been put into the hands of another to be divided between many persons, has been divided according to the theoretical plan, for he has no experience of any divisions of this sort, and he has had extended experience of divisions in which various deductions in the shape of squeezes were the prominent features. In like manner, it is very hard to make an arrangement by which one Chinese shall have charge of the food provision for others, in which, if close inquiry is made, it shall not appear that those who receive the food suppose that the one who provides it is retaining a certain proportion for his own use. The dissatisfaction in such cases may possibly be wholly suppressed, but there is no reason to think that the suspicion is absent because it does not manifest itself upon the surface. Indeed, it is only a foreigner who would raise the question at all, for the Chinese expect this state of things as surely as they reckon on friction in machinery, and with equal reason.

It is the custom of waiters in Chinese inns, upon leaving the room of a guest who has just paid his bill, to shout out each item of the account, not in order to sound the praises of him who has spent most money—as some travellers have supposed—but for the much more practical purpose of letting the other waiters know that the one who thus publicly declares the receipts is not secreting a portion of the gratuity, or " winemoney," which they invariably expect.

If any matter is to be accomplished which requires consultation and adjustment, it will not do in China, as it might
in any Western land, to send a mere message to be delivered
at the home of the person concerned, to the effect that such
and such terms could be arranged. The principal must go
himself, and he must see the principal on the other side. If
the latter should not be at home, the visit must be repeated
until he is found, for otherwise no one would be sure that the
matter had not been distorted in its transmission through other
media.

Frequent references have been made to the social solidarity
of the Chinese. In some cases the whole family or clan all
seem to have their fingers in the particular pie belonging to
some individual of the family. But into such affairs a person
with a different surname is, if he be a wise person, careful not
to intrude any of his fingers, lest they be burned. It is indeed
a proverb that it is hard to give advice to one whose surname
is different from one's own. What does this fellow mean by
mixing himself up in my affairs? He *must* have an object,
and it is taken for granted that the object is not a good one.
If this is true of those who are life-long neighbours and friends,
how much more is it true of those who are mere outsiders, and
who have no special relations to the persons addressed.

The character meaning " outside," has in China a scope and
a significance which can only be comprehended by degrees.
The same kind of objection which is made to a foreigner because he comes from an " outside " country, is made to a vil-
lager because he comes from an " outside " village. This is
true with much greater emphasis if the outsider comes from
no one knows where, and wants no one knows what. " Who
knows what drug this fellow has in his gourd?" is the inevitable inquiry of the prudent Chinese in regard to a fresh arrival.

If a traveller happens to get astray and arrives at a village

A Chinese Boy's School (Christian).

after dark, particularly if the hour is late, he will often find that no one will even come out of his house to give a simple direction. Under these circumstances the writer once wandered around for several hours, unable to get one of the many Chinese who were offered a reward for acting as a guide even to listen to the proposal.

All scholars in Chinese schools spend their time in shouting out their lessons at the top of their voices, to the great injury of their vocal organs, and to the almost complete distraction of the foreigner. This is " old-time custom," but if the inquiry for the reason be relentlessly pushed, one is told that without this audible assurance the teacher would suspect that his pupils were not devoting their exclusive attention to their lessons. The singular practice of making each scholar turn his back upon the teacher during the recitation is likewise due to the desire of the teacher to be certain that the pupil is not furtively glancing at the book held in the master's hand!

It is not every form of civilisation which emphasises the duty of entertaining strangers. Many of the proverbs of Solomon in regard to caution towards strangers gain a new meaning after actual contact with Orientals, but the Chinese have carried their caution to a point which it would be hard to surpass. A Chinese teacher employed by a foreigner to pick up children's ballads and sayings heard a little boy singing a nonsense song which was new to the teacher, who asked the little fellow to repeat the words, whereupon the child fled terror-stricken and was seen no more. He was a typical product of Chinese environment. If a man has become insane and has strayed away from home, and his friends scour the countryside, hoping to hear something of him, they know very well that the chances of finding traces of him are slight. If he has been at a particular place, but has disappeared, the natural inquiry of his pursuers would be, What did you do with him?

This might lead to trouble, so the safest way, and the one sure to be adopted if the inquirer is a stranger, is to assume total ignorance of the whole affair.

The same thing will not seldom happen, as we have learned by experience, when a Chinese stranger tries to find a man who is well known.   In a case of this sort, a man whose appearance indicated him to be a native of an adjacent province inquired his way to the village of a man of whom he was in quest.   But on his arrival he was disappointed to find that the whole village was unanimous in the affirmation that no such man was known there, and that he had never even been heard of.   This wholesale falsehood was not concocted by any deliberate prevision, for which there was no opportunity, but was simultaneously adopted by a whole villageful of people, with the same unerring instinct which leads the prairie-dog to dive into its hole when some unfamiliar object is sighted.

In all instances of this kind, the slight variations of local dialect afford an infallible test of the general region from which one hails.   A countryman who meets others will be examined by them as to his abode and its distance from a great number of other places, as if to make sure that he is not deceiving them.   In the same manner, scholars are not content with inquiring of a professed literary graduate when he " entered," but he will not improbably be cross-examined upon the theme of his essay, and how he treated it.   In this way it is not difficult, and is very common, to expose a fraud.   It is hopeless for a man to claim to be a native of a district the pronunciation of which differs by ever so little from his own, for his speech bewrayeth him.   Not only will a stranger find it hard to get a clue to the whereabouts of a man, his possible business with whom excites instantaneous and general suspicion, but the same thing may be true, as we have also had repeated occasion to know, in regard to a whole village.   The writer once sent several Chinese to look up certain other

Chinese who had been for a long time in a foreign hospital under treatment. Very few of them could be found at all. In one case a man who ventured to hold conversation with the strangers gave his surname only, which was that of a large clan, but positively refused to reveal his name, or "style." In another instance, a village of which the messengers were in search persistently retreated before them, like an *ignus fatuus*, and at last all traces of it disappeared, without its having been found at all! Yet once the strangers were probably within a mile or two of it, and in the case just referred to, the stranger who could not find the man for whom he was looking, proved to have been within ten rods of his dwelling at the time he was baffled.

The writer is acquainted with an elderly man who has a well-to-do neighbour with whom he was formerly associated in one of the secret sects so common in China. On asking him about this neighbour, whose house was at a little distance from his own, it turned out that the two men, who had grown up together and had passed more than sixty years in proximity, never met. "And why was this?" "Because the other man is getting old and does not go out much." "Why, then, do you not sometimes go to see him and talk over old times? Are you not on good terms?" The person addressed smiled the smile of conscious superiority, and shook his head. "Yes," he said, "we are on good terms enough, but he is well off, and I am poor, and if I were to go there it would make talk. Folks would say, What is he coming here for?"

A conspicuous illustration of the instinctive recognition by the Chinese of the existence of their own mutual suspicion is found in the reluctance to be left alone in a room. If this should happen, a guest will not improbably exhibit a restless demeanour and will perhaps stroll out into the passage, as much as to say, "Do not suspect me; I did not take your things, as you see; I put them behind me." The same thing is sometimes observed when a self-respecting Chinese calls upon a foreigner.

Nothing is so certain to excite the most violent suspicion on the part of the Chinese as the death of a person under circumstances which are in some respects peculiar. A typical example of this is the death of a married daughter. Although, as already mentioned, the parents are powerless to protect her while she lives, they are in some degree masters of the situation when she has died, provided that there is anything to which any suspicion can be made to attach itself. Her suicide is an occasion on which the girl's parents no longer adopt their proverbial position of holding down the head, but, on the contrary, hold their head erect, and virtually impose their own terms. The refusal to come to an understanding with the family of the girl under such circumstances would be punished by a long and vexatious lawsuit, the motive for which would be in the first instance revenge, but the main issue of which would eventually be the preservation of the "face" of the girl's family.

There is an ancient saying in China, that when one is walking through an orchard where pears are grown it is well not to adjust one's cap, and when passing through a melon patch it is not the time to lace one's shoes. These sage aphorisms represent a generalised truth. In Chinese social life it is strictly necessary to walk softly, and one cannot be too careful. This is the reason why the Chinese are so constitutionally reticent at times which seem to us so ill-chosen. They know as we cannot that the smallest spark may kindle a fire that shall sweep a thousand acres.

The commercial life of the Chinese illustrates their mutual suspicion in a great variety of ways. Neither buyer nor seller trusts the other, and each for that reason thinks that his interests are subserved by putting his affairs for the time being out of his own hands into those of a third person who is strictly neutral, because his percentage will only be obtained by the completion of the bargain. No transaction is considered as made at all, until "bargain money" has been paid. If the matter is a more comprehensive one, something must be put into writing, for "talk is empty, while the mark of a pen is final."

The chaotic condition of the silver market in China is due partly to the deep-seated suspicion which cash-shops entertain for their customers, and which customers cherish towards the cash-shops, in each case with the best grounds. Every chopped dollar in south China, every chopped piece of chopped silver in any part of China, is a witness to the suspicious nature of this great and commercial people; keen as they are to effect a trade, they are keener still in their reluctance to do so. The very fact that a customer, whether Chinese or foreign makes no difference, wishes to sell silver after dark is of itself suspicious, and it will not be surprising if every shop in the city should successively impart the sage advice to wait till to-morrow.

The banking system of China appears to be very comprehensive and intricate, and we know from Marco Polo that bank-bills have been in use from a very ancient period. But they are not by any means universal in their occurrence, and all of them appear to be exceedingly limited in the range of their circulation. The banks of two cities ten miles apart will not receive each other's bills, and for a very good reason.

The high rate of Chinese interest, ranging from twenty-four to thirty-six or more per cent., is a proof of the lack of mutual confidence. The larger part of this extortionate exaction does not represent payment for the use of money, but insurance on risk, which is very great. The almost total lack of such forms of investments as we are so familiar with in Western lands is due not more to the lack of development of the resources of the Empire, than to the general mistrust of one another among the people. " The affairs of life hinge upon confidence," and it is for this reason that a large class of affairs in China will for a long time to come be dissociated from their hinges, to the great detriment of the interests of the people.

A curious example of Chinese commercial suspicion was afforded a few years ago by a paragraph in the newspapers, giving an account of the condition of things in the Chinese colony in the city of New York. The Chinese organisation probably does not differ from that of other cities where the Chinese have established themselves. They have a Municipal Government of their own, and twelve leading Chinese are the officers thereof. They keep the money and the papers of the Municipality in a huge iron safe, and to insure absolute safety the safe is locked with twelve ponderous brass (Chinese) padlocks all in a row, instead of the intricate and beautiful combination locks used in the New York banks. Each one of the twelve members of the Chinese Board of Aldermen has a key to one of these padlocks, and when the safe is opened all twelve of them must be on hand, each to attend to the unlocking of his own padlock. One of these distinguished aldermen having inopportunely died, the affairs of the Municipality were thrown into the utmost confusion. The key to his padlock could not be found, and if it had been found no one would have ventured to take the place of the deceased, through a superstitious fear that the dead man would be jealous of his successor, and would remove him by the same disease of which he himself had died. Even the funeral bills could not be paid until a special election had taken place to fill the vacancy. This little incident is indeed a window through which those who choose to do so may see some of the prominent traits of the Chinese character clearly illustrated—capacity for organisation, commercial ability, mutual suspicion, unlimited credulity, and tacit contempt for the institutions and inventions of the men of the West.

The structure of the Chinese government contains many examples of the effects of lack of confidence. Eunuchs are an essentially Asiatic instance in point, and they are supposed to have existed in China from very ancient times ; but during the present dynasty this dangerous class of persons has been dealt with in a very practical way by the Manchus, and deprived of the power to do the same mischief as in past ages.

Another example of the provision for that suspicion which must inevitably arise when such inharmonious elements as the conquerors and the conquered are to be co-ordinated in high places, is the singular combination of Manchus and Chinese in the administration of the government, as well as the arrangement by which the president of one of the Six Boards may be the vice-president of another. By these checks and balances the equilibrium of the state machinery has been preserved. The censorate furnishes another illustration of the same thing, on an extended and important scale.

Those whose knowledge of the interior workings of the Chinese administration entitles their opinions to weight, assure us that the same mutual suspicion which we have seen to be characteristic of the social life of the Chinese is equally characteristic of their official life. It could not indeed be otherwise. Chinese nature being what it is, high officials cannot but be jealous of those below them, for it is from that quarter that their rivals are to be dreaded. The lower officials, on the other hand, are not less suspicious of those above them, for it is from that quarter that their removal may be at any moment effected. There seems the best reason to believe that both the higher and the lower officials alike are more or less jealous of the large and powerful literary class, and the officials are uniformly suspicious of the people. This last state of mind is well warranted by what is known of the multitudinous semi-political sects, with which the whole Empire is honeycombed. A District Magistrate will pounce down upon the annual gathering of a temperance society such as the well-known Tsai-li, which merely forbids opium, wine, and tobacco, and turn over their anticipated feast to the voracious "wolves and tigers " of his yamên, not because it is proved that the designs of the Tsai-li Society are treasonable, but because it has been officially assumed long since that they must be so. All secret societies are treasonable, and this among the rest. This generalised suspicion settles the whole question, and whenever occasion arises the government interposes, seizes the leaders, banishes or exterminates them, and thus for the moment allays its suspicions.

It is obvious that so powerful a principle as the one which we are considering must be a strong reinforcement of that innate conservatism which has been already discussed, to prevent the adoption of what is new. The census which is occasionally called for by the government does not occur with sufficient frequency to make it familiar to the Chinese, even in name. It always excites an immediate suspicion that some ulterior end is in view. How real this suspicion is, is illustrated by an incident which occurred in a village next to the one in which the writer lived. One of two brothers, hearing that a new census had been ordered, took it for granted that it signified compulsory emigration. It is customary in such cases to leave one brother at home to look after the graves of the ancestors, but the younger of the two, foreseeing that he must go, promptly proceeded to save himself from the fatigues of a long journey by committing suicide, thus checkmating the government.

It is a mixture of suspicion and of conservatism which has made the path of the young Chinese who were educated in the United States such a bed of thorns from the time of their return to the present day; it is the same fell combination which shows itself in opposition to the inevitable introduction of railways into China. Suspicion of the motives of the government will long prevent the reforms which China needs. More than thirty years ago, when the importance of the issue of small silver coinage was pointed out to a distinguished statesman in Peking, he replied—with great truth—that it would never do to attempt to change the currency of the Empire. " Were it to be tried, the people would immediately suppose that the government gained some advantage by it, and it would not work."

Great obstacles are invariably thrown in the way of the opening of mines, which, if properly worked, might make China what she ought to be, a rich country. The "earth dragon" below ground, and peculation and suspicion above it, are as yet too much for anything more than the most rudimentary steps of progress in this most essential direction. No matter how great advantages may be or how obvious, it is almost impossible to get new things introduced when an all-pervading suspicion frowns upon them. The late Dr. Nevius, who did so much at Chefoo for the cultivation of a high grade of foreign fruits in China, fruits which visibly yield an enormous profit, was obliged to contend against this suspicion at every step, and one less patient and less philanthropic would have abandoned the project in disgust. When profits are once assured this state of things of course gradually disappears. But it is very real when inquiries are set on foot like those by the Imperial Maritime Customs in regard to the raising of silk-worms or tea. How can those who are interested in these matters possibly believe, in defiance of all the accumulated experience of past ages, that the object of these inquiries is not a tax, but the promotion of production and the increase of the profits of skilled labour ? Who ever heard of such a thing, and who can believe it when he does hear it? The attitude of the Chinese mind towards such projects as this may be expressed in the old Dutch proverb, " Good-morrow to you all, as the fox said when he leaped into the goose-pen!"

It remains to speak of the special relations of this topic to foreigners. The profound suspicion with which foreigners are regarded is often accompanied by, and perhaps largely due to, a belief, deep-rooted and ineradicable, that foreigners are able to do the most impossible things with the greatest ease. If a foreigner walks out in a place where he has not been often seen, it is inferred that he is inspecting the *fêng-shui* of the district. If he surveys a river, he is determining the existence of precious metals. He is supposed to be able to see some distance into the earth, and to have his eyes on whatever is best worth taking away. If he engages in famine relief, it is not thought too much to suppose that the ultimate object must be to carry off a large part of the population of the district, to be disposed of in foreign lands. It is by reason of these opinions on *fêng-shui* that the presence of foreigners on the walls of Chinese cities has so often led to disturbances, and that the height of foreign buildings in China must be as carefully regulated as the location of a frontier of the Empire. The belief in the uniformity of nature appears to be totally lacking in China. Mr. Baber mentions a saying in Szechuan of a certain hill, that opium grows without, and coal within. But this is not simply a notion of the ignorant, for Professor Pumpelly declares that one of the high officials in Peking told him the same thing, and used the statement as an argument against the too rapid removal of coal deposits, the rate of the growth of which is unknown. It is said that the late statesman Wen Hsiang, having read Dr. Martin's " Evidences of Christianity," was asked what he thought of it, to which he replied that the scientific part of the work he was prepared to accept, but *the religious sections*, in which the affirmation is made that the earth revolves around the sun, were more than he could believe!

The whole subject of the entrance of foreigners into China is beyond the Chinese intellect in its present state of development. Seeing Baron von Richthofen ride over the country in what appeared to the people of Szechuan a vague and purposeless manner, they imagined him to be a fugitive from some disastrous battle. Many a Chinese, who has afterwards come to understand the foreign barbarian all too well, has at first sight of his form, especially if he chanced to be tall, been seized with secret terror. Many Chinese women are persuaded that if they once voluntarily enter a foreigner's dwelling the fatal spell will work, and they will be bewitched; if they are at last prevailed upon to enter, they will not on any account step on the threshold, nor look into a mirror when it may be offered to their sight, for thus they would betray away their safety.

A few years ago a young Chinese scholar from an interior province, where foreigners were practically unknown, was engaged with some difficulty to come to the premises of the writer to assist a new-comer in acquiring the language. He remained a few weeks, when he recollected that his mother was very much in need of his filial care, and left, promising to return at a fixed date, but was seen no more. During all the time that he was on the foreigner's premises, this astute Confucianist never once took a sip of tea, which was brought to him regularly by the servants, nor ate a meal on the place, lest he should imbibe besotment. When a foreign envelope was handed to him by another teacher, that he might enclose the letter which he had written to his mother assuring her that thus far he was safe, and when it was shown him how this same envelope was self-sealing, a little moisture being applied by the tongue, his presence of mind did not for an instant forsake him, and he blandly requested the *other teacher* to do the sealing, as he was not expert at it.

It is this frame of mind which leads to the persistent notions in regard to Chinese books printed by foreigners. There is a widespread conviction that they are drugged, and the smell of printer's ink is frequently identified as that of the " bewildering drug " which is embodied in their composition. Sometimes one hears that it is only necessary to read one of these books, and forthwith he is a slave to foreigners. A slightly different point of view was that taken by a lad of whom we have heard, who, having read a little way in one of these tracts, threw it down in terror and ran home, telling his friends that if one should read that book and tell a lie, he would inevitably go to hell! Sometimes colporteurs have found it impossible to give away these books, not, as might be supposed, because of any hostility to the contents, of which nothing was known and for which nothing was cared, but because it was feared that the gift would be made the basis on which to levy a kind of blackmail, in a manner with which the Chinese are only too familiar.

The same presupposition leads to a panic if a foreigner injudiciously attempts to take down the names of Chinese children, a simple process which has been known to be eminently successful in breaking up a prospective school. The system of romanising Chinese characters must in its initial stages meet this objection and suspicion. Why should a foreigner wish to teach his pupils to write in such a way that their friends at home cannot read what they say? All the explanations in the world will not suffice to make this clear to a suspicious old Chinese who knows that what has been good enough for the generations that have come before his children is good enough for them, and much better than the invention of some foreigner of unknown antecedents. It may almost be said that a general objection is entertained to *anything* which a foreigner proposes, and often for the apparent reason that he proposes it. The trait of " flexible inflexibility " leads your Chinese friend to assure you in the blandest but most unmistakable terms, that your proposal is very admirable and very preposterous.

Sarcasm is a weapon which, in the hands of a foreigner, is not at all to the taste of the Chinese. A foreigner whose knowledge of Chinese was by no means equal to the demands which he wished to make upon it, in a fit of deep disgust at some sin of omission or commission on the part of one of his servants, called him in English a "humbug." " Deep ranklea in his side the fatal dart," and at the earliest opportunity the servant begged of a lady whose Chinese was fully equal to the tax upon it, to be told what the dreadful word meant which had been thus applied to him. The mandarins who seized upon the blocks of Mr. Thom's translation of "Æsop's Fables" were in the same frame of mind as the Peking servant. These officials could not help perceiving in the talking geese, tigers, foxes, and lions some recondite meaning which could be best nipped in the bud by suppressing the entire edition.

Some of the most persistent instances of Chinese suspicion towards foreigners are manifested in connection with the many hospitals and dispensaries now scattered over so large a part of China. Amid the vast number of patients there are many who exhibit an implicit faith and a touching confidence in the good-will and the skill of the foreign physician. But there are many others, of whose feelings we know much less, except as the result of careful inquiry, who continue to believe the most irrational rumours in regard to the extraction of eyes and hearts for medicine, the irresistible propensity of the surgeon to reduce his patients to mince-meat, and the fearful disposition said to be made of Chinese children in the depths of foreign cellars. A year or two of experience of the widespread benefits of such an institution might be expected to dissipate such idle rumours as the wind disperses a mist; but they continue to flourish side by side with tens of thousands of successful treatments, as mould thrives in warm damp spots during the month of August.

The whole history of foreign intercourse with China is a

history of suspicion and prevarication on the part of the Chinese, while it doubtless has not been free from grave faults on the side of foreigners. It is a weary history to retrace, and its lessons may be relegated to those who are charged with the often thankless task of conducting such negotiations. But as it often happens that private persons are obliged to be their own diplomats in China, it is well to know how it should be done. We will give a sample case which is an excellent illustration. The question was about the renting of some premises in an interior city, to which a local official on various grounds took exception. The foreigner presented himself at the interview which had been arranged, clad in the Chinese dress, and armed with the necessary materials for writing. After the preliminary conversation the foreigner slowly opened his writing materials, adjusted his paper, shook out his pen, examined his ink, with an air of intense preoccupation. The Chinese official was watching this performance with the keenest interest and the liveliest curiosity. " What are you doing ? " he inquired. The foreigner explained that he was simply getting his writing materials in order—" only that and nothing more." " Writing materials! What for? " " To take down your answers," was the reply. The official hastened to assure his foreign guest that this extremity would by no means be called for, as *the premises could be secured!* How could this magistrate be sure where he should next hear of this mysterious document, the contents of which he could not possibly know?

China is a country which abounds in wild rumours, often of a character to fill the heart with dread. Within the past few years such a state of things has been reported among the Chinese in Singapore that coolies positively refused to travel a certain street after dark, on account of the imminent danger of having their heads suddenly and mysteriously cut off. The Empire is probably never free from such epochs of horror ; to those concerned the terrors are as real as those of the French Revolution to the Parisians of 1789. Infinite credulity and mutual suspicion are the elements of the soil in which these tearful rumours thrive, and on which they fatten. When they have to do with foreigners, long and painful experience has shown that they must not be despised, but must be taken in the early stages of their development. None of them could do serious harm if the local officials were only sincerely interested to stamp them out. In their ultimate outcome, when they have been suffered to grow unchecked, these rumours result in such atrocities as the Tientsin massacre. All parts of China are well adapted to their rapid development, and there is scarcely a province where they have not in some form occurred. For the complete removal of these outbreaks, the time element is as necessary as for the results of geologic epochs. The best way to prevent their occurrence is to convince the Chinese, by irrefragable object-lessons, that foreigners are the sincere well-wishers of the Chinese. This simple proposition once firmly established, then for the first time will it be true that "within the four seas, all are brethren."

CHAPTER XXV.

THE Chinese ideograph which is commonly translated "sincerity" is composed of the radicals denoting man and words. Its meaning lies upon the surface. It is the last in the series of the Five Constant Virtues enumerated by the Chinese, and in the opinion of many who are well acquainted with them it is in fact about the last virtue which in the Celestial Empire is likely to be met with on any considerable scale. Many who know the Chinese will agree with the observation of Professor Kidd, who, after speaking of the Chinese doctrine of "sincerity," continues: "But if this virtue had been chosen as a national characteristic, not only to be set at defiance in practice, but to form the most striking contrast to existing manners, a more appropriate one than sincerity could not have been found. So opposed is the public and private character of the Chinese to genuine sincerity, that an enemy might have selected it as ironically descriptive of their conduct in contrast with their pretensions. Falsehood, duplicity, insincerity, and obsequious accommodation to favourable circumstances are national features remarkably prominent." How far this judgment is justified by the facts of Chinese life we may be able better to decide when we shall have considered those facts in detail.

We have assumed that it is a reasonable theory, and one which we believe is supported by the opinion of competent scholars, that the Chinese of the present day do not differ to any great extent from the Chinese of antiquity. There can hardly be a doubt that the standard of the Chinese and the present standard of Western nations as to what ought to be called sincerity differ widely. He who peruses the Chinese Classics with a discerning eye will be able to read between the lines much indirection, prevarication, and falsehood which are not distinctly expressed. He will also find the Chinese opinion of Occidental openness condensed into the significant expression, " Straightforwardness without the rules of propriety becomes rudeness." To an Occidental there is a significance in the incident related of Confucius and Ju-pei, as found in the Confucian "Analects," which is not at all apprehensible to a Confucianist. The following is the passage, from Legge's translation: " Ju-pei wished to see Confucius, but Confucius declined to see him on the ground of being sick. When the bearer of this message went out at the door, Confucius took his harpsichord, and sang to it, in order that Ju-pei might hear." The object of Confucius was to avoid the disagreeable task of saying that the character of Ju-pei was not such that Confucius wished to meet him, and he took this characteristically Chinese way to do it.

The example of Confucius in this matter was followed by Mencius. Being a guest in a certain kingdom he was invited to court, but hoping that the king would honour him by the first call, Mencius alleged sickness, and the next day, to show that this was a mere excuse made a call elsewhere. The officer with whom Mencius spent the night held a long conversation with the Sage as to the merits of this proceeding, but the discussion between them turns exclusively on the question of propriety and precedent, and no reference whatever to the morality of lying for the sake of convenience. There is no apparent reason to suppose that this point was ever thought of by any of the persons concerned, any more than it is by a modern Confucian teacher who explains the passage to his pupils.

There is no doubt that the ancient Chinese were far in advance of their contemporaries in many other lands in the instinct of preserving records of the past. Their histories, however prolix, are undoubtedly comprehensive. Many Western writers seem to feel the greatest admiration for Chinese histories, and place unrestricted confidence in their statements. The following paragraph is taken from an essay by Dr. J. Singer, lector of the University of Vienna, translated and published in the *China Review*, July, 1888: " Scientific criticism has long ago recognised and in ever-increasing extent proved the historical reliability of the ancient documents of China. Richthofen, for instance, the latest and most thorough-going explorer of China, in discussing the surprisingly contradictory elements which make up the character of the Chinese as a people, contrasts their strict truthfulness in recording historical events and their earnestness in the search for correct knowledge, whenever statistical facts are concerned, with that absolute and generally sanctioned license in lying and dissimulation which prevails everywhere in China, in popular intercourse and in diplomatic negotiations." It should be borne distinctly in mind that historical accuracy may be exhibited in two widely different lines: the narration of events in due order and proportion, and the explanation of those events by an analysis of character and motives. It is said by those who have looked into Chinese histories most extensively, that while in the former particular these works are no doubt far in advance of the times in which they were written, in the latter particular they are by no means adapted to carry the impression of that scrupulosity which Dr. Singer supposes. Without expressing any opinion on a subject of which we have no special knowledge, we will merely call attention to the singular, if not unprecedented, circumstance that a nation which is affirmed to indulge in a license for lying, can at the same time furnish successive generations of historiographers who are reverent of the truth. Do not the same passions which have distorted the history of other lands operate in China? Do not the same causes produce in China the same effects as in the rest of the world ?

It is important to bear in mind that not only is the teaching of Confucianism greatly defective in the particular noted, but the practice of the great Master himself is not such as to commend historical fidelity. Dr. Legge, who does not lay much stress on " certain charges which have been made from unimportant incidents in the Sage's career," attaches great importance to the manner in which Confucius handled his materials in the " Spring and Autumn Annals," a work which contains the record of the kingdom of Lu for two hundred and forty-two years, down to within two years of Confucius' death. The following paragraphs are taken from Dr. Legge's lecture on Confucianism, published in his volume on " The Religions of China " : " Mencius regarded the *Ch'un Ch'iu* [" Spring and Autumn Annals "] as the greatest of the Master's achievements, and says that its appearance struck terror into rebellious ministers and unfilial sons. The author himself had a similar opinion of it, and said that it was from it men would know him, and also (some of them) condemn him. Was his own heart misgiving him when he thus spoke of men condemning him for the *Ch'un Ch'iu ?* The fact is that the annals are astonishingly meagre, and not only so, but evasive and deceptive. ' The *Ch'un Ch'iu*,' says Kung Yang, who commented on it, and supplemented it within a century after its composition, ' conceals [the truth] out of regard to the high in rank, to kinship, and to men of worth.' And I have shown in the fifth volume of my ' Chinese Classics ' that this ' concealing ' covers all the ground embraced in our three English words—ignoring, concealing, and misrepresenting. What shall we say to these things ? . . . I often wish that I could cut the knot by denying the genuineness and authenticity of the ' Spring and Autumn ' as we now have it ; but the chain of evidence that binds it to the hand and pencil of Confucius in the close of his life is very strong. And if a foreign student take so violent a method to enable him to look at the character of the philosopher without this flaw of historical untruthfulness, the governors of China and the majority of its scholars will have no sympathy with him, and no compassion for his mental distress. Truthfulness was one of the subjects that Confucius often insisted on with his disciples ; but the *Ch'un Ch'iu* has led his countrymen to conceal the truth from themselves and others wherever they think it would injuriously affect the reputation of the Empire or of its sages."

We have just seen that those who claim truthfulness for the Chinese in their histories are ready enough to admit that in China truth is confined to histories. It is of course impossible to prove that every Chinese will lie, and we have no wish to do so if it were possible. The strongest testimony on this point can be gathered from the Chinese themselves, whenever their consciences have been sufficiently awakened and their attention directed to the matter. Such persons are frequently heard to say of their race, as the South Sea Island chief said of his : " As soon as we open our mouths a lie is born." To us, however, it does not seem that the Chinese lie for the sake of lying, as some have supposed, but mainly for the sake of certain advantages not otherwise to be had. " Incapable of speaking the truth," says Mr. Baber, " they are equally incapable of believing it." A friend of the writer received a visit from a Chinese lad who had learned English, and who wished to add to his vocabulary an expression meaning " You lie." He was told the phrase, but cautioned not to use it to a foreigner, as the result would certainly be that he would be knocked down. He expressed unfeigned surprise at this strange announcement, for to his mind the words conveyed a meaning as harmless as the remark, " You are humbugging me." Mr. Cooke, the China correspondent of the London *Times* in 1857, speaking of the antipathy of Occidentals to be called liars, observes: "But if you say the same thing to a Chinaman, you arouse in him no sense of outrage, no sentiment of degradation. He does not deny the fact. His answer is, ' I should not *dare* to lie to your Excellency.' To say to a Chinaman, 'You are an habitual liar, and you are meditating a lie at this moment,' is like saying to an Englishman, 'You are a confirmed punster, and I am satisfied you have some horrible pun in your head at this moment.'"

The ordinary speech of the Chinese is so full of insincerity, which yet does not rise to the dignity of falsehood, that it is very difficult to learn the truth in almost any case. In China it is literally true that a fact is the hardest thing in the world to get. One never feels sure that he has been told the whole of anything. Even where a person is seeking your help, as, for example, in a lawsuit, and wishes to put his case entirely in your hands, nothing is more probable than that you will discover subsequently that several important particulars have been suppressed, apparently from the general instinct of prevarication and not of malice prepense, since the person himself must be the only loser by the suppression. The whole of anything does not come out till afterwards, no matter at what point you take it up. A person who is well acquainted with the Chinese will not feel that he understands a matter because he has heard all about it, but will rather take the items which he has heard and combine them with others, and finally call a council of the Chinese whom he trusts most and hold a kind of inquest over these alleged facts to ascertain what their real bearing probably is.

Lack of sincerity, combined with the suspicion which has been already discussed, accounts for the fact that a Chinese will often talk for a very great length of time, saying practically nothing whatever.   Much of the incomprehensibility of the Chinese, so far as foreigners are concerned, is due to their insincerity.   We cannot be sure what they are after.   We always feel that there is more behind.   It is for this reason that when a Chinese comes to you and whispers to you mysteriously something about another Chinese in whom you are much interested, you are not unlikely to experience a sinking sensation in the pit of the stomach.   You are uncertain whether the one who is speaking is telling the truth, or whether the character of the one of whom he is speaking has caved in. One never has any assurance that a Chinese ultimatum is ultimate.   This proposition, so easily stated, contains in itself the germ of multitudinous anxieties for the trader, the traveller, and the diplomatist.

The real reason for anything is hardly ever to be expected, and even when it has been given, one cannot be sure of this fact.   Every Chinese, the uneducated not less than others, is by nature a kind of cuttle-fish capable of distilling any amount of turbid ink, into which he can retreat with the utmost safety so far as pursuit is concerned.   If you are interviewed on a journey and invited to contribute to the travelling-expenses of some impecunious individual who hopes to exploit a new field, your attendant does not say, as you would do, " Your expenses are none of my affair, begone with you! " but " with a smile that is child-like and bland," he explains that your allowance of money is barely sufficient for your own use, and so you will be deprived of the pleasure of contributing to your fellow-traveller.   We have seldom met a Chinese gate-keeper who would say to a Chinese crowd, as a foreigner tells him to do, " You *cannot* come in here," but he will observe instead, that they must not come in, because the big dog will bite them if they do.

There are few Chinese who have any well-developed conscience on the subject of keeping an engagement. This characteristic is connected with their talent for misunderstanding, and with their disregard of time. But whatever the real reason for the failure, it is interesting to see what a variety of alleged reasons exist for it. The Chinese in general resemble the man who, being accused of having broken his promise, replied that it was of no consequence, as he could make another just as good. If it is a fault for which he is reproved, promises of amendment flow in limpid streams from his lips. His acknowledgments of wrong are complete—in fact, too complete, and leave nothing to be desired but sincerity.

A Chinese teacher who was employed in inditing and commenting upon Chinese aphorisms, after writing down a fine sentiment of the ancients, made an annotation to the effect that one should never refuse a request in an abrupt manner, but should, on the contrary, grant it in form, although with no intention to do so in substance. " Put him off till to-morrow, and then until another to-morrow. Thus," he remarked in his note, " you comfort his heart! " So far as we know the principle here avowed is the one which is generally acted upon by the Chinese who have debts for which payment is sought. No one expects to collect his debt at the time that he applies for it, and he is not disappointed ; but he is told most positively that he will get it the next time, and the next, and the next.

One of the ways in which the native insincerity of the Chinese is most characteristically manifested is their demeanour towards children, who are taught to be insincere without consciousness of the fact either on their own part or on the part of those who teach them. Before he is old enough to talk, and when he can attach only the vaguest significance to the words which he hears, a child is told that unless he does as he is bid some terrific object, said to be concealed in the sleeve of a grown person, will catch him. It is not uncom-

mon for foreigners to be put in the place of the unknown mon-
ster, and this fact alone would be sufficient to account for all
the bad words which we frequently hear applied to ourselves.
Why should not children who may have been affrighted with
our vague terrors when they were young, hoot us in the streets
as soon as they have grown large enough to perceive that we
are not dangerous but only ridiculous?

The carter who is annoyed by the urchins in the street yelling after his foreign passenger, shouts to them that he will capture several of them, tie them on behind his cart and carry
them off. The boatman under like provocation contents himself with the observation that he will pour scalding water
upon them. The expressions, "I'll beat you," "I'll kill you,"
are understood by a Chinese child of some experience to constitute an ellipsis for "Stop that!"

There is in Chinese a whole vocabulary of words which are
indispensable to one who wishes to pose as a "polite" person,
words in which whatever belongs to the speaker is treated
with scorn and contempt, and whatever relates to the person
addressed is honourable. The "polite" Chinese will refer to
his wife, if driven to the extremity of referring to her at all, as
his "dull thorn," or in some similar elegant figure of speech,
while the rustic, who grasps at the substance of "politeness,"
although ignorant of its formal expression, perhaps alludes
to the companion of his joys and sorrows as his "stinking
woman." This trait of Chinese etiquette is not inaptly presented in one of their own tales, in which a visitor is represented as calling clad in his best robes, and seated in the
reception-room awaiting the arrival of his host. A rat which
had been disporting itself upon the beams above, insinuating
its nose into a jar of oil which was put there for safe-keeping,
frightened at the sudden intrusion of the caller, ran away, and
in so doing upset the oil-jar, which fell directly on the caller,
striking him a severe blow, and ruining his elegant garments

with the saturation of the oil. Just as the face of the guest was purple with rage at this disaster, the host entered, when the proper salutations were performed, after which the guest proceeded to explain the situation. "As I entered your honourable apartment and seated myself under your honourable beam, I inadvertently terrified your honourable rat, which fled and upset your honourable oil-jar upon my mean and insignificant clothing, which is the reason of my contemptible appearance in your honourable presence."

That very few foreigners can ever bring themselves to give Chinese invitations in a Chinese way, goes without saying. It requires long practice to bow cordially to a Chinese crowd as one goes to a meal, and remark blandly, "Please all sit down and eat," or to sweep a cup of tea in a semicircle just as it is raised to the lips, and, addressing one's self to the multitude, observe with gravity, "Please all drink." Not less real is the moral difficulty of exclaiming at suitable situations, "*K'o-t'ou, k'o-t'ou,*" signifying, "I can, may, must, might, could, would, or should" (as the case may be) "give you a prostration"; or of occasionally interjecting the observation, "I ought to be beaten, I ought to be killed," meaning that I have offended against some detail of the rules of etiquette; or of stopping in the midst of a horseback ride, upon meeting a casual acquaintance, and proposing to him, "*I* will get off and *you* shall mount," quite irrespective of the direction in which you may be travelling, or the general irrationality of the procedure. Yet the most ignorant and uncultivated Chinese will frequently give these invitations with an air, which, as already remarked, extorts admiration from the most unsympathetic Occidental, who pays the unconscious tribute of him who cannot to him who can. Such little ceremonies, as we have had repeated occasion to observe, are enforced contributions on the part of individuals to society at large, that friction may be diminished, and he who refuses to contribute will be punished in a manner not the less real because it is oblique. Thus a carter who neglects to take his cue down from his head and descend from his cart when he has occasion to inquire the way, will not improbably be given a wrong direction, and reviled besides.

To be able to determine what is the proper thing to be done when Orientals offer presents, is in itself a science, and perhaps as much so in China as in other countries. Some things must not be accepted at all, while others must not be altogether refused, and there is generally a broad debatable land, in regard to which a foreigner can be sure of nothing except that, left to his own judgment, he will almost infallibly do the wrong thing. In general, offers of presents are to be suspected, especially those which are in any particular extraordinary. Of this class are those which are tendered on the occasion of the birth of a son, in reference to which the classical dictum, "I fear the Greeks, *even* bearing gifts," is universally and perennially appropriate. There is always something behind such an offer, and, as the homely Chinese proverb says of a rat dragging a shovel, the "larger end is the one that is behind," or, in other words, what is (virtually) required in return is much greater than what is given.

Of the hollowness of these offers many foreigners in China have had experience. We have ourselves had occasion to be but too familiar with the details of a case in which a theatrical exhibition was offered to a few foreigners by a Chinese village, as a mark of respect, of course with the implied understanding that it should be duly acknowledged by suitable feasts. When this honour was definitely declined, it was proposed to devote the funds, or rather a small part of them, to the construction of a building for public use, which, in the case of the first village, was actually done. No sooner was this agreed upon than eleven other villages, also deeply smitten with gratitude for famine relief and medical help, proceeded to send deputations to make on their part formal offers of theatrical exhibitions, which they were perfectly aware would be and must be declined. The representatives of each village received the intelligence of the refusal of these honours with the same sad surprise, each of them offered to divert the funds in question to the public building already referred to, and each one of them allowed the matter to drop at that point, and no further reference whatever was ever made to it by any one of them!

It is not foreigners only who are beset in this way. Rich Chinese who have had the misfortune to be made happy, are sometimes visited by their neighbours with congratulatory gifts of a trifling character, such as toys for a new-born heir, presents the total value of which is practically nothing, but which must be acknowledged by a feast—the invariable and always appropriate Chinese response. It is on occasions like this that the most inexpert in Chinese affairs learns to appreciate the accuracy of the Chinese aphorism, which observes, " When one is eating one's own, he eats till the tears come; but when he is eating the food of others, he eats till the perspiration flows." It frequently happens under such conditions that the host is obliged to assume the most cordial appearance of welcome, when he is inwardly fuming with rage which cannot possibly be expressed without the loss of his "face," which would be even more deadly than the loss of the food.

This suggests that large class of expressions which come under the general designation of "face-talk." That much of the external decorum with which foreigners are treated by Chinese in their employ, especially in large cities, is a mere external veneer, is easily seen by contrasting the behaviour of the same persons in public and in private. It is said that a Chinese teacher who is a model of the proprieties at his foreign master's house, is not unlikely to " cut him dead " if he meets the same master on the streets of Peking, for the reason that to notice him at that time would lead to a public recognition of the fact that the Chinese pundit is in some way indebted to the foreign barbarian for replenishing the rice-bowl of the Chinese—a circumstance which, however notorious, must not be formally admitted, especially in public. It is very common for a number of Chinese, on entering a room where there is a foreigner, to salute all the Chinese in the room by turn, and totally ignore the foreigner. A Chinese teacher is not unlikely to flatter his foreign pupil with the information that his ear is remarkably correct and his pronunciation almost perfect, and that he will soon surpass all his contemporaries in the acquisition of the language, while at the very same time the peculiar errors of the pupil are not improbably matter of sport between the teacher and his companions. In general, it may be taken for granted that the last person to set one right in matters of Chinese speech is the teacher who is employed for that purpose.

One of the ways in which the formal and hollow politeness of the Chinese manifests itself, is in voluntary offers to do what it is very desirable should be done, but which others cannot or will not undertake. If the offer comes to nothing we should not be disappointed, for it is not improbable that it was made with the definite knowledge that it could not be carried out, but the "face" of the friend who made the offer is assured. In like manner, if there is a dispute as to the amount of money to be paid at an inn, your carter will probably come forward as arbitrator, and decide that he will make up the difference himself, which he does by taking the amount required from your cash-bag. Or if he were to pay the money from his own funds, he would bring in his bill for the same, and if he was reminded that he offered of his own accord to make it up, he would reply, " Do you expect the man who attends the funeral to be buried in the coffin too? "

There is a great deal of real modesty in China notwithstanding appearances to the contrary, but it cannot for a moment be doubted that there is likewise a great deal of mock modesty, both on the part of men and of women. It is very common to hear it said of some disagreeable matter, that it is wholly unmentionable, that the words are totally unutterable, etc., when all parties are perfectly aware that this is a mere form denoting reluctance to express an opinion. The very persons who use this high-toned language would be ready enough to employ the foulest expressions of vituperation whenever they were excited by anger.

False modesty is matched by a false sympathy, which consists of empty words; but for this the Chinese are not to be blamed, as they have no adequate material out of which sympathy for others can be developed in any considerable quantities and for any length of time. But empty sympathy is not so repugnant to good taste as that mockery of sympathy and of all true feeling which contemplates death with boisterous merriment. Mr. Baber mentions a Szechuan coolie who burst into a delighted laugh at the spectacle of two dogs devouring a corpse on the tow-path. Mr. Meadows tells us that his Chinese teacher laughed till he held his sides at the amusing death of his most constant companion. It is no explanation of these strange exhibitions, often observed in the case of parents at the death of children of whom they were fond, that long grief has dried up its external expression, for there is a wide distinction between a silent grief and that rude mockery of natural feeling which offends the instincts of mankind.

It is, as we have had occasion to remark, several hundred years since foreigners began to have commercial relations with the Chinese. There have been multiplied testimonies to the business honesty of those with whom these relations have been held. Without generalising to a degree which might be precarious, it is safe to say that there must be a good basis for testimonies of this sort. As a specimen of what these testimonies are, we may quote the words of Mr. Cameron, Manager of the Hongkong and Shanghai Bank, on occasion of his farewell to Shanghai : " I have referred to the high commercial standing of the foreign community.   The Chinese are in no way behind us ourselves in that respect ; in fact, I know of no people in the world I would sooner trust than the Chinese merchant and banker.   Of course there are exceptions to every rule, but to show that I have good reasons for making such a strong statement, I may mention that for the last twenty-five years the bank has been doing a very large business with Chinese in Shanghai, amounting, I should say, to hundreds of millions of taels, and we have never yet met with a defaulting Chinaman."   Perhaps the best commentary on the statement just quoted is the fact that within three years after it was made, a Chinese compradore of the same bank in Hongkong so crippled it by losses for which it did not appear that there was any security that a million dollars were subtracted from the annual profits.

Whether there is an essent'al difference between Chinese business as conducted by wholesale and that by retail, we have no means of knowing.   But without abating in the least from the value of the testimonies to which reference has been made, it is a fair question whether a large part of results noted are not due to the admirable system of mutual responsibility already described—a system which Western nations would do well to imitate.   It is only natural that foreigners doing business with the Chinese should avail themselves to the fullest extent of such commercial safeguards as exist, and for such results as are thus attained the Chinese are unquestionably entitled to the fullest credit.   Yet after all such acknowledgments are made, it remains true, as testified by a vast array of witnesses, and by wide and long observation, that the commerce of the Chinese is a gigantic example of the national insincerity.

An interesting essay has been written by one who knew of what he was affirming, on the process by which in ordinary trade two Chinese each succeed in cheating the other. The relation of two such individuals is generally the relation between Jacob and Laban, or, as the Chinese phrase runs, it is the iron brush meeting the brass wash-dish. It is a popular proverb that to put a lad into trade is to ruin him. False weights, false measures, false currency, and false goods—these are phenomena from which it is difficult to escape in China. Even in the great establishments which put up conspicuous signs, notifying the public that they will here find "goods genuine, prices real," "positively no two prices," the state of things does not correspond to the surface seeming.

We by no means intend to affirm such a proposition as that there is no honesty to be found in China, but only that, so far as our experience and observation go, it is literally impossible to be sure of finding it anywhere. How can it be otherwise with a people who have so little regard for truth? A well-dressed scholar who meets a foreigner is not ashamed to affirm in reply to a question, that he cannot read, and then when a little book has been handed him to look at, he does not hesitate to slink away in the crowd without paying the three cash which is the cost. He has no sense of shame at such a proceeding, but rather a thrill of joy that he has circumvented the silly foreigner, who has so little astuteness as to trust a total stranger. It is very common for a man who is buying from a foreigner to give a cash less than the proper amount, alleging that he has not another cash with him. When he is informed that there is one in his ear at the moment, he takes it out with reluctance, feeling that he has been defrauded. In like manner a man who has spent "an old half-day" in trying to get something free of cost, on the ground that he is totally without money, will at last draw forth a string of a thousand cash, hand it to you with an air of melancholy, and request you to take out the proper amount. But if he is believed, and gets something for nothing, he departs with a keen joy in his heart, like that of one who has slain a serpent.

The solidarity of Chinese society finds one of its manifestations in the constant habit of borrowing what belongs to a relative, with or without a notification of the intention so to do. Many of the articles thus "borrowed" are at once put in pawn, and if they are wanted again the owners must redeem them. A Chinese boy in a mission school was detected in stealing money from the single lady who had charge of the scholars' rooms. Upon being confronted with irrefragable proof of his guilt, he explained, with sobs, that when at home he had always been in the habit of stealing from his mother, and that his foreign teacher was so much like an own mother to him that he was betrayed into stealing from her too!

While it is undoubtedly true that many of the evils which are so conspicuous in Chinese social life are to be found also in Western lands, it is of the utmost importance clearly to perceive the points of essential contrast. One of these we take to be that already mentioned, in that insincerity in China, while not always to be met with, is always to be looked for. Instances of this have been already cited in speaking of other topics, and others might be referred to at almost any length.

An interesting volume remains to be written by some one who has the requisite knowledge, on the theory and practice of Chinese squeezes—a practice which extends from the Emperor on his throne to the lowest beggar in the Empire. With that practical sagacity for which they are so deservedly noted, the Chinese have reduced this business to a perfect system, which can no more be escaped than one can escape the pressure of the atmosphere. Vicious and demoralising as the system is, it is not easy to see how it can be done away with, except by a complete reorganisation of the Empire.

The result of this state of things, and of the characteristics ot the Chinese which have led to it, is that it is very difficult for a foreigner to have to do with the Chinese in a practical way, and on any extended scale, and yet contrive to preserve his reputation—should he be so fortunate as to have one—as a "superior man." It is a proverb constantly quoted, and self-verifying, that carters, boatmen, inn-keepers, coolies, and middlemen, irrespective of any specific offence, all deserve to be killed on general principles. The relation of this class of persons and others like them to foreigners is peculiar, for it is known that foreigners will consent to a great deal of imposition rather than have a social typhoon, for which they generally lack both the taste and the talent; yet it is by the social typhoon that, in case of any supposed breach of equity on the part of Chinese towards Chinese, the social atmosphere is brought at last to a state of equilibrium.

He must be a rare man who has no blind side upon which those Chinese who choose to do so cannot get. Not to be too suspicious and not to be too confiding is a rare illustration of the golden mean. If one exhibits that just disapprobation towards insincerity which it seems to demand, the Chinese, who are shrewd judges of human nature, set it down to our discredit as a mark of "temper"; while if we maintain the placid demeanour of a Buddha absorbed in his Nirvana, a demeanour which is not easy for all temperaments at all times, we are at once marked as fit subjects for further and indefinite exactions. That was a typical Chinese who, being in foreign employ, saw one day a peddler on the street, vending little clay images of foreigners, cleverly executed and in appropriate costume. Stopping for a moment to examine them, he said to the dealer in images, "Ah, you play with these toys; I play with the real things."

It is unnecessary to do more than to allude in passing to the fact that the Chinese government, so far as it is knowable, appears to be a gigantic example of the trait which we are discussing. Instances are to be found in the entire history of foreign relations with China, and one might almost say in all that is known of the relations of Chinese officials to the people. A single but compendious illustration is to be found in those virtuous proclamations which are issued with such unfailing regularity, in such superlative abundance, with such felicity of diction, on all varieties of subjects and from all grades of officials. One thing only is lacking, namely, reality, for these fine commands are not intended to be enforced. This is quite understood by all concerned, and on this point there are no illusions. "The life and state papers of a Chinese statesman, like the Confessions of Rousseau, abound in the finest sentiments and the foulest deeds. He cuts off ten thousand heads, and cites a passage from Mencius about the sanctity of human life. He pockets the money given him to repair an embankment and thus inundates a province, and he deplores the land lost to the cultivator of the soil. He makes a treaty which he secretly declares to be only a deception for the moment, and he declaims against the crime of perjury." Doubtless there may be pure-minded and upright officials in China, but it is very hard to find them, and from the nature of their environment they are utterly helpless to accomplish the good which they may have at heart. When we compare the actual condition of those who have had the best opportunity to become acquainted with the Chinese Classics, with the teachings of these Classics, we gain a vivid conception of how practically inert they have been to bring society to their high standard.

"How many Chinese have you ever known whom you would implicitly trust?" This question must be understood to relate only to those who have come under no influences outside of regular Chinese education. Different replies will be given by different persons according to their experience, and according to their standard of judging of Chinese character. Most foreigners would probably reply, "A very few,"

" Six or eight," "A dozen," as the case may be. Occasionally the answer will be, " A great many, more than I can remember." But we must believe that intelligent and discriminating observers who can truthfully give the latter reply are exceedingly few in number.

It is always prudent to observe what things a people take for granted, and to act accordingly. As we have seen in the discussion of mutual suspicion as a factor in Chinese social life, the Chinese take it for granted that they are not to trust others, for reasons which they well understand. It is precisely this state of things which makes the future of China so full of uncertainty. The governing class as a whole is not the best but the worst in the Empire. An intelligent Taotai remarked to a foreigner that " the officials under the Emperor are all bad men and ought to be killed, but it would be of no use to kill us, as the next incumbents would be just as bad as we." The serpent, as the Chinese adage runs, knows his own hole, and it is a significant fact that the official class in China is profoundly distrusted by the class next below it, the mercantile. They know that the so-called " reformation " is but a superficial shell, which will soon scale off. A Chinese mason spending a vast amount of time smoothing the outside of chimneys and roofs which he has built badly with untempered mortar, and which he *knows* will smoke and leak at the first opportunity, is a type of many things in China.

There is wealth enough in China to develop the resources of the Empire, if there were but the confidence, without which timid capital will not emerge from its hiding-place. There is learning enough in China for all its needs. There is no lack of talent of every description. But without mutual confidence, based upon real sincerity of purpose, all these are insufficient for the regeneration of the Empire.

A few years ago the writer was consulted by an intelligent Chinese in regard to the possibility of doing something for the relief of a district that has great trouble with its wells, which are made in the usual Chinese way, and bricked up by a wall begun from the top and lowered as the well is deepened. But in this particular locality the soil is of such a character that after a time the whole ground sinks, taking the well and its brick lining with it, leaving only a hole, which eventually caves in and becomes dry. Like the attempt to remedy the evils of this unfortunate district in the province of Chihli is any prescription to cure the ills from which China is suffering, and has long suffered, which does not go deep enough to reach the roots of character. All superficial treatment will prove at last to be but burying cart-loads of excellent material in a Slough of Despond.

THE TEMPLE OF HEAVEN, PEKING.

CHAPTER XXVI.

POLYTHEISM, PANTHEISM, ATHEISM.

CONFUCIANISM, as a system of thought, is among the most remarkable intellectual achievements of the race. It is true that the Western reader cannot escape a feeling that much of what he finds in the Confucian Classics is jejune. But it is not merely by perusing them that we are to receive our most forcible impressions of what the Chinese Classics are and have been, but by contemplating their effects. Here is the Chinese race, by far the mightiest aggregation of human beings in any one nation on earth, " with a written history extending as far back as that of any other which the world has known, the only nation that has throughout retained its nationality, and has never been ousted from the land where it first appeared," existing, for aught that appears, in much the same way as in hoary antiquity. What is the explanation of this unexampled fact ? By what means has this incomputable mass of human beings, dwelling on the Chinese plains from the dawn of history until now, been controlled, and how is it that they appear to be an exception to the universal law of the decay and death of nations ?

Those who have investigated this subject most thoroughly are united in declaring that this result is due to the fact that, whereas other nations have depended upon physical force, the Chinese have depended upon moral forces. No student of history, no observant traveller who knows human nature, can fail to be impressed, to the point of deep awe, with the thought of the marvellous restraining power which Chinese morality has exerted upon the race from the earliest times until now. " It would be hard to overestimate," says Dr. Williams, "the influence of Confucius in his ideal princely scholar, and the power for good over his race which this conception has ever since exerted. The immeasurable influence in after-ages of the character thus portrayed proves how lofty was his own standard, and the national conscience has ever since assented to the justice of the portrait." "The teaching of Confucianism on human duty," says Dr. Legge, "is wonderful and admirable. It is not perfect, indeed. But on the last three of the four things which Confucius delighted to teach—letters, ethics, devotion of soul, and truthfulness—his utterances are in harmony both with the Law and the Gospel. A world ordered by them would be a beautiful world."

The entire freedom of the Chinese classical works from anything which could debase the mind of the readers is a most important characteristic which has been often pointed out, and which is in the greatest possible contrast to the literatures of India, Greece, and Rome. " No people," says Mr. Meadows, " whether of ancient or modern times, has possessed a sacred literature so completely exempt as the Chinese from licentious descriptions, and from every offensive expression. There is not a single sentence in the whole of the Sacred Books and their annotations that may not be read aloud in any family circle in England. Again, in every other non-Christian country, idolatry has been associated with human sacrifices and with the deification of vice, accompanied by licentious rites and orgies. Not a sign of all this exists in China."

The direct personal responsibility of the Emperor to heaven for the quality of his rule; the exaltation of the people as of more importance than the rulers; the doctrine that the virtuous and able should be the rulers, and that their rule must be based upon virtue; the comprehensive theory of the five relations of men to each other; the doctrine that no one should do to another what he would not have that other do to him—these points have stood out like mountain-peaks from the general level of Chinese thought, and have attracted the attention of all observers. In closing what we have to say of the Chinese, we wish to place emphasis upon the moral excellences of the Confucian system, for it is only by putting those excellences in their true light that we can hope to arrive at any just comprehension of the Chinese people. Those excellences have made the Chinese pre-eminently amenable to moral forces. The employment of the classical writings in the civil service examinations for successive ages has unified the minds of the people to a marvellous degree, and the powerful motives thus brought into play, leading every candidate for a degree to hope for the stability of the government as a prerequisite to his own success, has doubtless been a principal factor in the perpetuation of the Chinese people to this present time.

Whether the Chinese ever did have a knowledge of one true God is indeed a point of considerable interest. Those who have examined most critically the classical writings of the Chinese assure us that the weight of scholarship is upon the side of the affirmative. By others who have a claim to an independent judgment, this proposition is altogether denied. If the Chinese ever did recognise the true God, that knowledge has certainly been most effectually lost, like an inscription on an ancient coin now covered with the accumulated rust of millenniums. To us the question seems to be of very much less practical concern than some would make it, and for our present purposes it may be altogether ignored. What concerns us in our present inquiry is neither a historical nor a theoretical matter, but a practical one, to wit, What is the relation which exists between the Chinese and their divinities?

It is in some cases not difficult to trace the stages by which the heroes and worthies of antiquity from being honoured came to be commemorated, and from being merely commemorated came to be worshipped. All the gods of China may be said to have been dead men, and by the rite of ancestral worship it may be affirmed that in a sense all the dead men of China are gods. Temples are constantly erected by the consent of the Emperor, to men who while living had in various ways distinguished themselves. It is impossible to say that any one of these men may not in the slow evolution of ages rise to the highest place among the national divinities. There can be no doubt whatever that as a nation the Chinese are polytheistic.

That there is a tendency in man towards the worship of nature is a mere truism. The recognition of irresistible and unknown forces leads to their personification and to external acts of adoration, based upon the supposition that these forces are sentient. Thus temples to the gods of wind, thunder, etc., abound. The north star is an object of constant worship. There are temples to the sun and to the moon in Peking, in connection with the Imperial worship, but in some regions the worship of the sun is a regular act of routine on the part of the people in general, on a day in the second month which they designate as his "birthday." Early in the morning the villagers go out to the east to meet the sun, and in the evening they go out towards the west to escort him on his way. This ends the worship of the sun for a year.

An exceedingly common manifestation of this nature-worship is in the reverence for trees, which in some provinces (as, for example, in northwestern Honan) is so exceedingly common that one may pass hundreds of trees of all sizes, each of them hung with bannerets indicating that it is the abode of some spirit. Even when there is no external symbol of worship, the superstition exists in full force. If a fine old tree is seen standing in front of a wretched hovel, it is morally certain that the owner of the tree dare not cut it down on account of the divinity within.

It is often supposed that the Emperor is the only individual in the Empire who has the prerogative of worshipping heaven. The very singular and interesting ceremonies which are performed in the Temple of Heaven by the Emperor in person are no doubt unique. But it would be news to the people of China as a whole that they do not and must not worship heaven and earth each for themselves. The houses often have a small shrine in the front wall facing the south, and in some regions this is called the shrine to heaven and earth. Multitudes of Chinese will testify that the only act of religious worship which they ever perform (aside from ancestral rites) is a prostration and an offering to heaven and earth on the first and fifteenth of each moon, or, in some cases, on the beginning of each new year. No prayer is uttered, and after a time the offering is removed, and, as in other cases, eaten. What is it that at such times the people worship ? Sometimes they affirm that the object of worship is " heaven and earth." Sometimes they say that it is " heaven," and again they call it " the old man of the sky." The latter term often leads to an impression that the Chinese do have a real perception of a personal deity. But when it is ascertained that this supposed " person " is frequently matched by another called " grandmother earth," the value of the inference is open to serious question. In some places it is customary to offer worship to this " old man of the sky " on the nineteenth of the sixth moon, as that is his " birthday." But among a people who assign a " birthday " to the sun, it is superfluous to inquire who was the father of " the old man of the sky," or when he was born, for on matters of this sort there is absolutely no opinion at all. It is difficult to make an ordinary Chinese understand that such questions have any practical bearing.

He takes the tradition as he finds it, and never dreams of raising any inquiries upon this point or any other. We have seldom met any Chinese who had an intelligible theory with regard to the antecedents or qualities of "the old man of the sky," except that he is supposed to regulate the weather, and hence the crops. The wide currency among the Chinese people of this term, hinting at a personality, to whom, however, so far as we know, no temples are erected, of whom no image is made, and to whom no worship distinct from that to "heaven and earth" is offered, seems to remain thus far unexplained.

The word "heaven" is often used in the Chinese Classics in such a way as to convey the idea of personality and will. But it is likewise employed in a manner which suggests very little of either, and when we read in the commentary that "heaven is a principle," we feel that the vagueness of the term is at its maximum. To this ambiguity in classical use corresponds the looseness of meaning given to it in everyday life. The man who has been worshipping heaven, upon being pressed to know what he means by "heaven," will frequently reply that it is the blue expanse above. His worship is therefore in harmony with that of him who worships the powers of nature, either individually or collectively. His creed may be described in Emersonian phrase as "one with the blowing clover and the falling rain." In other words, he is a pantheist. This lack of any definite sense of personality is a fatal flaw in the Chinese worship of "heaven."

The polytheism and pantheism of the lower classes of Chinese are matched in the upper classes by what appears to be pure atheism. From the testimony of those who know most on this point, from the abundant surface indications, and from antecedent probability, we have no difficulty in concluding that there never was on this earth a body of educated and cultivated men so thoroughly agnostic and atheistic as the mass of Confucian scholars.* The phrase "antecedent probability" refers to the known influence which has been exerted over the *literati* of China by the materialistic commentators of the Sung Dynasty. The authority of Chu Hsi, the learned expounder of the Chinese Classics, has been so overwhelming that to question any of his views has long been regarded as heresy. The effect has been to overlay the teachings of the Classics with an interpretation which is not only materialistic, but which, so far as we understand it, is totally atheistic.

After the Yellow River emerges from the mountains of Shansi and Shensi, it continues its way for hundreds of miles to the sea. In successive ages it has taken many different routes, ranging through six or seven degrees of latitude, from the mouth of the Yang-tse-Kiang to that of the Peiho. But wherever it has flowed it has carried ruin, and has left behind it a barren waste of sand. Not unlike this has been the materialistic current introduced by the commentators of the Sung Dynasty into the stream of Chinese thought, a current which, having flowed unchecked for seven centuries, has left behind it a moral waste of atheistic sand, incapable of supporting the spiritual life of a nation. Taoism has degenerated into a system of incantations against evil spirits. It has largely borrowed from Buddhism to supplement its own innate deficiencies. Buddhism was itself introduced to provide for those inherent wants in the nature of man which Confucianism did little or nothing to satisfy. Each of these forms of instruction has been greatly modified by the others. Any kind of organisation which offers a method of practising virtue will be patronised by those who happen to be disposed to lay up a little merit, and to whom this avenue appears as good as

---

* Mr. Meadows remarks that every consistent Confucianist ought to be a blank atheist, but as human nature is seldom ideally self-consistent, many Confucianists either believe in the gods, or think that they do so.

any other. Any kind of a divinity which seems adapted to exert a favourable influence in any given direction will be patronised, just as a man who happens to need a new umbrella goes to some shop where they keep such goods for sale. To inquire into the antecedents of the divinity who is thus worshipped, no more occurs to a Chinese than it would occur to an Englishman who wanted the umbrella to satisfy himself as to the origin of umbrellas, and when they first came into general use.

It is not uncommon to meet with learned disquisitions upon the question as to the number of Buddhists and Taoists in China. In our view this question is exactly paralleled by an inquiry into the number of persons in the United Kingdom who use ten-penny nails as compared with the number of those who eat string-beans. Any one who wants to use a ten-penny nail will do so if he can obtain it, and those who like string-beans and can afford to buy them will presumptively consume them. The case is not different in China as regards the two most prominent " doctrines." Any Chinese who wants the services of a Buddhist priest, and who can afford to pay for them, will hire the priest, and thus be " a Buddhist." If he wants a Taoist priest, he will in like manner call him, and this makes him " a Taoist." It is of no consequence to the Chinese which of the two he employs, and he will not improbably call them both at once, and thus be at once " a Buddhist " and " a Taoist." Thus the same individual is at once a Confucianist, a Buddhist, and a Taoist, and with no sense of incongruity. Buddhism swallowed Taoism, Taoism swallowed Confucianism, but at last the latter swallowed both Buddhism and Taoism together, and thus " the three religions are one ! "

The practical relation of the Chinese to their " three religions " may be illustrated by the relations of an Anglo-Saxon to the materials of which his language is composed : " Saxon and

Norman and Dane are we; " but even were it possible to determine our remote origin, the choice of our words would not be influenced in the smallest degree by the extent to which we may happen to have Saxon or Norman blood in our veins. Our selection of words will be determined by our mental habits, and by the use to which we wish to put the words. The scholar will use many Latin words, with liberal admixture of the Norman, while the farmer will use mostly plain Saxon terms. But in either case the Saxon is the base, to which the other stocks are but additions. In China Confucianism is the base, and all Chinese are Confucianists, as all English are Saxons. To what extent Buddhist or Taoist ideas, phraseology, and practices may be superimposed upon this base, will be determined by circumstances. But to the Chinese there is no more incongruity or contradiction in the combination of the "three religions " in one ceremony, than there is to our thought in the interweaving of words of diverse national origin in the same sentence.

It is always difficult to make a Chinese perceive that two forms of belief are mutually exclusive. He knows nothing about logical contradictories, and cares even less. He has learned by instinct the art of reconciling propositions which are inherently irreconcilable, by violently affirming each of them, paying no heed whatever to their mutual relations. He is thus prepared by all his intellectual training to allow the most incongruous forms of belief to unite, as fluids mingle by endosmosis and exosmosis. He has carried "intellectual hospitality " to the point of logical suicide, but he does not know it, and cannot be made to understand it when he is told.

Two results of this mechanical union of creeds are very noteworthy. The first is the violence done to the innate instinct of order, an instinct for which the Chinese are especially distinguished, which is conspicuously displayed in the elaborate machinery of the carefully graded ranks of officials, from the first to the ninth, each marked by its own badge, and having its own special limitations. Something analogous to this might certainly have been looked for in the Chinese pantheon, but nothing of the sort is found. It is vain to inquire of a Chinese which divinity is supposed to be the greater, the " Pearly Emperor " or Buddha. Even in the " Temple-to-all-the-gods " the order is merely arbitrary and accidental, and subject to constant variations. There is no regular graduation of authority in the spirit world of the Chinese, but such utter confusion as, if found on earth, would be equivalent to chronic anarchy. This state of things is seen in a still more conspicuous manner in the " Halls of the Three Religions," where the images of Confucius, of Buddha, and of Laotze are displayed in a close harmony. The post of honour is in the centre, and this we should expect to be conceded to Confucius, or if not to him—since he made no claim of any kind to divinity—then to Laotze. There is good reason to think that this question of precedence has been in by-gone days the occasion of acrimonious disputes, but in nearly all the instances of which we happen to have heard, it has been settled in favour of Buddha, albeit a foreigner!

Another significant result of the union of all beliefs in China, is the debasement of man's moral nature to the lowest level found in any of the creeds. This is in accordance with a law akin to that by which a baser currency invariably displaces that which is better. All the lofty maxims of Confucianism have been wholly ineffective in guarding the Confucianists from fear of the goblins and devils which figure so largely in Taoism. It has often been remarked, and with every appearance of truth, that there is no other civilised nation in existence which is under such bondage to superstition and credulity as the Chinese. Wealthy merchants and learned scholars are not ashamed to be seen, on the two days of the month set apart for that purpose, worshipping the fox, the weasel, the hedgehog, the snake, and the rat, all of which in printed placards are styled " Their Excellencies," and are thought to have an important effect on human destiny.

It is not many years since the most prominent statesman in China fell on his knees before a water-snake which some one had been pleased to represent as an embodiment of the god of floods, supposed to be the incarnation of an official of a former dynasty, whose success in dealing with brimming rivers was held to be miraculous. This habit of worshipping a snake, alleged to be a god, whenever floods devastate China appears to be a general one. In districts at a distance from a river, any ordinary land-serpent will pass as a god and "no questions asked." If the waters subside, extensive theatrical performances may be held in honour of the god who has granted this boon, to wit, the snake, which is placed on a tray in a temple or other public place for the purpose. The District Magistrate, and all other officers, go there every day to prostrate themselves and to burn incense to the divinity. A river-god is generally regarded as the rain-god in regions adjacent to waterways, but at a little distance in the interior, the god of war, Kuan Ti, is much more likely to be worshipped for the same purpose ; but sometimes both are supplanted by the goddess of mercy. To a Chinese this does not seem at all irrational, for his mind is free from all presumptions as to the unity of nature, and it is very hard for him to appreciate the absurdity, even when it is demonstrated to him.

In connection with these prayers for rain, another curious and most significant fact has often been brought to our notice. In the famous Chinese novel called "Travels to the West," one of the principal characters was originally a monkey hatched from a stone, and by slow degrees of evolution developed into a man. In some places this imaginary being is worshipped as a rain-god, to the exclusion of both the river-god and the god of war. No instance could put in a clearer light than this the total lack in China of any dividing line between the real and the fictitious. To a Western mind causes and effects are correlative. What may be the intuitions of cause and effect in the mind of a Chinese who prays to a non-existent monkey to induce a fall of rain, we are not able to conjecture.

The gods of the Chinese being of this heterogeneous description, it is of importance to inquire what the Chinese do with them. To this question there are two answers: they worship them, and they neglect them. It is not very uncommon to meet with estimates of the amount which the whole Chinese nation expends for incense, paper money, etc., in the course of a year. Such estimates are of course based upon a calculation of the apparent facts in some special district, which is taken as a unit, and then used as a multiplier for all the other districts of the Empire. Nothing can be more precarious than so-called " statistics " of this sort, which have literally no more validity than that census of a cloud of mosquitoes which was taken by a man who "counted until he was tired, and then estimated."

There is very little which one can be safe in predicating of the Chinese Empire as a whole. Of this truth the worship in Chinese temples is a conspicuous example. The traveller who lands in Canton, and who perceives the clouds of smoke arising from the incessant offerings to the divinities most popular there, will conclude that the Chinese are among the most idolatrous people in the world. But let him restrain his judgment until he has visited the other end of the Empire, and he will find multitudes of the temples neglected, absolutely unvisited except on the first and fifteenth of the moon, in many cases not then, and perhaps not even at the New-Year, when, if ever, the Chinese instinct of worship prevails. He will find hundreds of thousands of temples the remote origin of which is totally lost in antiquity, and which are occasionally repaired, but of which the people can give no account and for which they have no regard.   He will find hundreds of square miles of populous territory in which there is to be seen scarcely a single priest, either Taoist or Buddhist.   In these regions he will generally find no women in the temples, and the children allowed to grow up without the smallest instruction as to the necessity of propitiating the gods.   In other parts of China the condition of things is totally different, and the external rites of idolatry are interwoven into the smallest details of the life of each separate day.

The religious forces of Chinese society may be compared to the volcanic forces which have built up the Hawaiian Islands. In the most northern and western members of the group the volcanoes have for ages been extinct, and their sites marked only by broken-down crater-pits now covered with luxuriant vegetation.   But on the southeastern member of the group the fires are still in active operation, and continue at intervals to shake the island from centre to circumference.   In some of the oldest parts of China there is the least attention paid to temple worship, and in some of the provinces which at the time of China's greatest glory were wild and barbarous regions, idolatry is most flourishing.   But it is easy to be misled by surface indications such as these.   It is quite possible that they may pass for more than they are worth, and before well-grounded inferences can be safely drawn the subject requires much fuller investigation than it has as yet received.

To "reverence the gods, but to keep at a distance from them," was the advice of Confucius.   It is not strange, therefore, that his followers at the present day consider *respectful neglect* to be the most prudent treatment for the multitudinous and incongruous divinities in the Chinese pantheon.   When contrasted with the Mongols or the Japanese, the Chinese people are felt to be comparatively free from the bias of religion.   It is common to see over the doors of temples the classical expression, " Worship the gods as if they were present." The popular instinct has taken at its true value the uncertainty conveyed in the words "as if," and has embodied them in current sayings which accurately express the state of mind of the mass of the people:

> "Worship the gods as if they came,
> But if you don't, it's all the same."

> "Worship the gods as if the gods were there,
> But if you worship not, the gods don't care."

One step beyond respectful neglect of the gods is *ceremonial reverence*, which consists in performing a certain routine in a certain way, with no other thought than that of securing certain external results by so doing.

The idea of solemnity appears to be foreign to the Chinese mind. We do not know how to speak of it without expressing an idea of what is merely decorum. All Chinese worship of Chinese divinities, of which we have ever been cognisant, has appeared to be either routine ceremonial, or else a mere matter of barter—so much worship for so much benefit. When "the old man of the sky" is spoken of as a being, and to be reverenced, the uniform presentation of this aspect, to the exclusion of all others, shows in a most decisive manner what the worship really is. "Because we have our food and clothes from him," is the reply when a Chinese is asked why he makes periodical prostrations to this "person." Even when the individual has no definite opinions as to the real existence of such a being, this does not prevent his conformity to the rite. The ancients did so, and he does as they did. Whether it is of any use "who knows?"

This habit of looking at religious ceremonial from a superficial standpoint is well illustrated in a couplet which is sometimes posted, in a semi-satirical sense, upon the pillars of a neglected shrine:

A Chinese Idol.

" When the temple has no priest, the wind sweeps the floor;
     If the building is without a light, the moon acts as lamp."

The gods are worshipped, just as in Western lands an insurance policy is taken out, because it is the safer way. " It is better to believe that the gods exist," says the popular saying, "than to believe that they do not exist;" that is, if they do not exist at all, there is no harm done; whereas if they do exist, and are neglected, they may be angry and revengeful. The gods are supposed to be actuated by the motives which are known to actuate men. It is a proverb that one who has a sheep's head (for a temple offering) can get whatever he desires, and also that those divinities, such as the "Three Pure Ones," who have nothing special to bestow, will always be poor, while the goddess of mercy and the god of war will be the ones honoured and enriched.

Not only do the Chinese base the argument for the worship of the gods upon the strictly hypothetical foundation, "it can do no harm, and it may do some good," but they go a step farther, into a region where it is totally impossible for an Occidental mind to follow them. They often say and appear to think, "If you believe in them, then there really are gods; but if you do not believe in them, then there are none!" This mode of speech (a mode of thought it can scarcely be called) resembles that of a Chinese who should say: " If you believe in the Emperor, then there is one; but if you do not believe in one, then there is no Emperor." When this analogy is pointed out, the Chinese are ready enough to admit it, but they do not appear to perceive it for themselves by any necessary process.

There are many Chinese worshippers who are to be seen making a prostration at every step, sometimes occupying very long periods of time in going on tedious and difficult pilgrimages. When asked what is their motive for submitting to these austerities, they will tell us that as there is so much false worship of the gods, it is necessary for worshippers to demonstrate by these laborious means that their hearts are sincere. Whatever may be said in regard to such exceptional instances, we have no hesitation in affirming that all that has been already said of the absence of sincerity among the Chinese, in their relations to one another, applies with even greater force to much of their worship.   The photograph of a group of priests belonging to a temple near Peking is a perfect masterpiece in the representation of serpentine cunning.   Men who have such faces live lives to correspond with their faces.

It is as true of the Chinese as it has been of other nations in heathenism, that they have conceived of their gods as altogether such as they are themselves, and not without reason, for many of the gods are the countrymen of those who worship them.   The writer once saw a proclamation posted in the name of the goddess of mercy, informing the world that representations had been made at the court of heaven to the effect that mankind were waxing very vicious.   The "Pearly Emperor" of the divinities, upon hearing this, was very angry, and in a loud tone reviled all the subordinate gods because they had failed to reform mankind by exhortation !   Human beings are supposed to be surrounded by a cloud of spirits, powerful for evil, but subject to bribes, flattery, cajolery, and liable to be cheated.   A Chinese is anxious to take advantage of the man with whom he makes a bargain, and he is not less anxious to take advantage—if he can—of the god with whom he makes a bargain—in other words, the god to whom he prays. Perhaps he purchases felicity by subscribing towards the repair of a temple, but he not improbably has his subscription of two hundred and fifty cash registered as a thousand.   The god will take the account as it stands.   While the temple is in process of repair a piece of red paper is perhaps pasted over the eyes of each god, that he may not see the confusion by which he is surrounded and which is not considered respectful.

If the temple is situated at the outskirts of a village, and is in too frequent use by thieves as a place in which to divide their booty, the door may be almost or even altogether bricked up, and the god left to communicate with the universe as best he can.

The familiar case of the kitchen-god, who ascends to heaven at the end of the year to make his report of the behaviour of the family, but whose lips are first smeared with glutinous candy to prevent his reporting the bad deeds which he has seen, is a typical instance of a Chinese outwitting his celestial superiors. In the same way a boy is sometimes called by a girl's name to make the unintelligent evil spirits think that he *is* a girl, in order to secure his lease of life. Mr. Baber speaks of the murder of female infants in Szechuan, whose spirits are subsequently appeased by mock money, which is burned, that it may be conveyed to them for their expenses! The temples to the goddess who bestows children, unlike most other temples, are often frequented by women. Some of these temples are provided with many little clay images of male children, some in the arms of their patron goddess, and others disposed like goods on a shelf. It is the practice of Chinese women, on visiting these temples, to break off the parts which distinguish the sex of the child and eat them, so as to insure the birth of a son. In case there are large numbers of little images, as just mentioned, it is with a view to the accommodation of the women who frequent the temple, each of whom will take an image, but it must be stolen and not openly carried off. In case the desired child is born, the woman is expected to show her gratitude by returning two other images in the place of that which she stole! Chinese sailors suppose that the dreaded typhoons of the China seas are caused by malignant spirits, which lie in wait to catch the junks as they navigate the dangerous waters. When the storm reaches a pitch of extreme violence, it is said that it is the habit of the mariners to have a paper junk made of the exact pattern of their own, and complete in all its details. This paper junk is then cast into the sea at the point of maximum disturbance, in order that the angry water-spirits may be deceived into thinking that this is the vessel of which they are in quest, and thus allow the real one to escape!

The custom prevails in many parts of China, upon occasion of the spread of some fatal epidemic like cholera, at the beginning of the sixth or seventh moon to hold a New-Year's celebration. This is with a view to deceiving the god of the pestilence, who will be surprised to find that he is wrong in his calculations as to the time of year, and will depart, allowing the plague to cease. This practice is so well understood that the phrase "autumnal second month" is understood to be a periphrasis for "never." Another method of hoodwinking a divinity is for a man to creep under a table upon which are placed offerings, and to put his head through a round hole made for that purpose. The god will think that this is a genuine case of offering a man's head in sacrifice, and will act accordingly. The man will withdraw his head, and enjoy his well-earned felicity.

In one case of which we happened to be cognisant, where a village decided to remove the gods from a temple and use it for a schoolhouse, they had hoped to pay a considerable proportion of the expenses of the alterations by the "silver" to be extracted from the hearts of the late gods. But the simple-minded rustics were not familiar with the ways of Chinese gods and of those who make them, who are like unto them; for when they came to search for the precious hearts they were not found right, but consisted simply of lumps of pewter! Cases no doubt occur in which the priests do conceal treasures in the images of their gods, and they are matched by corresponding cases in which the temples are robbed, and the gods either carried off bodily or pulverised on the spot.

Violent treatment of Chinese divinities on the part of those who might be expected to worship them, is by no means unknown. We have heard of an instance in which a District Magistrate tried a case which involved a priest, and by implication the Buddha which was the occupant of the temple. This god was summoned to appear before the magistrate and told to kneel, which he failed to do, whereupon the magistrate ordered him to be beaten five hundred blows, by which time the god was reduced to a heap of dust, and judgment was pronounced against him by default.

Nearly every year petitions are incessantly put up to the rain-god to exert his powers on the parched earth, which cannot be planted until there is a rainfall. After prayers have been long continued with no result, it is common for the villagers to administer a little wholesome correction by dragging the image of the god of war out of his temple and setting him down in the hottest place to be found, that he may know what the condition of the atmosphere really is at first hand, and not by hearsay only. The habit of exhibiting undisguised dissatisfaction with the behaviour of the gods is referred to in the current saying, "If you do not mend the roof of your house in the third or fourth moon, you will be reviling the god of floods in the fifth moon or the sixth."

We have heard of an instance in which the people of a large city in China, having been visited by an epidemic of great severity, decided that this was owing to the malevolent influence of a particular divinity of the district. Banding themselves together precisely as if the god were a living bully, they set upon him and reduced him to his original elements. Of the accuracy of this narrative we have no proofs except its currency, but that appears to be sufficient in itself. The whole proceeding is not inconsistent with the Chinese notions about gods and spirits.

In view of facts such as those to which we have been

directing the reader's attention, it might be most natural for one who was not familiar with the Chinese character, to draw the inference that it cannot be possible that the Chinese have any religion at all. This statement has indeed been often made in explicit language. In Mr. Meadows' work on "The Chinese and Their Rebellions," he quotes some of the too sweeping generalisations of M. Huc only to denounce them, affirming them to be "baseless calumny of the higher life of a great portion of the human race." Mr. Meadows is ready enough to admit that the Chinese are not attracted either to the bare results of centuries of doctrinal disputes or to the conduct of the nations which accept those results as their creed, but emphatically denies the assertion that the Chinese have "no longing for immortality, no cordial admiration of what is good and great, no unswerving and unshrinking devotion to those who have been good and great, no craving, no yearning of the soul to reverence something high and holy." Sir Thomas Wade, on the other hand, whose long familiarity with China and the Chinese might be supposed to entitle him to speak with authority on so plain a question as whether the Chinese have or have not a religion, has recently published his opinion as follows: "If religion is held to mean more than mere ethics, I deny that the Chinese have a religion. They have indeed a cult, or rather a mixture of cults, but no creed; innumerable varieties of puerile idolatry, at which they are ready enough to laugh, but which they dare not disregard."

Into the interesting and by no means easily answered question here raised we do not feel required to enter. It would be easy to discuss it at great length, but we are not certain that any light would be thrown upon it. In our view there is a practical method of approaching the matter, which will serve our purpose much better than abstract discussion. Taoism and Buddhism have greatly affected the Chinese, but the Chinese are not Taoists as such, neither are they Buddhists.

They are Confucianists, and whatever may be added to their faith, or whatever may be taken away by the other systems of thought, the Chinese always remain Confucianists. We shall close by endeavouring to show in what respects Confucianism comes short of being a religion such as the Chinese ought to have. In order to do this, we shall quote the language of a distinguished Chinese scholar, whose conclusions cannot be lightly set aside.

At the end of his "Systematical Digest of the Doctrines of Confucius," Dr. Ernst Faber devotes a section to The Defects and Errors of Confucianism, which are set forth, while at the same time it is acknowledged that there is in Confucianism much that is excellent concerning the relations of man, and many points in which the doctrines of Christian revelation are almost echoed. We quote the four-and-twenty points specified, adding here and there a few words of comment.

1. "Confucianism recognises no relation to a living god."

2. "There is no distinction made between the human soul and the body, nor is there any clear definition of man, either from a physical or from a physiological point of view."

The absence of any clear doctrine as to the soul of man is very perplexing to the foreign student of Confucianism. The ultimate outcome of its teaching, in the case of many of the common people, is that they know nothing about any soul at all, except in the sense of animal vitality. When a man dies, there is classical authority for the statement that his "soul" goes upwards towards heaven, and his "animal soul" goes into the earth. But a simpler theory is that so constantly advanced, and which is entirely harmonious with the agnostic materialism of the true Confucianist, that "the soul" or breath dissolves into the air, and the flesh into the dust. It is frequently quite impossible to interest a Chinese in the question whether he has three souls, one soul, or no soul at all. To him the elucidation of such a matter is invested with the same kind and degree of interest which he would feel in learning which particular muscles of the body produce the movement of the organ concerned in eating. As long as the process is allowed to go on with comfort, he does not care in the smallest degree by what name the anatomist designates the muscular fibres which assist the result. In like manner, as long as the Chinese has enough to do to look after the interest of his digestive apparatus, and that of those who are dependent upon him, he is very likely to care nothing either about his "souls" (if he has any) or about theirs, unless it can be shown that the matter is in some way connected with the price of grain.

3. "There is no explanation given why it is that some men are born as saints, others as ordinary mortals."

4. "All men are said to possess the disposition and strength necessary for the attainment of moral perfection, but the contrast with the actual state remains unexplained."

5. "There is wanting in Confucianism a decided and serious tone in its treatment of the doctrine of sin, for, with the exception of moral retribution in social life, it mentions no punishment for sin."

6. "Confucianism is generally devoid of a deeper insight into sin and evil."

7. "Confucianism finds it therefore impossible to explain death."

8. "Confucianism knows no mediator, none that could restore original nature in accordance with the ideal which man finds in himself."

9. "Prayer and its ethical power find no place in the system of Confucius."

10. "Though confidence is indeed frequently insisted upon, its presupposition, truthfulness in speaking, is never practically urged, but rather the reverse."

11. "Polygamy is presupposed and tolerated."

12. "Polytheism is sanctioned."

13. "Fortune-telling, choosing of days, omens, dreams, and other illusions (phœnixes, etc.) are believed in."

14. "Ethics are confounded with external ceremonies, and a precise despotic political form."

15. "The position which Confucius assumed towards ancient institutions is a capricious one."

16. "The assertion that certain musical melodies influence the morals of the people is ridiculous."

17. "The influence of mere good example is exaggerated, and Confucius himself proves it most of all."

If it be true, as Confucian ethics claim, that the prince is the vessel as the people are the water; that when the cup is round the water will be round, and when the dish is flat the water will be flat—it seems hard to explain how the great men of China have not exerted a stronger influence in the way of modifying the character of those who study their lives. If example is really so powerful as Confucianists represent, how does it happen that as seen in its effects it is so comparatively inert? The virtual deification of the "superior man," as mentioned below under No. 20, is matched by the entire absence of any mediator, as already pointed out under No. 8. No matter how "superior" the sage may be, he is obliged to confine himself to giving good advice. If the advice is not taken, he not only cannot help it, but there is no further advice given.

To us that has always appeared to be a singularly suggestive passage in which Confucius said: "I do not open up the truth to one who is not eager to get knowledge, nor help out any one who is not anxious to explain himself. When I have presented one corner of a subject to any one, and he cannot from it learn the other three, I do not repeat the lesson." The advice which he gives is for superior men only. Such advice is excellent, but it is by no means a prophylactic. When it has failed to act as such, then what is wanted is a restorative.   It is idle to stand over the traveller who, having fallen among thieves, is stripped and wounded, and to discourse to him of the importance of joining friendly caravans, of the unadvisability of sustaining serious lesions of the tissues, by which much blood is likely to be lost and the nervous centres injured. The wounded man, already faint from loss of blood, knows all that; indeed, he knew it all the while.   What he needs now is not retrospective lectures on the consequences of violating natural laws, but oil, wine, a place of refuge for a possible recovery, and above all, a wise and helpful friend.   For the physically disabled, Confucianism may at times do something; for the morally and spiritually wounded it does and can do nothing.

18. " In Confucianism the system of social life is tyranny. Women are slaves.   Children have no rights in relation to their parents, whilst subjects are placed in the position of children with regard to their superiors."

19. " Filial piety is exaggerated into deification of parents."

20. " The net result of Confucius' system, as drawn by himself, is the worship of genius, *i.e.*, deification of man."

21. " There is, with the exception of ancestral worship, which is void of any true ethical value, no clear conception of the dogma of immortality."

22. " All rewards are expected in this world, so that egotism is unconsciously fostered, and if not avarice at least ambition."

23. " The whole system of Confucianism offers no comfort to ordinary mortals, either in life or in death."

24. " The history of China shows that Confucianism is incapable of effecting for the people a new birth to a higher life and nobler efforts, and Confucianism is now in practical life quite alloyed with Shamanistic and Buddhistic ideas and practices."

Of the strange intermixture of different forms of faith in

China we have already spoken. That neither Confucianism nor either of its co-religions is capable of " effecting for the people a new birth to a higher life and nobler efforts " is well recognised by the Chinese themselves. This is strikingly shown in one of their fables, the literary authorship of which we have not ascertained.

According to this account, Confucius, Laotze, and Buddha met one day in the land of the Immortals, and were lamenting the fact that in those degenerate times their excellent doctrines did not seem to make any headway in the Central Empire. After prolonged discussion, it was agreed that the reason must be that while the doctrines themselves are recognised as admirable, human nature is inadequate to live up to them without a constant model. It was accordingly decided that each of the founders of these schools of instruction should materialise himself, go down to earth, and try to find some one who could do what it was so necessary to have done. This plan was at once carried into effect, and in process of time, while wandering about the earth, Confucius came on an old man of venerable appearance, who, however, did not rise at the approach of the sage, but inviting the latter to be seated, engaged him in a conversation on the doctrines of antiquity and the degree to which they were at that time neglected and practised. In his discourse the old man showed such profound acquaintance with the tenets of the ancients, and displayed such vast penetration of judgment, that Confucius was greatly delighted, and after a long interview retired. But even when the sage took his leave, the old man did not rise. Having found Laotze and Buddha, who had been altogether unsuccessful in their search, Confucius related to them his adventure, and recommended that each of them should in turn visit the sitting philosopher, and ascertain whether he was as well versed in their doctrines as in those of Confucius. To his unmixed delight, Laotze found the old man to be almost as familiar with the tenets of Taoism as its founder, and a model of eloquence and fervour.   Like Confucius, Laotze was struck by the fact that although maintaining a most respectful attitude, the old man did not rise from his place.   It was now the turn of Buddha, who met with the same surprising and gratifying success.   The old man still did not rise, but he exhibited an insight into the inner meaning of Buddhism such as not had been seen for ages.

When the three founders of religion met to consult, they were unanimously of the opinion that this rare and astonishing old man was the very one, not only to recommend each of the " three religions," but also to demonstrate that " the three religions are really one."   Accordingly they all three once more presented themselves before the old man in company with each other.   They explained the object of their previous visits, and the lofty hopes which the old man's wisdom had excited, that through him all three religions might be revived, and at last reduced to practice.   The old man, still seated, listened respectfully and attentively, and replied as follows: "Venerable sages, your benevolence is high as heaven and deep as the seas.   Your plan is admirably profound in its wisdom.   But you have made an unfortunate selection in the agent through whom you wish to accomplish this mighty reform.   It is true that I have looked into the books of Reason and of the Law, and into the Classics.   It is also true that I have a partial perception of their sublimity and unity.   But there is one circumstance of which you have not taken account.   Perhaps you are not aware of it.   It is only from my waist upward that I am a man; below that point I am made of stone.   My forte is to discuss the duties of men from all the various points of view, but I am so unfortunately constituted that I can never reduce any of them to practice."   Confucius, Laotze, and Buddha sighed deeply, and vanished from the earth, and since that day no effort has been made to find a mortal who is able to exhibit in his life the teachings of the three religions.

A comparison has often been made between the condition of China at the present time, and that of the Roman Empire during the first century of our era. That the moral state of China now is far higher than that of the Roman Empire then, scarcely admits of a rational doubt, but in China, as in Rome, religious faith has reached the point of decay. Of China it might be said, as Gibbon remarked of Rome, that to the common people all religions are equally true, to the philosopher all are equally false, and to the magistrate all are equally useful. Of the Emperor of China, as of the Roman Emperor, it might be affirmed that he is " at once a high-priest, an atheist, and a god "! To such a state has Confucianism, mixed with polytheism and pantheism, brought the Empire.

It has been well said that there is one thing which is worse than pure atheism, and that is entire indifference as to whether atheism is true. In China polytheism and atheism are but opposite facets of the same die, and are more or less consciously held for true by multitudes of educated Chinese, and with no sense of contradiction. Its absolute indifference to the profoundest spiritual truths in the nature of man is the most melancholy characteristic of the Chinese mind, its ready acceptance of a body without a soul, of a soul without a spirit, of a spirit without a life, of a cosmos without a cause, a Universe without a God.

CHAPTER XXVII.

THE REAL CONDITION OF CHINA AND HER PRESENT NEEDS.

THE Confucian Classics are the chart by which the rulers of China have endeavoured to navigate the ship of state. It is the best chart ever constructed by man, and perhaps it is not too much to say, with the late Dr. Williams, Dr. Legge, and others, that its authors may have had in some sense a divine guidance. With what success the Chinese have navigated their craft, into what waters they have sailed, and in what direction they are at present steering—these are questions of capital importance now that China is coming into intimate relations with so many Western states, and seems likely in the future to exert an influence increasingly great.

It has been said that " there are six indications of the moral life of a community, any one of which is significant; when they all agree in their testimony they afford an infallible test of its true character. These are: (1) the condition of industry; (2) the social habits; (3) the position of woman and the character of the family; (4) the organisation of government and the character of the rulers; (5) the state of public education; (6) the practical bearing of religious worship on actual life."

In the discussion of the various characteristics of the Chinese which have attracted our notice, each of the foregoing points has been incidentally illustrated, albeit incompletely and without that observance of proportion necessary in a full treatment of these topics. In a survey of the Chinese character the field of view is so extensive that many subjects must be passed by altogether. The characteristics which have been selected are intended merely as points through which lines may be drawn to aid in outlining the whole. There are many additional "characteristics" which ought to be included in a full presentation of the Chinese as they are.

The greater part of the illustrative incidents which have been already cited in exemplification of various "characteristics" of the Chinese have been mentioned because they appeared upon examination to be typical. They are like bones of a skeleton, which must be fitted into their place before the whole structure can be seen. It will not do to ignore them, unless perhaps it can be shown that they are not bones at all, but merely plaster-of-Paris imitations. It may indeed be objected that the true place of each separate bone has been mistaken, and that others which are important modifiers of the total result have not been adjusted to their proper places. This criticism, which is a perfectly just one, we not only admit but expressly affirm, declaring that it is not possible to gain a complete idea of the Chinese from selected "characteristics," any more than it is possible to gain a correct idea of a human countenance from descriptive essays on its eyes, its nose, or its chin. But at the same time we must remind the reader that the judgments expressed have not been hastily formed, that they are based upon a mass of observations far in excess of what has been referred to, and that in many cases the opinions might have been made indefinitely stronger, and still have been fully warranted by the facts. These facts are as patent to one who comes within their range as a North China dust-storm, which fills the eyes, the ears, the nostrils, the hair, and the clothing with an almost impalpable powder, often surcharging the atmosphere with electricity, and sometimes rendering lamps necessary at noonday. One may be very wrong in his theory of the causes of this phenomenon, but altogether right in his description of it. But there is this important difference between the observation of physical and of moral phenomena : the former force themselves on the attention of every human being, while the latter are perceived only by those whose opportunities are favourable, and whose faculties are directed towards the things that are to be seen.

The truth is that the phenomena of Chinese life are of a contradictory character, and whoever looks upon one face of the shield, ignoring the other, will infallibly judge erroneously, and yet will never come to a perception of the fact that he is wrong. The union of two apparently irreconcilable views in one concept is not an easy task, but it is often a very necessary one, and nowhere is it more necessary than in China, where it is so difficult to see even one side completely, not to speak of both.

Of the lofty moral quality of Confucianism we have already spoken. That it produces many individuals possessing a high moral character we are prepared to believe. That is what ought to be expected from so excellent a system of morals. But does it produce such characters on any considerable scale, and with any approach to uniformity? The real character of any human being can be discovered by answering three questions : What is his relation to himself ? What is his relation to his fellow-men ? What is his relation to the object of his worship ? Through these three fixed points the circle defining his true position may be drawn. Those who may have followed us thus far know already what replies we find in the Chinese of to-day to these test questions. His relations both to himself and to others are marked by an absence of sincerity, and his relations to others by an absence of altruism ; his relations to the objects of his worship are those of a polytheist, a pantheist, and an agnostic.

What the Chinese lack is not intellectual ability. It is not patience, practicality, nor cheerfulness, for in all these qualities they greatly excel. What they do lack is Character and

Conscience. Some Chinese officials cannot be tempted by any bribe, and refuse to commit a wrong that will never be found out, because "Heaven knows, earth knows, you know, and I know." But how many Chinese could be found who would resist the pressure brought upon them to recommend for employment a relative who was known to be incompetent ? Imagine for a moment the *domestic consequences* of such resistance, and is it strange that any Chinese should dread to face them ? But what Chinese would ever think of carrying theoretical morals into such a region as that ? When it is seen what a part parasitism and nepotism play in the administration of China, civil, military, and commercial, is it any wonder that Chinese gate-keepers and constables are not to be depended upon for the honest performance of their duties ?

He who wishes to learn the truth about the moral condition of the Chinese can do so by the aid of the Chinese themselves, who, however ready to cover their own shortcomings and those of their friends, are often singularly frank in confessing the weak points in the national character. Some of these descriptions of the Chinese by other Chinese have often served to us as reminders of a conversation upon which Carlyle dwells with evident enjoyment, in one of the volumes of his "Life of Frederick the Great." That monarch had a school-inspector, of whom he was rather fond, and with whom he liked to talk a little. "Well, M. Sulzer, how do your schools get on ? " asked the King one day. "How goes our education business ? " "Surely, not ill, your Majesty, and much better in late years," answered Sulzer. "In late years, why? " "Well, your Majesty, in former times, the notion being that mankind were naturally inclined to evil, a system of severity prevailed in schools ; but now, when we recognise that the inborn inclination of men is rather to good than to evil, schoolmasters have adopted a more generous procedure." "Inclination rather to good ! " said Frederick, shaking his old head, with a sad smile. "Alas, dear Sulzer, I see you don't know that damned race of creatures." (*Er kennt nicht diese verdammte Race.*)

Chinese society resembles some of the scenery in China. At a little distance it appears fair and attractive. Upon a nearer approach, however, there is invariably much that is shabby and repulsive, and the air is full of odours which are not fragrant. No photograph does justice to Chinese scenery, for though photography has been described as "justice without mercy," this is not true of Chinese photography, in which the dirt and the smells are omitted.

There is no country in the world where the symbol denoting happiness is so constantly before the eye as in China. But it requires no long experience to discover that it is a true observation that Chinese happiness is all on the outside. We believe it to be a criticism substantially just that there are no homes in Asia.

In contemplating the theory of Chinese society, and the way in which that theory is reduced to fact, we are often reminded of those stone tablets to be seen at the spot where the principal highways cross streams. The object of these tablets is to preserve in "everlasting remembrance" the names of those by whom the bridges were erected and repaired. Sometimes there are half a dozen such stones in immediate proximity, in various stages of decay. We are much interested in these memorials of former dynasties and of ages long gone by, and inquire for the bridge the building of which they commemorate. "Oh, that," we are told, "disappeared generations ago—no one knows when!"

A few years ago the writer was travelling on the Grand Canal, when a head-wind prevented further progress. Strolling along the bank, we found the peasants busily engaged in planting their fields. It was May, and the appearance of the country was one of great beauty. Any traveller might have admired the minute and untiring industry which cultivated such wide areas as if they were gardens. But a short conversation with these same peasants brought to light the fact that the winter had been to them a time of bitter severity. Floods and drought having in the previous year destroyed the crops, in every village around people had starved to death—nay, were at that moment starving. The magistrates had given a little relief, but it was inadequate, sporadic, and subject to shameful peculations, against which the poor people had no protection and for which there was no redress. Yet nothing of all this appeared upon the surface. Elsewhere the year had been a prosperous one, the harvests abundant and the people content. No memorial in the Peking *Gazette*, no news item in the foreign journals published in China, had taken account of the facts. But ignorance of these facts on the part of others certainly had no tendency to alter the facts themselves. The people of the district continued to starve, whether other people knew it or not. Even the flat denial of the facts would not prove an adequate measure of relief. *À priori* reasoning as to what the Chinese ought to be is one thing; careful observation of what they actually are is quite another.

That many of the evils in Chinese society the existence of which we have pointed out are also to be found in Western "nominally Christian lands," we are perfectly aware. Perhaps the reader may have been disappointed not to find a more definite recognition of this fact, and some systematic attempt at comparison and contrast. Such a procedure was in contemplation, but it had to be given up. The writer's acquaintance with any Western country except his own is of an altogether too limited and inadequate character to justify the undertaking, which must for other reasons have failed. Let each reader make his own running comparisons as he proceeds, freeing himself as far as he may be able from "the bias of patriotism," and always giving the Chinese the benefit of the doubt. After such a comparison shall have been made, the very lowest result which we should expect would be the ascertained fact that the face of every Western land is towards the dawning morning of the future, while the face of China is always and everywhere towards the darkness of the remote past. A most pregnant fact, if it is a fact, and one which we beg the reader to ponder well; for how came it about?

The needs of China, let us repeat, are few. They are only Character and Conscience. Nay, they are but one, for Conscience *is* Character. It was said of a famous maker of pianos that he was " like his own instruments—square, upright, and grand." Does one ever meet any such characters in China?

At the close of the biography of one of the literary men of England, who died but a few years ago, occurs the following passage, written by his wife: " The outside world must judge him as an author, a preacher, a member of society; but they only who lived with him in the intimacy of everyday life at home can tell what he was as a man. Over the real romance of his life, and over the tenderest, loveliest passages in his private letters, a veil must be thrown; but it will not be lifting it too far to say, that if .in the highest, closest of earthly relationships, a love that never failed—pure, passionate, for six-and-thirty years—a love which never stooped from its own lofty level to a hasty word, an impatient gesture, or a selfish act, in sickness or in health, in sunshine or in storm, by day or by night, could prove that the age of chivalry has not passed away forever, Charles Kingsley fulfilled the ideal of a ' most true and perfect knight to the one woman blest with that love in time and to eternity."

The fairest fruit of Christian civilisation is in the beautiful lives which it produces. They are not rare. Hundreds of records of such lives have been produced within the present generation, and there are thousands upon thousands of such lives of which no public record ever appears. Every reader must have known of at least one such life of single-hearted devotion to the good of others, and some have been privileged to know many such, within the range of their own experience. How are these lives to be accounted for, and whence do they draw their inspiration ? We have no wish to be unduly sceptical, but after repeated and prolonged consideration of the subject, it is our deliberate conviction that if the forces which make the lives of the Chinese what they are were to produce one such character as Mrs. Kingsley represents her husband to have been, that would be a moral miracle greater than any or all that are recorded in the books of Taoist fables. No human institution can escape from the law, inexorable because divine: " By their fruits ye shall know them." The forces of Confucianism have had an abundant time in which to work out their ultimate results. We believe that they have long since done all that they are capable of doing, and that from them there is no further fruit to be expected. They have achieved all that man alone can do, and more than he has done in any other land, under any other conditions. And after a patient survey of all that China has to offer, the most friendly critic is compelled, reluctantly and sadly, to coincide in the verdict, " The answer to Confucianism is China."

Three mutually inconsistent theories are held in regard to reform in China. First, that it is unnecessary. This is no doubt the view of some of the Chinese themselves, though by no means of all Chinese. It is also the opinion adopted by certain foreigners, who look at China and the Chinese through the mirage of distance. Second, that reform is impossible. This pessimistic conclusion is arrived at by many who have had too much occasion to know the tremendous obstacles which any permanent and real reform must encounter, before it can even be tried. To such persons, the thorough reformation of so vast a body as the Chinese people appears to be a task as hopeless as the galvanising into life of an Egyptian mummy. To us, the second of these views appears only less unreasonable than the first; but if what has been already said fails to make this evident, nothing that could here be added would be sufficient to do so.

To those who are agreed that reform in China is both necessary and possible, the question by what agency that reform is to be brought about is an important one, and it is not surprising that there are several different and inharmonious replies.

At the very outset, we have to face the inquiry, Can China be reformed from within herself? That she can be thus reformed is taken for granted by those of her statesmen who are able to perceive the vital need of reformation. An instance of this assumption occurred in a recent memorial in the Peking *Gazette*, in which the writer complained of the inhabitants of one of the central provinces as turbulent, and stated that a certain number of competent persons had been appointed to go through the province, to explain to the people the maxims of the Sacred Edicts of K'ang Hsi, by which vigorous measure it was apparently expected that the character of the population would in time be ameliorated. This explanation of moral maxims to the people (originally an imitation of Christian preaching) is a favourite prescription for the amendment of the morals of the time, in spite of the barrenness of results. When it fails, as it always does, there is nothing to be done but to try it over again. That it must fail, is shown by the longest experience, with every modification of circumstances except in the results, which are as nearly as possible uniformly *nil*. This has been sufficiently shown already in the instructive allegory of the eloquent old man whose limbs were stone.

But if mere precept is inert, it might be expected that example would be more efficient. This topic has also been previously discussed, and we need recur to it only to point out the reason why in the end the best examples always fail to produce the intended results. It is because they have no power to propagate the impulse which gave them life. Take, for instance, the case of Chang Chih-tung, formerly Governor of Shansi, where he is reported to have made the most vigorous efforts to put a stop to the practice of opium-smoking among the officials, and opium-raising among the people. How many of his subordinates would honestly co-operate in this effort, and what could possibly be effected without such co-operation ? Every foreigner is compelled to recognise his own comparative helplessness in Chinese matters when the intermediaries through whom alone he can act are not in sympathy with his plans for reform. But if a foreigner is comparatively helpless, a Chinese, no matter what his rank, is not less so. The utmost that can be expected is that when his purpose is seen to be inflexibly fixed, the incorruptible official will carry everything before him (so far as external appearances go), as a cat clears an attic of rats, while the cat is there. But the moment the official is removed, almost before he has fairly gone, the rats are back at their work, and everything goes on as before.

That a Chinese statesman should cherish hopes of personally reforming his country is not only creditable to him, but perfectly natural, for he is cognisant of no other way than the one which we have described. An intelligent British official, who knows "the terrible *vis inertiæ* of Oriental apathy and fatalism—that dumb stupidity against which Schiller says even the gods are powerless"—and who knows what is involved in permanent "reform," would have been able to predict the result with infallible precision. In referring to certain abuses in southwest China, connected with the production of copper, Mr. Baber remarks : " Before the mines can be adequately worked, Yunnan must be peopled, the Lolos must be fairly treated, roads must be constructed, the facilities offered for navigation by the upper Yang-tse must be improved—in short, China must be civilised. A thousand years would be too short a period to allow of such a consummation, unless some force from without should accelerate the impulse." * To attempt to reform China without "some force from without," is like trying to build a ship in the sea; all the laws of air and water conspire to make it impossible. It is a principle of mechanics that a force that begins and ends in a machine has no power to move it.

Between Tientsin and Peking there is a bend in the Peiho, where the traveller sees half of a ruined temple standing on the brink of the bank. The other half has been washed

---

* These significant words of the late Mr. Baber have recently received a striking confirmation from a memorial in the Peking *Gazette* of August, 1890, from T'ang Chiung, Director of Mines in Yunnan, who makes a report in regard to the condition of the works and the output. He states that " a great deal of illicit mining is carried on by the people, and the officials are afraid of the consequences of asserting their rights despotically. A plan has, however, been devised of buying up the copper privately mined by the natives at a low price, and thus taking advantage of the extra labour by a measure at once profitable and popular. In this way the memorialist thinks the mines will work well, and will give no excuse for the intrusion of outsiders." The rescript merely orders the Board of Revenue to "take note."

In a postscript memorial the Director informs the Emperor that ten thousand catties of copper are bought monthly from the illicit workers of the private mines, and that the labourers " are not paid wages, but are supplied with oil and rice." In conclusion he " describes the whole state of the mines as highly satisfactory."

It is not every day that an official of the rank of governor officially informs an Emperor that the laws of his Empire are constantly and deliberately violated by large numbers of persons with whom the magistrates dare not interfere, but whom, on the other hand, they mollify with oil, rice, and a sum of money sufficient to induce them to part with their stolen copper; and that in consequence of this defiance of the Emperor and his officials, the condition of the Emperor's mines is " highly satisfactory." No wonder the Board of Revenue was invited to " take note "!

away. Just below is an elaborate barrier against the water, composed of bundles of reeds tied to stakes. Half of this has been carried away by the floods. The gods stand exposed to the storms, the land lies exposed to inundation, the river is half silted up, a melancholy type of the condition of the Empire. There is classical authority for the dictum that "rotten wood cannot be carved." It must be wholly cut away, and new material grafted upon the old stock. China can never be reformed from within.

It is not long since the idea was widely entertained in the lands of the West that China was to be regenerated by being brought into "the sisterhood of nations." The process by which she was introduced into that "sisterhood" was not indeed such as to give rise to any well-founded hopes of national regeneration as a consequence. And now that the leading nations have had their several representatives at Peking for more than thirty years, what beneficial effect has their presence had upon the evils from which China suffers? The melancholy truth is that the international relations of the great powers are precisely those in which they appear to the least advantage. The Chinese are keen observers; what have they perceived in the conduct of any one of the states of the West to lead to the conviction that those states are actuated by motives more elevated than those which actuate the Empire which they wish to "reform"? And now that China is herself becoming a "power," she has her hands fully occupied in playing off one set of foreign interests against another, without taking lessons of those who are much more concerned in "exploiting" China than in teaching her morals. If China is to be reformed, it will not be done by diplomacy.

There are not wanting those who are firmly persuaded that what is needed by China is not merely admission into the family of nations, but unrestricted intercourse, free trade, and the brotherhood of man. The gospel of commerce is the

panacea for China's needs ; more ports, more imports, a lower
tariff, and no transit taxes.   Perhaps we do not hear so much
of this now as two or three decades ago, during which time
the Chinese have penetrated more fully than before into Aus-
tralia and the United States, with results not always most
favourable to " unrestricted intercourse " and the " brotherhood of man."   Have there not also been loud whispers that
Chinese tea and Chinese straw-braid have been defective in
some desirable qualities, and has not this lack been partly
matched by defects in certain articles imported into China
from the lands of the West?

As an auxiliary of civilisation, commerce is invaluable, but
it is not by itself an instrument of reform.   Adam Smith, the
great apostle of modern political economy, defined man as " a
trading animal " ; no two dogs, he says, exchange bones.   But
supposing they did so, and supposing that in every great city
the canine population were to establish a bone exchange, what
would be the inevitable effect upon the character of the dogs?
The great trading nations of antiquity were not the best nations, but the worst.   That the same is not true of their modern successors is certainly not due to their trade, but to wholly
different causes.   It has been well said that commerce, like
Christianity, is cosmical in its aim ; but commerce, like the
rainbow, always bends towards the pot of gold.

It is sufficient to point to the continent of Africa, with its
rum and its slave traffic, each introduced by trading and by
Christian nations, and each an unspeakable curse, to show
that, taken by itself, there is no reformatory influence in commerce.

There are many friends of China well acquainted with her
condition, whose prescription is more comprehensive than any
of those which we have named.   In their view, China needs
Western culture, Western science, and what Mr. Meadows
called " funded civilisation."   The Chinese have been a cul-

tured nation for millenniums. They had already been civilised for ages when our ancestors were rooting in the primeval forests. In China, if anywhere on the globe, that recipe has been faithfully tried. There is in culture as such nothing of a reformatory nature. Culture is selfish. Its conscious or unconscious motto is, " I, rather than you." As we daily perceive in China, where our boasted culture is scouted, there is no scorn like intellectual scorn. If Chinese culture has been unable to exert a due restraining influence upon those who have been so thoroughly steeped in it, is it probable that this result will be attained by a foreign exotic ?

Of science the Chinese are unquestionably in the greatest need. They need every modern science for the development of the still latent resources of their mighty Empire. This they are themselves beginning clearly to perceive, and will perceive still more clearly in the immediate future. But is it certain that an acquaintance with science will exert an advantageous moral influence over the Empire ? What is the process by which this is to take place ? No science lies nearer to our modern advancement than chemistry. Would the spread of a general knowledge of chemistry in China, therefore, be a moral agency for regenerating the people ? Would it not rather introduce new and unthought-of possibilities of fraud and violence throughout every department of life ? Would it be quite safe, Chinese character being what it is, to diffuse through the Empire, together with an unlimited supply of chemicals, an exact formula for the preparation of every variety of modern explosives ?

By "funded civilisation" are meant the material results of the vast development of Western progress. It includes the manifold marvels resulting from steam and electricity. This, we are told, is what China really needs, and it is all that she needs. Railways from every city to every other city, steam navigation on her inland waters, a complete postal system, national banks, coined silver, telegraphs and telephones as nerves of connection—these are to be the visible signs of the new and happy day for China.

Perhaps this was the half-formed idea of Chang Chih-tung, when in his memorial on the subject of railways he affirmed that they will do away with many risks incidental to river transport, "such as stealing by the crew." Will the accumulation, then, of funded civilization diminish moral evils ? Do railways ensure honesty in their employés, or even in their managers ? Have we not read "A Chapter of Erie," showing how that great highway between states was stolen bodily, the stockholders helpless, and "nobody to blame " ? And will they do these things better in China than it has as yet been possible to be sure of having them done in England or in America ? Is funded civilisation an original cause by itself, or is it the effect of a long train of complex causes, working in slow harmony for great periods of time ? Would the introduction of the ballot-box into China make the Chinese a democratic people, and fit them for republican rule ? No more will funded civilisation produce in the Chinese Empire those conditions which accompany it in the West, unless the causes which have produced the conditions in the West are set in motion to produce the like results in China. Those causes are not material, they are moral.

How is it that with the object-lessons of Hongkong, of Shanghai and other treaty ports before them, the Chinese do not introduce "model settlements " into the native cities of China ? Because they do not wish for such changes, and would not tolerate them if they were introduced. How is it that with the object-lesson of an honest administration of the Imperial Maritime Customs before their eyes for nearly a third of a century, the government does not adopt such methods elsewhere ? Because, in the present condition of China, the adoption of such methods of taxation of Chinese by Chinese

is an absolute moral impossibility. British character and conscience have been more than a thousand years in attaining
their present development, and they cannot be suddenly taken
up by the Chinese for their own, and set in operation, like a
Krupp gun from Essen, mounted and ready to be discharged.

The forces which have developed character and conscience
in the Anglo-Saxon race are as definite and as certain facts of
history as the landing of Julius Cæsar in Britain, or the invasion of William the Conqueror. These forces came with
Christianity, and they grew with Christianity. In proportion
as Christianity roots itself in the popular heart these products
flourish, and not otherwise.

Listen for a moment to the great advocate of culture, Mat-
thew Arnold: " Every educated man loves Greece, owes gratitude to Greece. Greece was the lifter-up to the nations of
the banner of art and science, as Israel was the lifter-up of the
banner of righteousness. Now the world cannot do without
art and science. And the lifter-up of the banner of art and
science was naturally much occupied with them, and conduct
was a plain, homely matter. And this brilliant Greece per-
ished for lack of attention to *conduct;* for want of conduct,
steadiness, character. . . . Nay, and the victorious revelation
now, even now, in this age, when more of beauty and more of
knowledge are so much needed, and knowledge at any rate
is so highly esteemed—the revelation which rules the world
even now is not Greece's revelation, but Judæa's; not the
pre-eminence of art and science, but the pre-eminence of
righteousness."

In order to reform China the springs of character must
be reached and purified, conscience must be practically en-
throned, and no longer imprisoned in its own palace like the
long line of Japanese Mikados. It is a truth well stated by
one of the leading exponents of modern philosophy, that " there
is no alchemy by which to get golden conduct from leaden

instincts." What China needs is righteousness, and in order to attain it, it is absolutely necessary that she have a knowledge of God and a new conception of man, as well as of the relation of man to God. She needs a new life in every individual soul, in the family, and in society. The manifold needs of China we find, then, to be a single imperative need. It will be met permanently, completely, only by Christian civilisation.

GLOSSARY OF TECHNICAL TERMS.

BOY, a term used by foreigners in China to denote the head-servant, irrespective of his age.

CATTY, a Chinese pound, equal by treaty to one and one-third pounds avoirdupois.

COMPRADORE, a steward or agent.

FÊNG–SHUI, literally, "wind-water." A complicated system of geomantic superstition, by which the good luck of sites and buildings is determined.

K'ANG, a raised platform of adobe or of bricks, used as a bed, and heated by means of flues.

K'O TOU, or *KOTOW,* the act of prostration and striking the head on the ground in homage or worship.

LI, a Chinese measure of length, three or more of which equal an English mile.

SQUEEZE, a forced contribution exacted by those through whose hands the money of others passes.

TAEL, a weight of money equivalent to a sixteenth of a Chinese pound; an ounce.

TAOTAI, an officer of the third rank, who is intendant of a circuit.

YAMEN, the office and residence of a Chinese official.

INDEX.

ImTheStory.com

Personalized Classic Books in many genre's

Unique gift for kids, partners, friends, colleagues

Customize:

- Character Names

- Upload your own front/back cover images (optional)

- Inscribe a personal message/dedication on the
  inside page (optional)

Customize many titles Including
- Alice in Wonderland
- Romeo and Juliet
- The Wizard of Oz
- A Christmas Carol
- Dracula
- Dr. Jekyll & Mr. Hyde
- And more...

CPSIA information can be obtained
at www.ICGtesting.com
Printed in the USA
BVOW08s1340260617

487714BV00009B/155/P

9 781313 838009